LIFE LESSONS

KH

Est. 1979

THE ROAD TO BECOMING THE
BEST VERSION OF MYSELF

HEALTH IS WEALTH

ALL RIGHT, ALL RIGHT, ALL RIGHT

LIVE, LOVE & LAUGH

WENT TO WORK
BEFORE I WENT TO WORK

SUCCESS IS A MINDSET

THERE'S ALWAYS MORE

I CAN'T MAKE THIS UP

Life Lessons

KEVIN HART

WITH NEIL STRAUSS

37INK

ATRIA

NEW YORK   LONDON   TORONTO   SYDNEY   NEW DELHI

37INK

ATRIA

An Imprint of Simon & Schuster, Inc.
1230 Avenue of the Americas
New York, NY 10020

Disclaimer: I'm perfect. So if you feel that there are any inaccuracies in the chronology or details of this book, it's not because I remembered some things wrong or have a drinking problem. It's because my memory is better than everyone else's, except for the times when it isn't because I'm busy looking to the future. All perfect people have this problem. Don't take my word for it: Read all the incredible quotes on the back cover and then take my word for it. I'm also a nice person, so I changed some names and identifying details (and created a composite or two) to protect people who are less perfect than me. Thanks for reading the tiny print at the beginning of this book. No one but you looks at these things, you know. That's because you're perfect too.

P.S. I may or may not have been drinking when I wrote this disclaimer.

Copyright © 2017 by Kevin Hart

For photo credits, see page 380.

All rights reserved, including the right to reproduce this book or portions thereof in any form whatsoever. For information address Atria Books Subsidiary Rights Department, 1230 Avenue of the Americas, New York, NY 10020.

First 37 INK/Atria Books hardcover edition June 2017

37INK / ATRIA BOOKS and colophon are trademarks of Simon & Schuster, Inc.

For information about special discounts for bulk purchases, please contact Simon & Schuster Special Sales at 1-866-506-1949 or business@simonandschuster.com.

The Simon & Schuster Speakers Bureau can bring authors to your live event. For more information or to book an event contact the Simon & Schuster Speakers Bureau at 1-866-248-3049 or visit our website at www.simonspeakers.com.

Interior design by Laurie Griffin

Manufactured in the United States of America

10 9 8 7 6 5 4 3 2 1

Library of Congress Cataloging-in-Publication Data has been applied for.

ISBN 978-1-5011-5556-7
ISBN 978-1-5011-5558-1 (ebook)

To my mom, my rock, my angel.

I am who I am because of you. My commitment to my craft and to becoming the best version of myself is all because of you. The lessons that you've given me are beyond priceless.

For that, I thank you.

Let him who would move the world first move himself.

—*Socrates*

A sliding board can't be slid on
if you ain't got on the right pants.

—*Chocolate Droppa*

CONTENTS

MANDATORY INTRODUCTION   1

LIFE LESSONS FROM DAD   3

Don't do what I do, do what I would tell you to do if I wasn't doing the stupid stuff I did.

LIFE LESSONS FROM MOM   21

Hard lessons are only hard to the weak who can't survive them... and to me.

LIFE LESSONS FROM SCHOOL   47

No matter what you may think, education is important and you need it and you can't succeed without it—unless you're talented and intelligent and figure out another path.

LIFE LESSONS FROM WORK   79

People with calluses work hard, but some people with soft hands work even harder because they got themselves to a level where they can take care of their hands.

LIFE LESSONS FROM PASSION   107

Putting all your eggs in one basket will lead to the birth of chickens that you will have to eat. What I'm trying to say by this is love what you do, which of course means... What are we talking about again? This writing stuff is tough sometimes. Just read the section.

LIFE LESSONS FROM APPRENTICESHIP 129

You need a teacher, because those who can't do, teach. So if you wanna learn something, go to someone who can't do it. Dammit, I think I wrote this one wrong.

LIFE LESSONS FROM THE GRIND 163

Without the grind, there is no reward. Think about it: What kind of sex have you ever had that hasn't started with a nice grind? I'll wait.

LIFE LESSONS FROM TRANSITION 185

The toughest transition is the transition to understanding that being yourself is all you need to be.

LIFE LESSONS FROM OPPORTUNITIES 213

The only way to prepare for what you want is to believe that what you want is coming tomorrow . . . or maybe the day after that. If not, then it will come pretty soon. If it hasn't come by that point, then you should change your want before you waste any more time. Shit, I'm talking to YOU, Tanya.

LIFE LESSONS FROM OBSTACLES 235

Sometimes you got to take three steps back to know that there's a lot more steps you can still take backward.

LIFE LESSONS FROM LOSS 253

If you experience loss, it doesn't mean you lost. It means you've been blessed with an opportunity to take a moment, realize how special someone or something has been to you, and go through new doors that were closed to you before. No jokes here. Just wisdom.

LIFE LESSONS FROM INDEPENDENCE 273

Waiting for other people to make your dreams come true is like waiting for a bus on a corner where there's no bus stop. Sometimes the bus driver may feel bad for you and stop anyway, but usually he'll speed right past and leave you standing there like an idiot.

LIFE LESSONS FROM TEAM BUILDING 287

I know I just said that you gotta do things alone, but make sure you do things alone with a team. That may not seem like it makes sense, but it makes total sense once you've read this section. And if it still doesn't make sense, I suggest you get a team to help you understand it.

LIFE LESSONS FROM BREAKTHROUGH 317

Don't do drugs. Instead, prove everyone who doubted you wrong. It's a bigger high. If this sounds self-centered, that's because it is. I'm a selfish guy. How else would it be possible to write a book this big about myself?

LIFE LESSONS FROM SUCCESS 341

You don't need my advice anymore. If you're successful, then it's your turn to give the advice. Unless you lose your success, in which case you gotta start over at chapter one.

EPILOGUE:
LIFE LESSONS FROM LEGACY BUILDING 365

One day you won't be here, but your legacy will. Even if the earth is gone, you contributed to that. If you'd done something different, maybe the planet would have survived another minute, another year, another millennium. Everything you do matters. So treat it like it matters.

ACKNOWLEDGMENTS 377

I CAN'T
MAKE
THIS
UP

MANDATORY INTRODUCTION

This introduction is mandatory.

That means you have to read it.

You can't just skip ahead to the sex scenes.

Because in order to get the most out of this book, there are three important words you're going to need to know and understand.

The first word is: "Huh?"

It's pronounced short and sharp, as if someone just hit you in the stomach. Typically, it's spoken while pulling your neck back, raising your eyebrows, and quickly scanning the room to make sure everything looks normal and you're not in some weird-ass dream.

The dictionary definition of the word is: "Did you just say what I think you said? Because it literally makes no sense and my mind can't process it right now, so I'm going to have to ask you to repeat it." It's the kind of thing you might say when your dad comes home bleeding and tells you that someone hacked him up with an axe.

(This really happened, people. I can't make this up.)

The second word is: "What?"

This is pronounced with a silent "t," and it generally follows a few seconds after a *Huh*. It's spoken with your mouth contorted into a look of disgust and your forehead creased, while looking at someone like they're batshit crazy.

It is short for: "What the hell did you just say? Because I only asked you to repeat the crazy shit you just said, and now you're adding some even crazier shit on top of it. My ears can't believe what they're hearing right now."

It's the kind of thing you might say when your dad, whose head is busted open and wrapped in a blood-soaked towel, assures you that he's fine and doesn't need to go to the hospital and just wants to lie down for a little bit.

The third word is: "Okay."

It's spoken with a shoulder shrug, a side-to-side shake of the head, and a roll of the eyes. It means: "I can't even begin to fathom your reality, but I've decided to just accept it and move on."

It's what you say when a *Huh* and a *What* have gotten you nowhere, and you're starting to think that maybe you actually are stuck in a dream and shouldn't eat pizza before bedtime anymore. Like when your dad tells you that the reason someone hacked him up with an axe was because he was jealous of his skills as a refrigerator repairman.

This all may seem unbelievable to anyone who hasn't met my father, but this is the honest-to-God truth. In life, you can choose to cry about the bullshit that happens to you or you can choose to laugh about it.

I chose laughter.

These are the stories behind the jokes, and a few lessons I've figured out about life, success, family, and relationships along the way.

Actually, I'm still working on the relationships part, but the rest I got down.

Life Lessons

FROM DAD

Don't do what I do, do what I would tell you to do
if I wasn't doing the stupid stuff I did.

Visiting Dad in prison with my older brother

1

BIRTH OF A SEX SYMBOL

My life began with one of the biggest lies men tell women:

"I'll pull out, I promise."

Those were the words that turned into me.

Of course, my dad had no intention of pulling out. He wasn't planning on knocking up my mom either. He just never learns from his mistakes.

The first mistake happened eight years earlier. His name was Robert Kenneth, my older brother. Our parents had just met back then, so Dad was able to get away with bigger lies:

"My nuts done got squashed in a bike accident. I can't do nothing with them."

That's really what he told her. I can't make this up.

When my mother found out she was pregnant, she beat the hell out of my dad.

His other lines were: "I'm just gonna put it in a little and leave it there. I just wanna be close to you." And then there was the classic, "I'm just gonna rub you with it. I promise I won't put it in."

I'm surprised there are just two of us.

Though if you count all the other women he did this with, there are something like eleven of us with six different women. At least one of them is my age too.

He definitely didn't learn from his mistakes.

———

My mom and dad met when he was working for Bell Telephone and she was a cashier at a Shop N Bag grocery store next door. From the moment he laid eyes on her—"a fine, petite country girl with big hips," as he put it—my dad started begging her to go on a date. This went on every day for a year.

My dad wasn't persistent because he was in love with her. He was a player. He probably had thirty women all over town he was using the same lines on. My mom just held out longer. As my dad always tells me, even though I definitely don't need to hear it, he had to "con her out of her drawers" because she'd never had sex before.

They never married, though they stuck it out together, probably because Kenneth was born a year after they started seeing each other. But they were like oil and water: My mom was bossy; my dad hated being told what to do. My mom didn't party; my dad did. My mom didn't believe in fighting; my dad believed fighting made you a man. My mom couldn't stand the smell of cigarettes, weed, or alcohol; my dad stank of all three. My mom believed that sex was a sacred thing; my dad didn't believe anything was sacred, *especially* sex.

When Mom found out she was pregnant with me, my father was picking up Kenneth from school.

"Spoon," my mom's sister Patsy yelled from inside the house when my father and Kenneth came home. My dad's full name is Henry Witherspoon, but everyone called him Spoon, and my brother was nicknamed Little Spoon.

"Yes, ma'am."

"Come here."

My father walked up the steps.

Aunt Patsy didn't budge. "Get in here!"

That's when my father knew he was in trouble.

"What did you do?" she asked as soon as he walked inside.

"What you talkin—"

"Nancy is pregnant, and she crying."

"Naw, Nance ain't pregnant!"

"Go tell *her* that. She waiting on you."

My dad hung his head and accepted his fate. He walked apologetically into the bedroom, and got cussed out royally. Usually, he could say "I love you" to calm her down. Whether he meant it or just used it as a strategy to appease her, no one knew. But this time, it didn't do him any good, and he went to sleep that night with her still going off on him, saying how this pregnancy was going to destroy her life. She'd just gone back to school and completed a computer programming class, so she was focused on a fresh start, not fresh diapers.

When my dad woke up the day after finding out I was on the way, Mom wouldn't speak to him. She didn't say another word to him for the next three weeks.

And that's how I came into this world: My life began as a lie. I was unwanted. My mother cried when she found out I existed. And I sat there stewing in her anger for months in the womb.

At least, that's one way to look at it. Here's another way.

My life began with passion, with my father's unrelenting desire for my mother. Even though I was unplanned, my mother made the commitment to having me and raising me right. And I inherited her commitment to hard work, and my father's unique sense of humor, bottomless optimism, and ability to get his way.

Life is a story. It's full of chapters. And the beauty of life is that not only do you get to choose how you interpret each chapter, but your interpretation writes the next chapter. It determines whether it's comedy or tragedy, fairy tale or horror story, rags-to-riches or riches-to-rags.

You can't control the events that happen to you, but you can control your interpretation of them. So why not choose the story that serves your life the best?

2

BLESSED LIFE OF A GENIUS

Though no one spoke about it, I always knew I was an accident. It would have been obvious to anyone who looked at my mom's photo albums.

Me: Mom, where was y'all at here?
Mom: I think that's when we went to some island in Florida.
Me: Huh? How'd y'all get island money?
Mom: That was before you were born. We took a family trip to Key West.
Me: What's Key West? (*Turns page.*) Mom, what's that tree Kenneth is swinging on?
Mom: Oh, that was our poplar tree. Your father built a swing on that tree.
Me: A swing? Okay.

I kept turning pages, asking where they were in different photos since I'd never had the luxury of traveling. I asked about the sharp suit Dad was wearing and about Mom's fancy hairdo. I saw my brother eating cake and holding ice cream in pictures, sitting next to Dad, who looked healthy, with firm muscles and good hair. They looked so happy and well-off.

Then I came along.

As soon as I was born, the pictures in the photo album changed. There were no tree houses or wooden swings or new bicycles. Dad didn't have sharp clothes. Mom's hair wasn't done. There were no more trips. Everything got a little more . . . poor.

Me: How come the furniture went away when I came around?
Mom: We had to cut back, son.

The only nice thing I ever got back then was a dog.
We lived on Fifteenth Street and Erie Avenue, in the heart of North Phila-

delphia. It was a tough area where shit happened consistently. One afternoon, my dad came home with a huge Labrador. I couldn't believe it. I was so happy, I couldn't stop screaming. I fell in love with that dog instantly.

"What's this, Spoon?" my mom asked when she saw it. There was a note of skepticism in her voice. "You got a dog?"

"I bought a dog for the boys," my dad said with forced nonchalance. "They been talking about a dog."

This dog wasn't a puppy. It was full-grown, with a tongue as big as my arm and fur that looked like old paper that had been left in the sun too long. It was probably seven. But it didn't matter to my brother and me. We'd been wanting a pet for so long.

We named him Tramp and brought him into our room to play. He was on the bed, licking our faces, when the doorbell rang.

I walked over to take a look. There was a man and a woman I hadn't seen before.

"You took our dog," they said.

"Your *what*?" my dad asked, as if he'd never heard anything so preposterous.

"You took our dog," they repeated. "She got loose and was running down the street, and the neighbors saw you take her and bring her here."

"What's going on?" My mom jumped in. "I thought you said you bought this dog."

"I did," my dad protested. I could see his wheels spinning as he quickly thought of a lie. "A friend of mine had it. I gave him money for it."

"Coco," the woman called.

The dog came bounding out of my room, stopped at her feet, and nuzzled against her leg.

They walked out of the house with their pet, and that was one of my earliest memories: getting and losing my first dog, all within fifteen minutes.

I suppose that was also my first life lesson: What's here today may be gone later today. Nothing is permanent.

Especially my father.

On a day I was too young to remember, he disappeared for four years.

My dad happens to be here with me as I'm writing this, and he wants to explain for the first time why he went away. So I'm going to slide over and let him onto the keyboard.

Here are a few words from Henry Witherspoon on what he feels happened at that time. Buckle up and prepare to enter the mind that shaped and molded me.

Go ahead, Dad.

3

FOUR YEARS GONE

by Henry "Spoon" Witherspoon

All right, all right, all right!

I guess I gotta tell this story. For my son Kevin—I'd do anything in the world for him.

Because he's my son. Who I'd do anything in the world for.

First of all, you ever deal with a public defender? I don't recommend it. I was this motherfucker's first case.

Kev, is it okay to use *motherfucker* in your book?

Kev?

Fuck it.

Here's what happened:

Now, I come up on my bike to this house, and they shootin' dice. So I shot dice. I'm gambling, but I got short.

I said, "Let me go home and grab some more money. I'll be right back."

When I come back, it's dark. I get up there, I don't pay this place no mind. I'm in a game. I know where we ain't, but I ain't really paying attention to where we *at*.

All I know is that the windows are boarded up. Shit, I knew people that lived in houses with windows boarded up, so that don't mean nothing to me.

I knock on the door. Ain't nobody answering. Makes sense: They got a game going on.

I go in. I think, *Hey, the lights are out.* I'm half-high. Actually, I'm whole high.

The whole of me is high.

I take a few steps and I trip over something. I feel around and it's a body. I don't know if it's alive or dead or sleeping or high. I pull it to the door to see what the situation is cause there ain't no light in there.

Suddenly, a cop opens the door. I ask him to help me. Next thing I know, I'm handcuffed.

That's what happened. This is God's honest truth, Kev.

I figure the cop had seen me walk into the building. Now, this cop gave a statement that he looked through the window and saw me having sex with this body I was dragging.

Mind you, the body was alive, and *he* told me it was a woman.

But that ain't even possible. How do you see through this piece-of-shit boarded-up window into a totally dark house? I couldn't even tell myself if it was a man or a woman.

They got this girl in court eighteen months later cause she didn't wanna come. They had me sitting in the detention center that whole time. When she got there, she told 'em, "I don't know what happened. I don't know him. Never seen him before. I don't even know how I got there. I was drinking."

There's no way I should have gone to jail, but I did. I went to jail for a rape that I didn't commit.

These are straight-up facts, Kev. You know Nancy and her sisters. They wouldn't be speaking to me if it had happened. They told me they were sitting next to these cops while they was out in the waiting room, and the cops were concocting the story that they wanted to tell.

So I wind up getting four to eight years. Them's the kind of charges, though they let me go home before my four years were up.

So here I go coming home from the roughest penitentiary in Pennsylvania, and Nancy is expecting me to be one way, but I done changed.

She hoping I'll be a perfect husband now. She still trying to run my life and pick my friends. She wanting me to get a job when won't nobody hire me with that jail time. She wanting too many changes too fast. But I had to be as rough as these people in this jail to survive. I got harder, you see. And I couldn't turn that shit on and off like it's a lightbulb or something. She didn't understand.

What you don't know, Kev, is that one day I come in and I'm trying to talk to her, and I guess she had a lot of pent-up anger in her. She started hollering and cussing and getting in my face. I'm macho, and I'm not gonna let myself be spoken to that way. So I grabbed her and I told her she better listen.

She broke away and ran to the bed. Reached under her side between the mattress and the springs and pulled out a hammer of mine that I hadn't seen in a couple of weeks.

I think on my feet. I looked at this and I told her, "Now, if you raise that hammer at me, I'mma beat the shit out of you."

That kind of toned her down with that hammer. But at the same time, it let me know how far we had gone and how unhappy I'd made this woman. Right then and there I knew that this shit was over. So I just said, "To hell with this. We done." And I go on 'bout my business.

4

ALL ABOUT MY AMAZING SHOULDERS

When most parents want to break bad news to their kid, they sit them down, place a hand over theirs, get real serious, and have a heart-to-heart talk. My dad never did that.

Instead, he would appear out of nowhere and start laying heavy shit on me in an offhand, matter-of-fact way, like he was talking about what he ate for breakfast.

Dad: Hey, you got a brother and sister. Your brother is the same age as you.
Your sister is a little older. They been around for a long time.
Me: Huh?
Dad: You heard me. Go over there and say hi to your brother, and he'll say hi back.
Me: Who?
Dad: That's your brother right there on the corner. I forgot to tell you. Just go.
Me: All right.
Dad: Also, me and your mother ain't together no more. I'm leaving the house.
Me: Wait, what?
Dad: Look, I still want to come by from time to time. I just gotta get out.
Nance and I ain't seeing eye to eye.
Me: Okay. I'm gonna cry, Dad. This one kinda hurts a little bit.
Dad: You'll be all right. Don't be a bitch.
Me: Okay.

I held the tears back. I wanted to show my dad that I could handle this information. It still hurt, of course, but I refused to let it hurt for long.

To this day, my brother thinks I got over it so quickly because I was young and he protected me. But I think that I was born with a gift: the shoulder shrug. For as long as I can remember, I've had the ability to shoulder-shrug things—to just accept them, say "okay," and get on with my life. The opposite of shoulder-shrugging would be to get depressed or angry and to hold on to those emotions for the rest of my life. But for whatever reason, whether it was because my father was matter-of-fact about the heaviest stuff or God put something in me, I've been able to take in all kinds of experiences and information and process them without holding on to any negative emotion afterward, even at a young age.

It upset Kenneth a lot more. He still remembers my mom chasing my dad with a knife after he broke the news—as well as my dad's last words when he left: "I wasted two good nuts on ya ass, Nance."

5

THE SELFLESS LOVE OF A FATHER

When he walked out, my dad promised that I'd still see him. For a while, I did—and I remember every single time, because the scariest and most heart-stopping things in my childhood *all* happened under the supervision of my father. Nearly every memory of my dad is of him exposing me to a violent or dangerous situation.

He didn't do it on purpose. It was just the way he lived his life. And by being with him, I lived that life too.

MEMORY #1

For one of our first adventures after he left, Dad picked my brother and me up at Mom's apartment. We asked where we were going.

His answer: "We're just going somewhere."

When you're a kid, there are a thousand questions that come up at this point: Where's *somewhere*? How long will we be there? Who else is going? What are we gonna do?

But my dad never gave us opportunities for questions. He didn't act or think like any other person I'd ever met, so he could have been taking us anywhere.

And this day, he had something special planned: He took us to what looked like a pond in New Jersey to rent a motorboat so we could go fishing. While we were on the water, I asked if I could drive, and he said, "Go ahead, Kev, I don't see why not."

A few reasons why not might have included the fact that I was eight, I'd never been in a boat before in my life, and I'd never driven anything besides a bike. But my dad didn't live in the world of reason. He was a firm believer in the "go ahead" school of parenting; whatever we asked to do, he'd just say "go ahead."

He handed me the tiller like I'd been a boat captain my whole life and I started driving. No more than a minute passed before I heard him saying, "Better slow up. You gonna hit that boat."

He didn't reach out to grab the tiller from me. He just sat there, cool as can be, repeating, "You better slow up." "Boy, you ain't slowing up."

I was frozen in place with my hand on the throttle, and I couldn't remember which direction slowed the boat. I guessed and turned the handle to my right. I guessed wrong.

The boat sped up and—*bam!*—smacked into another boat.

I destroyed both boats. All my dad had to say was, "Dammit, boy, you done did this one bad."

He didn't seem surprised. He didn't even seem pissed off. It was like I'd knocked over a cheap vase. He told the guy we rented the boat from, "My son done fucked the boat up, so we'll figure it out."

As best I can tell, what my dad figured out was to never go back there again.

MEMORY #2

The next time I remember being with my dad, my brother and I were walking along a street in our neighborhood with him. I'll never know where he was taking us, because out of nowhere, a group of guys jumped him.

My brother and I stood there, shocked, as they started pummeling Dad. "Go run home," my dad told us coolly between punches, as if we were leaving him with friends. "I'll meet you back there. Go ahead! I'll be all right."

So we went home and sat in the kitchen terrified, hoping he'd come back alive. An hour or so later, he strolled in the door covered in blood and casually asked, "You all right? You want something to eat?"

He didn't even mention the fight. It was as if nothing had happened.

The only other time I saw him that bloody was after he got hit by that axe.

I asked him about it much later, and he explained that he went to the home of someone named Mr. Jimmy. There was a man underneath the refrigerator who'd been struggling to repair it for two hours. My dad said, "Move out the way," and fixed it. The next thing he knew, the other repairman chopped him with an axe, presumably for taking the job away.

This is how my father concluded the story: "Coincidentally, a couple of weeks later, that sucka was found dead. I don't know nothing about it."

This is how I responded: "Dad, I don't want to know nothing about it either."

MEMORY #3

My mom was out and my cousins Anthony and Darryl were over. They were with my father, who was visiting and watching a video that my mom wouldn't allow me to see. My father was asleep and snoring, but everyone else was laughing. It sounded like more happiness than I'd ever heard in the house.

I peeked around the corner and saw my cousins losing their shit. I looked to the screen and saw a man dressed in red leather, standing alone and holding a microphone. He was just gesturing and speaking, and my cousins were in hysterics. I didn't know before that a movie could be just one person speaking—and still be so funny.

I wanted to laugh too. But I had to stay quiet so I could watch. I remember being at school afterward and hearing older kids reciting from that movie, *Eddie Murphy Delirious*, and feeling good about myself because I knew what they were talking about.

My parents were both big fans of stand-up comedy: Dad loved Redd Foxx, Robin Harris, and Richard Pryor. Mom would only listen to clean comedians, like Sinbad and Bill Cosby. I have vague memories of watching videos of these comics on stage telling jokes. I had no idea back then that my life would come full circle and I'd have a career doing the exact thing that brought my parents so much joy.

THE LAST MEMORIES

One afternoon, my brother and I were in the schoolyard shooting hoops. When my dad met us there, he overheard my brother talking about how good he was at basketball, so Dad challenged him to a game.

The thing is, my dad's not athletic in any way, shape, or form. But he's desperate and ruthless, and in a sport with no referee, that's an advantage. So he started playing jailhouse basketball, fouling my brother hard and elbowing him in the face. My brother, who was confused and angry that Dad was being so aggressive with him, won easily anyway.

After the game, Dad walked off, then returned ten minutes later holding his pit bull on a chain. He looked hard at my brother, said, "Sic 'im, Fats," and then let go of the chain.

Now, we'd heard of this pit bull because he was legendary in the neighborhood. My dad had taught him to snatch pocketbooks: He'd send Fats after some woman and she'd start running. He'd charge after her, knock her off balance, grab her purse in his fangs, and then follow my dad for a few blocks until the coast was clear, and my dad could take the pocketbook from him and go through it.

As soon as we saw that dog, my brother and I took off running, climbing a nearby fence and clinging to the top while Fats barked and snarled below. This dog was not playing; it was full-on vicious. My dad just stood there and laughed.

"He ain't gonna bite you," he yelled up at us. "Stop acting like bitches."

To this day, I can't comprehend why he'd sic an attack dog on his own kids just because he lost at basketball. The only reason I can think of is that, in his mind, Dad never loses, so he had to win in some way.

As my mom found out about these adventures, she became more and more reluctant to let my dad pick us up from school or take us pretty much anywhere. He'd beg and plead with my mom: "Yo, I'm sick of not being able to do anything for my kids."

Eventually, he wore her down, and she let him take me to camp. She would soon regret this.

Instead of asking my mom for information about the camp, my dad picked me up in his car and asked, "You know where you gotta go to camp at?"

Overconfident, even back then, I said, "Yep."

"All right, let's go."

My dad began driving, and at every intersection, he'd ask, "Which way do I turn?"

I'd point very confidently: "That way."

Eventually, completely by chance, we came upon a school. "This it?"

"Yep."

He stopped, and before I jumped out of the car, he gave me a pep talk.

"Hey, man, we all got big dicks. So listen, you gonna be cool for the rest of your life."

"What are you talking about, Dad?"

"Listen, you see this long dick here?" He gestured to the outline in his sweatpants. He never wore drawers, so he was always flowing loose. "You gonna grow one too, so you never gotta worry about nothing."

"Uh, okay, Dad."

I jumped out of the car. He didn't wait until I got inside or he saw an adult. He and his long dick just peeled off and sped away.

I walked in, carrying a brown sack with my lunch in it. A priest came up to me and asked what I was there for. I was in some kind of Catholic summer school.

He brought me to an office, and nobody there could figure out who I was. They kept checking different sheets of paper and records. Time passed. "Just eat your lunch while we figure this out," one of the priests told me.

Eventually, he figured it out: "Son, you don't go here."

They asked who dropped me off, and I said it was my dad.

"Where is he?"

"I don't know his address."

"What about your mom?"

Unfortunately for my dad, I knew her number at work. They called her, and my mom got in touch with my dad and cussed him out. For some reason, my father couldn't pick me up, so the priest walked me back to my dad's house.

As soon as my dad saw us, he said, "Son, you told me that's where you went to camp. You gotta stop doing that!"

In his mind, he was never at fault; it was always something stupid *I* did. Maybe that's how I learned to have a sense of humor about myself.

After all this, I could have gotten angry: What kind of dad lets an eight-year-old drive a motorboat basically unsupervised? What kind of dad sics a dog on his kids after losing at basketball? What kind of dad leaves a kid outside a random church and just takes off, without even checking to make sure it's the right place? What kind of dad makes so many enemies that people fight him in the streets when he's with his children? His craziness could have landed me in the hospital or the grave. Fuck him, and fuck anyone else who's on a power trip like that.

I could have taken that road and thought those things.

At every moment in life, there is a fork in the path you are on. And you can choose to go right or you can choose to go left. Every right you take leads you closer to your best possible destiny; every left leads you further away from it. These forks are not just decisions that lead to *actions*, like saying *yes* to a job offer, but thoughts that lead to *beliefs*, like blaming your father for ruining your life.

Your life today is the sum total of your choices. So if you're not happy with it, look back at your choices and start making different ones. Even if you are struck by lightning and injured, you made choices that led you to that spot at that particular time—and you get to choose how you feel about it afterward. You can be angry at the bad luck that you got struck or grateful for the good luck that you survived.

I've made a lot of rights that led me to where I am today, and choosing to appreciate my crazy-ass father was one of them. I also made a lot of lefts in the following years that hurt and limited me. One of my goals in life is to learn from my lefts so I can take more rights.

I never made it to camp that day with my dad. When he took me home after the whole mess, he warned, "I'm about to hear your mother's mouth when I get home. So after I drop you off, I don't know when the next time I'm gonna see you again will be because your mother's gonna be trippin.'"

He was right: After my mom shut the door on him that day, she didn't give him another chance to take me anywhere else. The door to childhood adventure was closed for good.

But that was my right-hand path.

Life Lessons

FROM MOM

Hard lessons are only hard to the weak who
can't survive them ... and to me.

Christmas with Mom

6

THUG LIFE

I've never done hard drugs, I've never been part of a gang, I've never smoked a cigarette. And I've only stolen one thing in my life, which cost less than fifty cents.

This is not because I didn't want to do these things.

It's because my mother wouldn't let me.

Growing up, I was terrified of her. She was more intimidating than any gang. So there was never a life of crime in the cards for me.

Nancy Hart was four foot ten with a healthy Afro and a beautiful smile, but just one look at her when that smile faded would put the fear of God into anyone—except my dad, because even God wouldn't put the fear of God into him. She had more strength and fight in her than any woman I've met since, with such a high level of stubbornness that you could assemble the leading experts in the world to tell her she was wrong about something, and she'd silence them within minutes—and probably have them doing chores for her too.

After my dad left when I was eight, it was just me, her, and my brother. We lived in a three-story walk-up. My brother and I climbed those stairs so often, we had them memorized: fifteen steps to the second floor and sixteen from there to our floor; thirty-one stairs in all.

Our apartment was small and cramped: The front door opened into the kitchen, where my mom had laid strips of upside-down duct tape next to the sink to catch roaches. Past that, there was a bathroom and a short hallway with one door, which led to my mother's room. My brother and I slept on a bunk bed in the hallway across from her door. At the end of the corridor, there was a tiny sitting area. We couldn't afford bookshelves, so everything was displayed in boxes and crates stacked on top of each other.

With Dad gone, my brother began filling in the caretaker role for me—in all the right and wrong ways. My mom gave him a fair amount of freedom, and he would come and go as he pleased. But just like Dad, he constantly butted heads with my mom. If he talked back, stayed out too late, or came home fucked up in any way, my mom would grab a belt in a heartbeat—unless she was in the kitchen. We knew not to make trouble when she was there, because then she'd grab a pan. And she would make sure it hurt.

We lived in an area where anything that wasn't locked up was stolen, and anything that *was* locked up was stolen. You had to lock your locks up at night. My brother soon became part of the problem. Any mistake you could make as a teenager, he made. He joined a gang. He robbed people. He dealt drugs.

On the day he started dealing, he came home as proud as can be. His chest was puffed out, his jaw was set, and his eyes were steely. He then made a gesture I'd never seen him make before: He tilted his head upward and a little to the side, until his chin was pointing at me, like he was a Mafia boss.

"Look," he began in a confident voice. "I know Dad ain't around. It's just me, you, and Mom. So I'm letting you know I got us."

"Huh?"

He winked at me. A slow wink, a do-you-have-something-stuck-in-your-eye wink, a teenager-who-thinks-he's-grown-up-and-has-life-figured-out wink. "I got us," he continued. "So if you need anything, you come to big brother and I'll take care of it, knowwhatimsayin."

Then he raised his right hand and summoned me with his finger. This motherfucker really thought he was Scarface. "C'mere."

I walked over obediently. He pulled out a small wad of cash and peeled off a one-dollar bill. The wad was probably *all* one-dollar bills. "Get yourself something," he said magnanimously. "Treat yourself to some chips."

Up to that point, I had no idea what was going on. But as soon as I saw that dollar, I didn't care. My brother was giving me money, and that was cool. "Thanks," I responded. "Love you, man."

He put on a pair of shades and left the house.

––––––––

The next day, my mom found his drug stash. He'd hidden it inside the grill at the bottom of the refrigerator. It was the worst place he could possibly have chosen to hide something, because the kitchen was my mom's world. She knew where everything was and where everything belonged.

After listening to her rage against my brother, I left the front door of the house open so I could alert him when he came home.

When I heard him climbing the steps a few hours later, I looked hard at him and rolled my eyes in Mom's direction. I shook my head no. I waved my hands frantically. I made an X with my arms. I eye-rolled, head-shook, hand-waved, and arm-Xed all at once. I did everything I could without making a sound to set off my mom. And this fool still had no idea what I was talking about, so he walked right through that door and to his doom.

As soon as she heard him, Mom marched to the door and yelled, "Oh, you selling drugs in this damn house?" She raised a pan in the air, ready to bring it down on his skull. Suddenly—and I'd never seen him do this before—he dodged the blow and socked her in the ribs.

Time froze, and the three of us stood frozen in silence, each with a different *oh shit* look on our face. The next thing I heard was my mother's voice yelling, "I'm gonna kill ya!" She grabbed not just one but a handful of knives from the kitchen drawer.

My brother wheeled around and leapt down what seemed like the entire flight of stairs. Suddenly, I heard a whoosh in the air. My mom had thrown a knife at him.

She scrambled down the stairs after him, throwing knives until he was a speck on the horizon of the block.

My brother didn't return home that night or the next day. My mom had my uncle Albert, who was an iron worker, put bars on the window to keep him from climbing up and sneaking in. Eventually, Kenneth called Aunt

Patsy, told her he was staying with a friend, and asked her to help calm my mom. She didn't succeed.

"He can't be here," my mom raged. "If he so much as puts one foot inside this house, I'm gonna kill him."

Time heals all wounds, and after a few weeks, she begrudgingly let him return. That was the end of his drug-dealing phase. I was happy to have him back—and lucky too, because he would soon teach me an important lesson.

7

THE LEGEND OF FREEBALL

I have a reputation as a guy you don't want on your side in a fight, because as soon as it looks like someone's about to be hit, I run. I like keeping my teeth inside my mouth.

At least, that's my reputation. And it's pretty much my fault, because it's part of the sense of humor that comes with being five foot four. But it's not how I live my life, thanks in large part to my brother.

My lesson in fighting began at football practice, where a teammate kept picking on me. He called me ugly and dirty, and talked shit about my mom. It was meaningless kid stuff, like saying that my mom had an Afro, which she did, but the issue was the tone in which he said it. Kids can say anything in a mocking, singsong voice, and make it sound uncool. "You have *ears*. Nyah-nyah-na-nyah-nyah, you have *eee-ars* and they're on the side of your *fay-ace!*" So it got under my skin. I told my brother, and he said, "You don't let nobody pick on you."

I agreed, but I still didn't do anything about it. I was hoping my brother would. A few weeks later, Kenneth came to one of our games and watched the kid harassing me. "What'd I tell you?" my brother said while I was on the bench. "Don't let nobody mess with you. Go stand up for yourself."

When the game ended, I walked up to the kid and grabbed the face mask of his helmet. Then I dragged him across the field until the mask came off, at which point I began hitting him in the face. When I was done, he was crying. The coach walked over and said, "Y'all be men and shake hands." We shook hands, and he never talked shit again.

I would have thought that a fight would escalate things. But the fact that it stopped the bullying taught me a lesson: Defend yourself at all times. Don't let nobody mess with you. If you don't stand up to them, they'll just keep bullying you, and it will get continually worse as they push to the edge of what they can get away with. However, if you stand up to them, and they feel fear after knowing what you're capable of, they'll find someone else to belittle. Even if you lose or get beat up, at least you can go to bed at night knowing you're not the kind of person who tolerates being pushed around.

I'm grateful that my brother taught me to stick up for myself, rather than knocking out that kid himself. It empowered me. My father, on the other hand, liked to fight my battles for me. He'd randomly appear at my games drinking a forty, then fall asleep. If there was a call he didn't like, he'd come roaring onto the field with the forty in his hands, his dick swinging in his sweatpants, pressing against everyone's face he passed in the stands. Then he'd yell at the coaches and the referee, threatening to kill them.

It was a type of protection that was more embarrassing than helpful. Around school, they nicknamed my brother "Forty" because of it. I was always worried they'd nickname me "Freeball."

At school, where my brother and father weren't around to either help or hurt me, there was another bully. He was a big kid with a cast on his arm. He'd constantly stick his fingers in my face and knock my books onto the ground.

One afternoon, I decided that it was time to end it. We were in the hallway, and I snuck up on him and punched him in the face. When he tried to hit me back, I grabbed his cast and banged it against the wall as hard as I could. He started crying, and I was sent to the principal's office and suspended.

I came home and told my mom everything. I expected her to be furious, but to my surprise, her first response was sympathetic. "You should always stand up to bullies," she said. "But you need to find other ways besides fighting. I can't support violence."

I still thought I was going to get a whupping, but maybe even she saw the irony of hitting me in order to teach me not to hit other people, so she grounded me instead.

Today, I've passed my brother's lesson on to my kids and taught them to stick up for themselves and each other. "If someone is threatening to hurt you, and they're bigger than you, pick up something and knock them in the head with it. Your problems will be gone."

That may sound like a violent message, but stopping a bully is different than being a bully. The real message is: You are somebody. You matter. And no one is allowed to take away your right to your property, your right to your safety, or your right to be yourself. Those are things that should be defended.

I've also taught my kids what I learned from my mother: that fighting is a last resort. It's always better to defuse fights through reason and humor when possible. After those incidents, I didn't get bullied much. And when someone wanted to start a fight, I learned to de-escalate it just by asking, "What are you doing? Why do you wanna fight and mess up the day? All that's gonna happen is we'll both get punished, so let's see if we can find a better way to work this out."

Occasionally, however, when I got real worked up, my logic failed me. Once, as I was wheeling my mom's clothes to the laundromat in a shopping cart, an older kid called me a pussy. I stopped to de-escalate, and when that didn't work, I informed him that his mother was a pussy. I ended up getting whupped by him and his friends. As I lay on the ground getting kicked, I wondered whether I really needed to stick up for myself *every* time. When it comes down to choosing between your life and your pride, I'll keep my life.

———

Soon after this, my brother followed my dad's footsteps out of the house.

There are many horrible and stupid ways you can fuck up as a kid, but one of the worst is doing anything to people who can't defend themselves, like babies or senior citizens. One afternoon, my brother tried to snatch a purse from an old lady. When she wouldn't let go of it, he punched her in the stomach. Even then, she wouldn't give up the purse. A few people noticed and started chasing my brother. He ran all the way home, which wasn't too smart, because the cops knew just where to find him and arrest him.

This was the last straw for my mom. She refused to help him after that. The next time she spoke to him, she said she wanted to take him to the library. She took him to court instead and had him emancipated. In my brother's own hearing afterward, the judge gave him the option of either going to a juvenile detention center or enlisting in the military.

So at age seventeen, just shy of finishing high school, my brother left for Army basic training and, ultimately, Schofield Barracks in Honolulu.

And then there were two.

8

MAMA'S BOY

Some single mothers put their oldest remaining son in the role of man of the house after Dad leaves. They'll teach him to take care of everything that their husband used to so there's no interruption of service.

Not my mom. The way she saw it, she'd been too lenient with my brother. She'd given him too much independence and let him run wild in the streets. As a parent, you can't compete with the streets. The streets will win every time. It's all there—women, money, drink, drugs, and, most powerful of all, other kids who appear to have the one thing your child wants more than anything: the freedom to do whatever the hell they want.

So my mom figured that if she could keep me off the streets, then I wouldn't turn out like my father and brother. She became relentless about making sure I had no free time to snatch purses, deal drugs, join a gang, or think any independent thoughts. I was the last man standing in that house, so this wasn't just an idea or experiment of hers. This became the first of her three purposes in life.

The second purpose was her job in the IT department of the University of Pennsylvania, and the third was the church. She'd always believed in God, but after my brother left, she became *religious*. Despite how hard she worked and how little she made, she began tithing to the church, ushering at services, and attending Bible study groups.

You'd think that religion would make someone more gentle and compassionate, because that's a big message of the Bible. And this may be true for some people when it comes to how they treat their friends. But it doesn't necessarily apply to how they treat their children, because another message of the Bible is that there are serious consequences for breaking the rules.

Mom was tough to begin with, but now she was righteous and holy. All the stress and anger she used to have about what my brother and father were doing turned into stress and anger about what I was *not* going to do. She set up a routine of structured, systematic, and supervised movement that she imposed on my life.

If I stepped even slightly out of line, I got hit with her open hand, fist, belt, shoe, slipper, even sections of plastic Hot Wheels track. She used to leave those tracks lying around the house just so they'd be convenient to punish any infraction. I have no doubt that all this came from a place of love, but it was a love so controlling that I felt envious of the neglected kids in school.

Her routine for me went like this: We woke up at six in the morning. I left to catch the school bus at seven o'clock and got to school at eight. When school ended at three, I went straight to an extracurricular activity like basketball. Because my mom was working and couldn't pick me up until evening, she did some research and found out that the Philadelphia Department of Recreation had a swim team that practiced most weekdays until half past eight. So she signed me up to swim after basketball.

The timing was so tight that if I didn't catch the bus and the train and make it to swim practice on time, she'd know that I was doing something I wasn't supposed to be. The schedule she designed didn't leave room for anything but hustle. That's where it all began.

My mom was particularly proud of having found the swim team, because she couldn't think of a single swimmer who'd ever been a criminal, which made it that much better in her eyes. I swam and swam and swam until I was over it, and still had to keep swimming until I graduated high school.

After practice every day, my mom picked me up, brought me home, and sat me down to do homework. When I finished, she fed me, checked my work, and made me redo parts that weren't good enough for her. Then she drew me a bath and put me to bed too exhausted to do anything but sleep.

On weekends, she didn't let me out of her sight. Either I went to swim meets or I tagged along with her to work, church, shopping, friends' homes, and Bible study groups. Whatever the events and obligations in her life happened to be, I was the guy who had to do them with her. There was no escape—no hanging out with friends, no room for any error, no nothing on my own. When a friend wanted to go to a movie, or a classmate invited me to his birthday party, or I wanted to watch an afternoon television show, if it didn't fit into my mom's plans, it wasn't happening.

What made this schedule even tougher was that my mom didn't believe in driving. She was a firm advocate of public transportation. "It's there for a reason," she'd always say. "Wherever it is that you want to be, we can get there."

She could have been a mathematician. She had every weekend planned out according to the bus schedule: "We're gonna take SEPTA at this time. Then we walk twelve minutes so we can catch the 15, which will come in exactly five minutes. The 15's gonna take us to the El, the El will take us to the subway, and we'll be back home by nine o'clock tonight."

On Saturdays, when she wanted to go shopping, we'd often get up at seven in the morning so we could get to the mall with the cheapest discounts by that afternoon. I hated this most of all in the winter, when we'd have to march around the city and wait at poorly sheltered bus stops in the freezing cold.

Once we got to the mall, Mom had a whole new schedule and set of rules. "Don't ask me for nothing," she'd warn. "You know what we're here for. We're gonna get what we gotta get and then we're gonna go."

If I was good and didn't ask for anything, sometimes she'd get me a slushy or a slice of pizza to get me hyped about carrying her shopping bags home. The transportation jigsaw puzzle on the way back was even worse, because I had to do it loaded down with bags. These days sometimes took up to six hours of preparation and transportation just to spend an hour at the mall.

Back then, all this drove me mad with frustration. But as I write about it today, I'm not complaining. I actually appreciate it. Unbeknownst to her, Mom was preparing me for the grind ahead. As I'm working on this book, for example, I'm in my trailer on the set of a movie. This is what my day was like yesterday:

When I woke up, I ran for ninety minutes. I lifted weights for another hour. Then I had to pack my stuff to switch hotel rooms. After that, I had lunch, followed by three back-to-back meetings that lasted another hour and a half. From there, I went straight to the lobby to take a van to the movie set. I got there at four in the afternoon. I didn't start shooting my scene until midnight. That scene only took fifteen minutes, and then I waited another two hours to shoot for twenty minutes. I waited another hour and a half until a production assistant told me they didn't need me anymore, at which point I caught a van back to the hotel and went to bed just after four in the morning.

In other words, I'm pretty much doing the same thing I did as a kid. I'm living a tightly organized and structured routine, except instead of getting to the mall, I'm spending twelve hours on set just to shoot for thirty-five minutes.

If I complained about this or threw a tantrum, I probably wouldn't be working today. Instead, this schedule is something I easily accept, because it's always been a part of my life. It turns out that the things I hated most as a child are the same things that serve me the most as an adult.

9

SNAPPING FUCKING PEAS

"**H**ey, Nance," one of my aunts was telling my mother on the phone. "You know, Shirrel's having everyone over for dinner tomorrow. Want us to swing by so we can pick you and Kevin up on the way?"

I stood next to the phone, thinking, *Please, please, Mom, say yes. Say yes. Say yes.*

It would save hours of time and aggravation if my aunt gave us a ride. But I couldn't say this out loud because if I uttered even a word, as soon as she got off the phone, Mom would pop me.

One of the things my mom hated most was when it looked to others like her household was out of control. I'd tried begging her to accept a ride once before, and her response was to pause, smack me around, and snap, "Don't you embarrass me. You shut your mouth when I'm talking."

Hoping for the impossible, I dropped down next to her and waited, only to hear her tell my aunt, "No, we're okay. I don't need y'all to pick us up. We're gonna take the bus."

The goddamn bus. I could recite every advertisement on that fucking bus by heart.

I walked to my bed, using every ounce of willpower to keep myself from kicking something. "How'd you get so stupid?" I yelled into the pillow. "Why don't you wanna get a ride nowhere? Stupid! Stupid! Stupid!"

Family dinner began at six in the evening, so we left the house at ten in the morning. We started then not because the commute to the middle of nowhere in West Oak Lane was so long, but because . . . I don't fucking know why. When we arrived, the only person at the house was my cousin Shirrel, who was twenty years older than me. Her husband, Preston, was out getting groceries, and their kids were in the street playing.

Eventually, my aunts Hattie, Patsy, and Mae arrived, which meant I was now sitting around with five old ladies, bored out of my skull, hoping they'd let me go outside and play. But instead they put me to work in the kitchen.

Some people cook with love. I prepared the food with hate, muttering angrily under my breath the whole time.

Me: *You got me in here snapping fucking peas. Ain't nobody else here. I'm hanging out like an idiot for four hours before the dinner. This is bullshit.*

Mom: Kevin, wash that pot out for your aunt.

Me: Yes, Mom. *I'll wash your pots. I'll wash your pots with my piss. See how you like those snap peas a little soggy.*

Of course, I couldn't actually work up the nerve to sabotage the food or rebel in any way. I washed pots, cleaned greens, and cooked while my mom talked and laughed with her sisters in the living room. Eventually, other relatives arrived, and my cousin Preston came home. He went straight upstairs to watch *Die Hard*.

"Hey, your aunt said to take that vinegar upstairs and give it to your cousin," my mom yelled soon after.

"*Why don't she just take it to Preston her own damn self?*" I muttered under my breath.

Then I realized that if I took the vinegar upstairs, I could watch some of the movie with him.

I climbed the stairs, but the moment I crossed the threshold of his room, Preston yelled, "Hey! What are you doing? Boy, get outta here."

"I have your vinegar."

"So they got you down there in that kitchen doing a bunch of shit?" he laughed.

"Can I stay up here with you?"

"No! Put that on the table and get out of here."

I did as he asked, then sat at the top of the stairs so I could at least listen to the movie. "Boy, what are you doing?" he barked after a couple of minutes. "Get back down there with the women."

I went back down there with the women. (Sometimes you don't realize how pathetic your own life is until you see it staring back at you on the page of your book.)

As I set the table just before dinner, fed up from the work, I thought about the long bus trip we'd have to take home in the cold that night. That's when I decided to make my move.

I pulled my aunt Patsy aside and whispered, "Don't tell my mom that I'm asking you, because if she finds out, she's gonna get mad at me. But please don't let her make us catch the bus. When we leave, it's gonna be late, and we'll be out there so long in that cold."

Then I pulled my cousins aside and pleaded with them as well, working all the angles. When they told me that they got me, I breathed a sigh of relief.

During the meal, once everyone started drinking, one of my older cousins said, "Nancy, that boy don't want to be on that bus tonight. Let us take you home."

"No, he's fine. Kevin, ain't you fine?"

"Yeah." *No, no, no, no.*

"We should get outta here now anyway so we can get home at a reasonable hour."

The dinner wasn't even over, and she made us leave. It made no sense to me. I was so mad, but I couldn't show it because I didn't want to get smacked all the way home. The after-hours bus schedule was so sparse, we didn't end up getting home until the middle of the damn night.

Today, I understand why she wouldn't accept a ride: She didn't want to be a burden to anyone. Her heart was so big that she'd rather be out in the cold at night for four hours than inconvenience someone for half an hour.

It was always just us—one hundred percent fucking us. And there was no hope for me to experience anything different, because her convictions and her patterns were set in stone.

Back then, I saw her as the worst, meanest person ever. I was irritated that she'd been much more lenient with my older brother. Anything he wanted to do, she'd say "all right." Anything I wanted to do, she'd say "no." When I'd complain that it wasn't fair, she'd respond: "Well, look what happened to Kenneth. I made a mistake doing that with him. I'm not making that mistake with you."

And that was why I never really rebelled. I saw where the road of not listening to my mom went. But I never saw examples of what happened on the other road. So I made the decision to suck it up, listen to my mom, and make the best of the situation.

As a single mother just getting by, she never let me know how hard it was for her to spend so much time and money looking after me. Even though we didn't live in the best of apartments and our neighborhood was pretty rough, my mom made sure that we lived clean and had food on the table.

Her attitude was: *I'll figure it out by myself. I'll find a way to pay for his swimming, put money away for his education, donate to the church, pay our rent, and keep the electricity on.*

Throughout my whole childhood, I only saw her reach out to one person for help: Ms. Davis.

10

CONFESSIONS OF A LADIES' MAN

Ms. Davis was old. Really old.

She lived by herself. She was one of those sweet, powder-smelling, church-going ladies who filled their houses with dogs and cats after their husband and children left or passed away.

Not long after my brother went into the military, my mom asked her for the only favor I'd ever heard her request. She had no other choice. There were gaps of time after school or basketball practice when my mom had to be at work, and she couldn't risk losing her job by leaving early—or losing me by leaving me unsupervised.

"Can you look after Kevin when I'm at work?" my mom asked Ms. Davis one day. "I don't want him on the street, so can you make sure he's at your house and doing homework, and I'll pick him up as soon as I get off work? I'll give you something for your time."

It turned out to be a good deal for Ms. Davis. This is how a typical afternoon of babysitting went:

Ms. Davis: See this here stamp? Notice how it doesn't have any black marks on it. I'm trying to find stamps like these. So any mail that you see with a clean stamp on it, take that stamp off and put it to the side so I can use it when I send stuff out.

Me: You want me to take stamps that have already been used off the mail and put them to the side so you can stamp new stuff?

Ms. Davis: Exactly. And when you're done, go clean off all those steps over there.

Me: What steps?

Ms. Davis: The steps down to the basement. I don't go in there. I don't do nothing in there, but them steps are dirty. They're filthy.

Me: Why you want me to clean 'em if you don't go down there?

Ms. Davis: Boy, you go wash those steps or I'll speak to your mother.

Me: Yes, ma'am.

There was so much shit in that basement, it looked like a city garbage dump. I made more than a fort out of the junk down there; I built a high-end, multiple-room clubhouse, using old cushions and blankets as walls. I hid out there as much as possible to avoid doing more useless chores for her.

That was where I first saw a naked woman. I found a *Playboy* in a pile of clutter, so I took it to the reading room in my clubhouse, where I had a little chair set up. I devoured every square inch of that magazine. As I was reading, I'd hear Ms. Davis calling around the house and outside the front door for me. I'd yell back, "I'm all right."

And I was all right.

Even though I've seen pictures of my mom's mother holding me when I was a baby, I don't remember meeting my grandparents much. So Ms. Davis became my play grandmother. I began thinking of her pets as my own, bringing them down to my clubhouse to hang out. I was a lonely mama's boy living in an imaginary world created out of boredom and blankets.

However, thanks to Ms. Davis, I learned a skill that would serve me well in life: charm. She constantly threatened to tell my mom if I stepped out of line or didn't listen to her. And if she said anything to my mom that remotely implied wrongdoing on my part, I'd get a whupping I'd never forget. One time, when Ms. Davis told my mom I hadn't done my homework, Mom turned red and began reaching for something to smack me with. There was nothing nearby except for her key ring, which had a small canister of Mace on it. I'll never forget the feeling of looking at it and thinking, *God, please don't let her Mace me. Please don't let her be angry enough to Mace me.*

Since preventing a beating was a matter of survival I learned to use charm to manipulate Ms. Davis. It turned out to be one of the first things in life to come easy for me.

One day, I went on a bike ride outside Ms. Davis's house, and I pedaled around the corner and out of her sight. When I came back, she threatened to tell my mom, and I had to escalate to Stage 5 on the Charming Manipulation Scale (CMS) to shut that down. The stages were, as follows:

Stage 1: *Plead.* "Can you please not tell my mom?"
Stage 2: *Elicit pity.* "She's going to whup me so hard. She just doesn't understand what it's like to be a kid."

Stage 3: *Engage empathy.* "If you had been out there with me, you would have done the same thing."

Stage 4: *Appeal to values.* "I saw Tao on the corner and I thought he could help me with my homework."

Stage 5: *Appeal to self-interest.* "I'll clean your back room if you don't tell."

Stage 6: *Run out of angles.* Get ass whupped.

When Ms. Davis said, "Boy, if you take that bike around the corner one more time, I *will* speak with your mama," I knew I'd succeeded. You never wanted to get to Stage 6.

11

HOT STUFF

The only relief from the monotony of being under my mom's control was spending time with my dad. But between how rarely she let him see me and how rarely he remembered to see me, that wasn't very often.

The great thing about my dad, though, was that he'd get me cool shit.

At one point, I wanted to be a professional BMX rider. It was the biggest thing in the neighborhood; all the popular kids were tricking their bikes out. So I asked my mom for one.

"Sure, you can get a bike," she said. I was shocked.

That shock didn't last long. The next day, she came home with a tricycle.

Mom: I got you this, because those new bikes aren't safe.

Me: Thanks, Mom. *A goddamn tricycle? You think I'm gonna go outside pedaling this, with my ass dragging on the sidewalk, while all my friends are doing wheelies and jumps and shit? This ain't even a bike.*

The next time I saw my dad, I told him what had happened. "You want a bike?" he asked. "I'll get you a brand-new, genuine BMX bike."

Later that day, he brought me a six-speed Huffy Sonic 6. It had a shield over the handlebars with a gear shifter behind it. If you pulled the brake up real fast, it would even spin out. It was exactly what I wanted.

"Go ahead, boy," he said. "Go ride that bike."

I couldn't believe it. This was the greatest day of my life.

I came home with my new bike early that evening, all hyped up.

Me: Mom! Dad got me the Sonic 6. It's outside. Wait till you see it.

Mom: Uh-uh, you ain't playing with that! It's stolen. Where he at?

Me: I think he's talking to somebody on the corner.

Mom: Well, you tell him to take that back.

Me: . . .

Mom: You go tell him. Or do you want *me* to tell him?

She marched downstairs with me under one arm and the bike dragging from the other.

My dad saw the approaching storm and instantly went on the defensive. "Nancy, don't start that stuff."

"My boy ain't playing with that. It's hot!"

That was the expression she always used: *It's hot!*

So no Sonic 6 for me. No nothing, ever, for me.

In Mom's defense, when I cooled off the next day, I realized that the bike hadn't come with a price tag, instructions, stickers, or anything that an item sold in a store would normally have.

Not long after that, my dad came by with a trash bag full of my favorite action figures. They weren't in packages, of course. They were just lying mangled in that bag. I was starting to notice that nothing he got me ever came in a box or with a price tag or wrapped in plastic. But it didn't matter.

Me: Mom! Look, look. Dad got me Lex Luthor. Michael Jackson! Oh my God, He-Man!

Mom: That stuff is hot!

Me: But Mom . . .

Mom: Put that stuff back in the bag, tie it up, and give it to me right now!

I returned them to the bag, tied it up, and gave it to her obediently.

She put it outside the door and called my dad. "You come get that hot shit. That shit is smoking at the top of the stairs right now. I don't want it in this apartment."

My dad always got me the perfect gifts, even if they were all stolen. But my mom, who spent actual money, always managed to screw it up. No matter what I wanted to get to fit in with the other kids in school, she always managed to buy something that would make me an outcast instead.

At that time, just like nearly every other kid, I looked up to Michael Jordan. He wore compression shorts underneath his basketball shorts, so some of the kids on my team began dressing the same way.

I made the mistake of saying to my mom, "For Christmas, I wanna get those basketball tights that go under your shorts, like Michael Jordan wears."

"That's it? That's what you want for Christmas?"

"Yes, please!"

When Christmas rolled around, there was a small package from my mom waiting for me under our miniature tree. I tore open the gift wrap, threw the lid off the box, and saw . . . girls' tights.

They were spandex, and *really* tight—not even remotely close to what Michael Jordan wore.

I put them on, just in case she knew something I didn't, and checked them out in the mirror. I looked like I was going to ballet class.

"What are these supposed to be?" I asked my mom.

"You said tights. They couldn't find your size nowhere, so I got you these. Boy, wear those tights, trust me."

I trusted her and wore them under my shorts to the next game.

"What kinda tights is those, Kev?" one of my teammates asked. "Those ain't for basketball, that's for sure."

"Uh-huh, yeah they are. You don't know what you're talking about."

"Let me see." He reached for the label, and I dodged him. I dodged everyone that day.

People say that when it comes to gift-giving, it's the thought that counts. Don't believe them. It's the gift that counts.

12

HORSEFACE AND JAMMIN' JOE

Every kid reaches a breaking point, where he or she says, "All right, I know you're the parent and you're an adult, but I'm gonna speak my mind."

My moment was in seventh grade. My friend's dad was taking him and some other kids to Clementon Park on a Saturday afternoon. The amusement park wasn't that far away, but my mom didn't know the kid or his parents, so she refused to let me go.

That's when I decided, *I'm gonna go for it. Whatever happens, happens, but enough is enough.*

I could feel the lump forming in my throat as I got ready to stand up to her for the first time and make my voice heard.

Mom: I don't know what these people are about. I'm not letting you go off with a bunch of strangers to get left behind accidentally or get caught up in gang activities.

Me: He's my friend. He's a good person. So is his dad. They would never do that.

Mom: I said *no* and I mean no. End of discussion.

Me: I-I-I'm sick of this. I don't want to be here anymore! I don't want to live here! I want to live with Dad. He lets me do whatever I want.

Mom: Then go.
Me: Huh?
Mom: Go live with your dad.
Me: What?
Mom: You heard me. If that's what you want, you're free to go.
Me: Okay, cool.

I couldn't believe my luck. I was finally free. I'd be able to go to movies and birthday parties and play outside with friends like a normal kid. Plus, maybe my dad could find me another Sonic 6.

I stuffed my clothing into a shopping bag and grabbed my basketball. Then she took me to my dad's house in South Philly and left me there.

When I looked up at the building, half the windows either were broken or didn't have shades. The place looked abandoned. I walked up the stairs, only to find that my dad's apartment made ours look like a mansion in comparison. It was a single room with ratty furniture and a bare lightbulb hanging from the ceiling. The small space was packed with people and animals and smoke and empty beer bottles and trash all over the floor.

"Kev!" Dad yelled when I entered, like I'd just arrived at a party. "You remember your aunt Antoinette, and your cousins Alton, Pat, Grant, Jammin' Joe, and Horseface. And of course, Uncle Don and Uncle Ray Ray. And my buddies Tank and Jo-Jo."

Not a single one of those people looked familiar. I took a step forward and stepped in shit from some kind of animal. I didn't know what kind, because there were creatures all over the place: dogs, cats, birds, snakes, rats.

Where my mom was all about structure, my dad had no sense of order at all. With his apartment's yellowing walls, stench of body odor, stale cigarette smoke, and animal droppings, it felt like I'd entered the armpit of the world.

When night fell, there was no actual dinnertime. There was just food lying around, which you had to grab before someone else did. When I got tired, I went to take a bath, but the apartment didn't have hot water. I had to heat water on a kerosene heater, then dump it into the tub.

I went to sleep in that room, which was still filled with animals, dubious relatives, and friends of my dad's. There was barking, snoring, and elbows and knees poking me. I could barely sleep. At seven in the morning, I untangled myself, crept out of the room, found the phone, and called my mom.

"Can I come back home?" She didn't seem surprised to hear from me.

An hour later, she picked me up at my dad's house and walked me home. As she did, she spoke sternly: "You're either gonna respect my rules and respect my word, or you're not gonna live under my roof. It's that simple."

I thought about her ultimatum. There was no middle ground between my parents. I could either choose a comfortable dictatorship or I could choose uncomfortable anarchy. I could follow in my brother's footsteps or stay on the other path. There was only one decision I could make.

"Yes, Mom."

In retrospect, I realize that she had known all along exactly what was going to happen and how things would play out. It was like a poker game, and she played her hand perfectly.

She could have written a book on reverse psychology. Once, after a friend of mine was caught smoking, she asked if I smoked too. I told her truthfully that I'd never smoked and had no interest, because Dad smoked cigarettes and I hated the smell. "If I ever see a single sign that maybe you've smoked a cigarette," she warned, "you're gonna sit in front of me and I'm gonna make you smoke five packs of cigarettes right there. You'll be so disgusted by smoking that you'll never want to pick up a cigarette again."

After I left my dad's house that morning, carrying my basketball and clothes in defeat, I wasn't the same. I had learned a valuable lesson that would last me a lifetime:

It's easy to complain about your life—how tough it is, how unfair it is, how stressful it is, how everyone else has it much better. But if you step into the life of someone you envy for just a day, you'll discover that everyone has their own problems, and they're usually worse than yours. Because your problems are designed specifically for you, with the specific purpose of helping you grow.

Experiencing a lifestyle without structure, discipline, values, strictness, and work ethic taught me to appreciate them a little more. Instead of just seeing the things my mom was taking away from me, I began to see the things she was giving me.

I didn't flip all the way from resentment to appreciation, but I began that slow process. And logically, no other response to the ups and downs of life makes sense besides gratitude. You are already in your experience. So you can either resent and resist it, and make it that much less enjoyable, or you can accept it and find *something* positive in it.

I accepted that I was stuck with my mom, so I may as well make the best of it. At times, that meant trying to sneak around behind her back to get what I wanted. But that didn't last long either. Unfortunately, I didn't have the ability to outsmart my mother.

I learned this the hard way.

Life Lessons
FROM SCHOOL

*No matter what you may think, education is
important and you need it and you can't
succeed without it—unless you're talented and
intelligent and figure out another path.*

The bowl cut

13

SECRETS OF AN INTERNATIONAL PLAYBOY

I had a tough time with girls.

The reason is because my mom used to cut my hair.

"I'm not paying nobody to do what I can do," she said. My mom would put a bowl over my head, grab the clippers, and go around my head one time, against the grain, and that was my haircut. Once, I looked in the mirror afterward, and there were these random bald patches. I looked like a Lego figure after you unsnap the hair from it.

Meanwhile, she used to go to the hair salon to get shape-ups and trims. To this day, I don't understand this shit. My brother actually began his entire life of crime because he wanted a haircut and couldn't figure out any way to get money for it besides stealing.

On my right-hand path, I realized that I could set up a barter system with my mom. The secret was to find something that was more important to her than twelve dollars for a haircut. And that something was my grades.

One day, in middle school, when I got good grades on my report card (which for me were Bs), my mom gushed:

Mom: I'm proud of you. What do you want as a reward? Name anything.
Me: All I want is a haircut from a barbershop.
Mom: I can just cut it for you.

Me: Please, I'm begging you: Let me go to the barbershop. I just want to experience a professional barber one time.

Mom: Okay, Kevin—but don't get used to it.

The next day, I went to school, saw the popular girl I liked, and with the confidence that only a hairstyle not cut by your mama can bring, said, "Hey."

To my complete surprise, she replied, "Hi." That was the first time she ever spoke to me.

"I got a haircut," I told her, like an idiot.

She smiled.

And that was enough for me. I decided that looking good made the world revolve around you. To this day, I still remember the name of the guy who cut my hair: Greg.

Thank you, Greg.

Two weeks later, the haircut had grown out and I was right back where I started. When I asked my mom for money to get my hair cut, she refused: "I'm not giving you twelve dollars for something I can do myself right now. Come over here. It'll just take five minutes."

"That's what I'm afraid of," I muttered as I submitted to another bowl cut.

Consequently, I never had girls beating down my locker. I damn sure remember who did have them though: Hakim. Girls loved Hakim. And I was pissed off about that—until I realized the secret to his success. It was pubic hair.

"Hey, you got hair on your dick yet, man?" Hakim asked one day.

Most guys my age seemed to be sprouting pubic hair and their confidence was growing in tandem. You were no longer a boy once you got that new growth. You were a fucking man.

So of course I told him, "Yeah, I'm already good down there."

"Let's see," he said.

He lowered his waistband and proved that, yes, he did indeed have some fuzz.

If I didn't back up my words by flashing some fuzz, Hakim would tell everyone. My already dismal chances with girls would hit a new low. I had to think quickly.

I dropped a notebook on the ground. As Hakim bent to pick it up, I reached my hand to the back of my head and pulled out a few strands.

Then, as Hakim was standing up, I reached into my waistband and pretended to pull the loose hair out.

"Oh, Kev's got hair," Hakim exclaimed. "He's got hair!"

And my middle school life was saved.

I ended up doing that maneuver so often in the following years, I'm surprised I had any hair left on my head.

"How y'all getting it?" I kept asking friends, trying to be casual about it. "What y'all doing? Putting grease on it or something?"

I tried everything to spark some growth. I put hair oil on the area. I put shaving cream on it. I put fertilizer on it. I prayed to God.

But nothing worked: I didn't get pubic hair until I was almost eighteen years old.

Being the last person to grow pubic hair in my class was probably the biggest stress I dealt with in my childhood. It was worse than my mom controlling my every movement, worse than my brother getting arrested and joining the military, worse than anything my dad did.

And the fucked-up thing is, I waited what seemed like my whole life to get pubic hair, then as soon as I got it, women started saying, "You gotta shave that shit off."

I guess to be a man, you just gotta be able to prove you can grow it. And once you know you can, you're supposed to get rid of it. Is there a life lesson in this? Probably not. At times, life is random if not downright stupid.

14

PACKING THAT MEAT

Eventually, I realized it wasn't pubic hair that got you the girls. I'd been so naïve. Girls didn't care about that. They cared about things that were more important—things that really mattered, things that made a difference. They cared about big dicks.

After hearing two girls talking about the size of Hakim's dick, I leapt into action: The next day, I came to school in my brother's old sneakers.

They were two sizes too big for me. But I knew that as soon as the girls saw how big my feet were, they'd think about the monster I was packing higher up.

"Yo, Kev, what's going on?" my friend Jabbar asked. "Your feet are big as shit."

"Shhh," I told him. "I'm dealing with it, you know. What you want me to do?"

I flopped all over school like I was the man that day—except during basketball practice. I couldn't run in those flippers, so my sneakers on the court looked nothing like the ones I wore during school.

I hoped no one would notice the difference. But I think they did, because pretty soon, everyone started calling me "Flip."

Fortunately, I have an optimistic disposition. So when fake pubic hair and big shoes didn't get me anywhere with the ladies, I decided to do the one thing that no teenage girl could resist: join a boy band.

NKOTB, Boyz II Men, New Edition—all these boy bands were poppin'. So I told my friend Jabbar that we should be poppin' too.

"I'm telling you, we'll make it," I elaborated. "We're both talented, and we got great voices."

The first problem was my premise: We weren't talented, and we had horrible voices. But we had a great dream, and who's going to say no to a child's dream?

The second problem was that between school and all the extracurricular programs my mother had enrolled me in, I had no free time to rehearse. I solved that one by practicing with Jabbar in Ms. Davis's yard. We were there nearly every afternoon for a month, very seriously working on the lyrics and choreography of our first hit single.

It was a song that we were sure would take the teenage girls of the nation by storm. We stood side by side, then shuffled a step to the right, and I sang, "Gonna love you up." Then we moved back to the center, and he sang, "Gonna love you down." And finally, we shuffled a step to the left and both sang, "Gonna love you always."

"Oh man, that's it!" I clapped him on the back when we completed that song. "We're gonna do this. Kev and Jabbar: album dropping everywhere this summer."

"I'm gonna get me my own house with all that money," Jabbar replied.

We probably spent more time bigging each other up than singing. Our album was going to be called *Didn't Make It*. It was a prophetic title.

It seemed like whatever I did to be cool only brought me more ridicule. The problem is that in most cases, what it takes to be cool in middle school is money. And we didn't have much. We couldn't afford the Malcolm X jackets that kids were wearing after the movie came out. We couldn't afford the Air Jordans. We couldn't afford the nice Starter jackets. All these phases came and went, and I just watched them pass by.

The only thing I had was my personality, and back then, it wasn't enough. I worked my way down from the most popular girls, who were dating the star quarterback or star point guard or track-and-field star (basically anyone with the word *star* attached), to the lonely girls who hung out in the library. When I worked up the courage to ask one of the cute but overlooked library girls to a movie, she responded, "No, that's not really my thing. I'm into books."

"Of course, I get it," I said, and slunk away.

So that was it: I'd burned through pretty much the entire female population of school. But fortunately, I lived in the city, so there were other options in the neighborhood. My first big crush was a girl named Tamika. She lived in another neighborhood, but would come to visit someone on my block, so I started talking to her.

One day my dad stopped by and saw me talking to her. I was so proud:

Me: Dad, I want you to meet Tamika.

Dad: I don't know about this one, Kev. Something about her teeth—

Me: Dad, she's right here!

Dad: All right, all right. Did you at least get your dick wet yet?

Me: I don't know what you're talking about. Just stop.

Dad: Naw, you ain't *never* had your dick wet.

Me: We're gonna go.

Dad: Aw, you ain't gonna be no faggot. Show her that long dick!

Despite my dad's lack of a filter, I eventually got her phone number and managed to convince her to go on a date with me.

The next problem was my mom: There was no room in her schedule for this date. The only way I could make it work was to play hooky during school.

It took me two weeks to convince Tamika to ditch her classes too. Once I did, we wandered around my neighborhood talking until someone spotted us, called my mom, and asked: "Is your son supposed to be in school today? Because I think I see him walking down the street right here."

She popped up on me and whupped my ass on the spot, flinging me all over the place in front of Tamika.

The saddest thing is, it wouldn't be the most embarrassing beating I got from my mom. That would happen the following year, when I started high school.

15

TIME TRAVELING

For the first thirteen years of my life, I was one of the taller kids in my class. Then in eighth grade, I stopped growing. My peers surpassed me on the height axis until I was the shortest in class, but in my mind, I was still a giant among teenagers. I even thought that, just maybe, the NBA was in my future.

When freshman year of high school began, a notice went up at George Washington High School: There were going to be tryouts for the varsity basketball team on Wednesday at six in the morning. There was nothing I wanted more than to play varsity basketball and get my career started.

Though my mom had signed me up for practically every team in a thirty-mile radius, she didn't actually care about sports. She just cared about keeping me off the streets and on her schedule. In those days, that schedule included taking the school bus, which didn't pick me up early enough in the morning to get to tryouts.

"You're not leaving the house at that hour to make any tryouts," she informed me. "You'd have to catch public transportation. It's not safe that early. You're not doing it."

I don't think I'd ever been as mad at her as I was that day. I loved basketball too much to miss my one shot at making the varsity team. So I devised a plan.

I studied the bus schedule and determined that the best bus to take was at 4:07 a.m. Then, the night before tryouts, I crept around the house while my mom was sleeping and meticulously set every clock forward by two hours. If there was something that had a time on it, from the VCR to her watch, I set it forward.

At four in the morning, her alarm clock clicked over to 6:00 a.m. and started buzzing. I was already awake and ready to sprint to the bus stop.

"Okay, Mom, I'm going to school." I stepped into my sneakers and stuffed my homework into my book bag. Then I got to that bus stop, made it to tryouts, and gave it my all.

By third period, I was feeling pretty proud of myself for pulling this off. I was joking with a friend in history class, waiting for the teacher to enter the room, when I noticed a familiar head on the other side of the glass panel in the classroom door.

It was *her*.

There is no fear like the terror I had of my mom in that moment.

As I sat there, with my heart clenched and my mouth suddenly dry, the door opened. The principal entered, with my mom right behind him.

"Kevin," he said. "Your mom is here to pick you up."

My classmates were instantly jealous. They thought I was getting to leave school early. As I weaved between desks, they all said goodbye and patted me on the back like I was the man. Meanwhile, I was trying not to shit my pants.

With every step I took toward that door, I saw my mom's control over her rage slip. By the time I was two paces from the door, she had her belt off. My whole body trembled as I took the next step. Suddenly—*thwack! Thwack! THWACK!*—she started beating my ass in front of the whole class.

The kids who had been jealous just a moment before started laughing and making fun of me. I cried up a storm as she whupped me out the door and into the hallway. She was such a high level of pissed off, even the principal was trying to get her to stop.

He didn't succeed. My mom beat me all the way out of the building and to the bus stop. Then she calmed down for a moment. But taking a break gave her an opportunity to think again about what I'd done, and a minute later, she had that belt whistling through the air again.

"Had me at work two damn hours early!" *THWACK! THWACK!* "Wasn't a goddamn soul in sight!" *THWACK!* **THWACK!**

(Up to that point, the worst beating I'd gotten was a few years earlier, after my first and last time shoplifting. I'd taken a pack of Starbursts from a store, because all the kids were eating them and I wanted to know what they tasted like. She caught me trying to open one on the train and smacked the hell out of me. Then she made me go back to the store, return the Starbursts, and apologize, as she whacked me the whole time. The fucked-up thing about it is I never got to taste a Starburst.)

When the bus finally arrived, she had to pause for a second to pay the fare. Then she found a reason to get mad at me again. "Sit down!" Before my butt even landed on the seat, she hit me again and yelled, "I said sit!"

Any excuse there was to hit me, she found it that day. "Don't you look at me like that!" *Thwack!* "Stop crying, boy!" *THWACK!* "I said STOP CRYING!"

My dad, despite all the violence I witnessed around him, only hit me one time. And even then, all he did was put his hand on the top of my head and smack his hand. With my mom, on this particular day, it got to the point where she was slapping the shit out of me over things that were out of my control. When we were close to our stop, we got up and walked to the doors. The bus braked and I stood on the steps, waiting for the doors to open. All of a sudden, behind me, she boomed, "Get off the bus!" *THWACK! THWACK!* The doors weren't even open yet.

I was grounded for three months after that. Since I'd pretty much been grounded my whole life anyway, I couldn't really complain. Especially since I made the team.

16

BECOMING ELITE

Never quit. That was the message that our varsity basketball coach, Calvin Jones, constantly drilled into our heads. He never got angry and yelled at us like other coaches did. Instead, he related to us and cared for us, and he became a mentor to me and many of the other guys.

My goal on the team was to be part of the starting lineup, but there were several players who were much better than me. Coach Jones would constantly tell me not to be comfortable sitting on the bench. But he also refused to let me start out of pity. Instead, he tried to instill in me the will to do better, the will to win, and the will to work hard for all of it.

It was effective, at least as far as basketball was concerned. When my mom brought me to work with her on the weekends, I'd go to the UPenn gym and play until she came to get me at five o'clock. All that basketball and swimming—playing in different leagues and gyms, meeting kids of all races and backgrounds, and traveling to so many different places in the state to compete—probably taught me how to communicate, understand, and get along with all different kinds of people.

However, the more I got into basketball, the less excited I got about swim team. Not only had my mom been making me do it for the last five years, but, in her tireless effort to keep me busy, when they offered a lifeguarding course, she signed me up for that too. I hated swimming, and I decided to stop trying.

It was a serious team, which was later the subject of a film, *Pride,* along with our coach, Jim Ellis. According to him, we were the first black swim team in our league to compete nationally. My teammates were very competitive and were not only winning medals, but getting As and Bs in school.

Meanwhile, I was just barely passing classes. My academic philosophy was that less is best; my job was to show up and not fail. So I started applying the same philosophy to swimming: I was there to move my arms and legs in the water and get by. At meets, I'd be the last one flailing in the pool. I'd get out, and no one would care. They'd just be waiting for me to finish so they could start the next race.

Of course, my mom responded to this minor act of rebellion perfectly.

"You wanna go and not try, that's on you," she said after another one of my shitty meets. "But you're still gonna go. So you can swim and be good or you can swim and not be good. But either way, you're still gonna be swimming."

I stuck with my plan. Around the pool, they had team pictures from different competitions. There were kids diving off starting blocks, holding up gold medals, and celebrating victories. I'd been on the team longer than most of the other kids, and there was just one photo of me, crouching by the side of the pool and adjusting my goggles. I looked awkward and suspicious, like I was cheating by slipping some kind of chemical in my goggles. Everyone used to joke about that picture. I was the joke of the team.

After a while, I started to realize that I wasn't hurting my mom by not trying. I was only hurting myself. Everything she did always put me in a position to recognize that.

The feeling of being left out—of watching everyone else celebrate and talk about winning—began to outweigh whatever little satisfaction I took in sucking. So I decided to start trying to become a better swimmer and earn some of those gold medals.

Unfortunately, that backfired too. By the end of the season, I started winning races, and my coaches saw potential in me. They moved me up to the highest level they had: the Elites. And now, instead of practicing once a day, I was practicing twice a day because these Elite motherfuckers were going after college scholarships and training for the Junior Olympics.

It was too much swimming. By trying to get out of it, I ended up having to do twice as much of it. Maybe that's another reason I so rarely rebelled against my mom: After every battle for freedom, I somehow ended up with less of it.

17

GETTING HARD

My mom's plan of keeping me busy eventually backfired in a way she never expected: All those extracurricular athletics made me strong.

Eventually, her beatings didn't hurt anymore. I stopped crying like I used to. The whuppings became more about her—to help her feel as if she was doing her job as parent and disciplinarian. Meanwhile, I was starting to have angry outbursts and explosions of temper. I wasn't a little boy anymore, and the degree of restriction she imposed wasn't healthy for a teenager. I had friends on the swim team who were leading responsible lives without parental discipline, and it was time for my mom to let go a little as well.

For the most part, I'd lived by her rules and hadn't joined a gang or snatched purses. So I began to advocate for my freedom, telling my mom whenever I could that she needed to start relaxing, that I could stay out of trouble without her help, that I could take care of myself.

She didn't take too kindly to my parenting advice. So when she whupped me or yelled at me, I'd wait a few days until it blew over, then readdress why going in a different direction might be more beneficial for both of us.

Usually, this only set her off again. One day, she was whupping my ass for having the nerve to tell her how to be a parent. When she got tired from hitting me and paused to catch her breath, I said, "You had enough?"

I couldn't believe the words that had just come out of my mouth. They signified that something was new, something had changed—the power dynamic was shifting. I knew it. She knew it. And it pissed her off.

"Oh, you wanna be a smart-ass?" She gasped the words between huffs and puffs as she mustered the strength to hit me even harder. She didn't want to show weakness.

A few days later, I complained again about her strict schedule, and she raised her fist and punched me in the arm. Her knuckles cracked against my tricep. When I walked away, I saw her shaking her hand in pain. That's when the beatings stopped.

She continued to give me verbal beatings, but she knew that short of stabbing, shooting, or Mace-ing me, there was nothing she could physically do anymore to harm me. "As long as you're under my roof, you're under my rules," she reminded me the next time she got upset at me.

"Well, I'm gonna get out from under this roof as soon as I can," I shot back.

She then made a promise that I held on to like a gold bar for the rest of high school: "When you're eighteen and you graduate high school, you can do whatever you want."

"Great!"

"But if you're still living under my roof at that time, you're gonna be going to college. You're not gonna be doing nothing in my house."

After that, she started to loosen her controls little by little. I knew that each new freedom was a test, and I'd pass it by showing respect for her rules and gratitude for her leniency. Even though some of these freedoms seemed huge to me at the time, they were more like quarter turns of a screw. Instead of picking me up at Ms. Davis's house, for example, she'd call when she was leaving work and let me walk home on my own to meet her.

When she let me go to a friend's birthday party one Saturday night, I felt like a prisoner being allowed into the sunshine for the first time in fifteen years. And I made damn sure to get back home on time. I knew if I was late, it might not happen again.

18

MY POWERS OF OBSERVATION AMAZE EVEN ME

Then, one day, we got robbed.

The weekend before, my mom and I had been out doing something very rare: shopping for school clothes. She took me to Burlington Coat Factory and Marshalls to get discounted jeans, shirts, and sweaters. She even got me my first semi-cool pair of shoes: Eastlands, brown leather boots with nice stitching that everyone was wearing in school. It was one of the greatest days of my teenage life.

That Monday, I left Ms. Davis's house as usual and walked home. As I was climbing the thirty-one steps, I looked at our door, and it looked back at me. Something seemed off. It was the hinges! They'd been removed. I screamed, "Oh, shit!" I looked around. No one was in sight.

I pulled open the door. Actually, I sort of pulled and lifted; it was more of an obstacle now than a door. I stuck my head in and yelled, "Mom!" Now, I knew my mom wasn't there, but I figured that would scare the thieves and murderers that I was sure had invaded my house.

After all, nothing scares a grown-ass man more than someone yelling "Mom!" in a whiny voice.

I walked inside, still yelling "Mom!" That was my weapon. *I don't need no gun. I got my mom.*

That was when it dawned on me that the apartment only had one door, so where were these criminals gonna run if they heard me and panicked? Straight at me. I stopped yelling.

This plan wasn't really well thought out. But you don't plan for these things. They just happen.

So I'm walking inside now, slowly, scanning for anything suspicious or out of place. Scanning, searching, examining. The hallway looked like it always looked. No one had taken the ceiling or made the walls wider. I don't know what the fuck I was expecting to see in the hallway.

I kept walking, scanning, examining. And then I backtracked and saw it: the stove. There was a pot of half-eaten grits on the stove. I knew it wasn't my mom's, because no one leaves a dirty dish in her kitchen. It was now pretty clear what had happened: Someone had broken into my house and cooked grits. I had a cook-and-run situation on my hands.

Suddenly, a new and bigger fear raced through my mind: This sneaky cooking motherfucker could have taken my new Eastlands too. That would be the equivalent today of someone breaking into my house and stealing half a million dollars' worth of jewelry, which actually happened. Honestly, it would be worse—at least the jewelry was insured. My Eastlands weren't, and I was convinced my previous lack of Eastlands was all that had separated me from every girl I liked in school.

I ran to the back room, my heart pounding. There they were: my precious Eastlands. I picked them up, just in case someone was hiding and waiting until I left to snatch them. Then I entered my mom's room.

Her middle drawer was open, and her stockings, underwear, and bras were on the floor and clearly tampered with. Now I had more than a cook-and-run situation on my hands. I had a situation on my hands that . . . I didn't even want to think about. That's not shit I ever want to think about.

I suddenly remembered that she hid her money in that drawer. So someone had taken our door off the hinges, entered my mom's bedroom, opened the exact drawer where she kept her money, snatched it, and then cooked grits in the kitchen.

At least whoever committed this heinous act knew nothing about shoes.

Shit, what if they got my new shirts?

I ran back to check. My school clothes were still there, so I stuffed them into my book bag just in case the thieves came back for them, because of course that must have been their real objective, before they got too hungry to see it through. I ran back to Ms. Davis's house and asked if I could use the phone.

Once I got my mom on the line, I broke the news, "I think we've been robbed."

To this day, I still don't know why I used the words "I think."

I don't know why I ran back to my babysitter's house either, rather than just use the phone at home.

And I don't know why I asked my mom to pick me up instead of meeting her in front of our house.

I don't know why I did a lot of things.

This was all new to me, okay? It was my first time being robbed. No one gets robbed perfectly the first time. It takes experience to get good at it: to not touch stuff and dust for fingerprints and bring in tracker dogs and do DNA tests on the grits and all the shit that championship-level victims do.

"It was your father." Those were the first words my mom said when she came to get me. She had stopped by the house first. "I got something for his ass." She balled up her fist, her face filled with a level of fury I hadn't seen since I'd set the clocks back.

She noticed me hugging my bursting-full book bag to my chest like my life depended on it and gave me a sympathetic smile. "Oh, honey, no one's gonna wanna steal that stuff."

She knew everything. That's how good she was.

"How do you know it was Dad?" I was still imagining a cabal of criminals that had followed us home from Burlington Coat Factory.

"That fool went straight for the middle drawer. Nobody else knows about that but you, me, your brother, and your father. So who else was it? Your brother's in Hawaii."

"Okay."

"People don't just rob you and cook. You bet your ass it was your father. His favorite damn food is grits."

She vented on the whole walk home. But I had my Eastlands. I had my new shirts. I had my new jeans. Everything had turned out fine.

I called my dad the next day. This was the entirety of the conversation:

Me: Mom said you robbed us.

Dad: She don't know what she's talking about, boy. Let me call you back.

A small part of me believed him, because I didn't think it was possible for my own father to do something so low. I didn't hear from him again until he called three weeks later. "Where you at, Dad?" I asked. "When are you coming to visit me?"

"Oh, you know I want to see you, son. I just got a lot going on right now. I'll see you in a couple weeks. Don't you forget about your dad now, you hear?"

A couple of weeks passed, and I didn't see him. He just called to check in on me and promised to see me again. This happened over and over, until he stopped calling.

Then one afternoon, I finally saw him. I was sitting on the train, and my dad walked through the door at the end of the car. I exclaimed, "Dad?!"

He looked me dead in the eye, then turned around and ran back into the car he came from. I sat there, confused. That night, I wrote my brother a letter. "I think I saw Dad on the train, and he ran away from me."

Two weeks later, I received my brother's reply: "Dude, don't worry about it. Dad's on drugs. He's not thinking right. He didn't mean anything by it."

Huh? I felt dizzy and sick to my stomach. At a family party that night, I asked our relatives and friends about my brother's accusation. Evidently, everyone in the world knew this piece of information but me.

The World: Hey, man, it's true. Your dad's on drugs.

Me: Why didn't anyone tell me?

The World: We're telling you now. He's on drugs, real bad.

Me: Don't you think that's something I should have known?

The World: Just don't give him no money, cause if you do, it's going to drugs.

Me: Did you know Dad was on drugs, Mom?

Mom: Yeah, I knew.

Me: Aunt Patsy?

Aunt Patsy: Yeah, everybody knows. Now you know too. So don't give him anything.

Me: Okay.

As usual, I shoulder-shrugged it. But years later, I had an opportunity to speak with him again about robbing us. The conversation went like this . . .

19

TRUTH, JUSTICE, AND THE HART WAY

THE TIME: *The present, Father's Day*

THE PLACE: *Orlando, Florida, vacation rental home*

THE SIZE: *20,300 square feet bigger than my childhood home*

Writer: Maybe you can help solve a mystery. Did you ever break into your son's home and take stuff?

Dad: No.

Kevin: If my mom were here, she would argue this man down right now.

Dad: Nah, I didn't do that.

Kevin: I'll never forget it. She said, "It was your father."

Dad: Listen, here's the thing: With Nance, anything that was wrong was *always* me.

Kevin: All arrows pointed to you on that one. Who else is gonna come into the house and cook your favorite food?

Dad: Listen, there's nothing I won't admit, because back then it wasn't me, it was that demon. So if I did something, I'd tell you. But ain't nobody gonna beat my butt over something I didn't do.

Kevin: Come on, Dad.

Dad: I ain't do it. The only thing I ever did was back before, with your brother. I brought him home one time and your mom wasn't there. I wasn't gonna leave him in the hall, so I went ahead and took the door off the hinges to let him in.

Kevin: (*To writer.*) See, he used the same method of getting in. Let me tell you something about my dad. He'll give you every hero story in the world, but we all know the reality of it.

Dad: Boy, you think people gonna pay you for talking about me like this? Knock yourself out. Ain't nothing wrong with my self-esteem.

Kevin: . . .

Dad: Let me tell you something about this boy here. Nancy sheltered him and his brother. And I understand that. That's part of a mother's love. Me, I knew that I had to get them out in the streets. So they gonna get robbed, they might get beat up, whatever. I wanted them to be exposed—give them some survival skills. That's what I did. And in doing that, they saw some stuff.

Kevin: Oh, we saw some stuff all right.

Dad: Not enough stuff.

20

FREAKY TALES

Everyone was talking about sex in the gym locker room.

They'd done it in the car with this girl, at this other girl's house when her parents were out, with this one girl during a movie.

After a while, I couldn't contain myself: "Wait a minute—hold on. Huh? Everybody here done this? I'm the only one who hasn't?"

I was a sophomore, and it was time to figure out this whole sex thing. I didn't want to be the only virgin in high school.

One of my close friends on the basketball team was named Khalil. He was a year older than me, a great player, and, most importantly, popular with the girls. Because I was hanging out with him, other kids thought that I might possibly be cool. And I began to believe that if he was popular with girls, then I could be too.

To make that happen, however, I first had to do the one thing that every human being must do at some point in their lives, otherwise they haven't really lived: accept myself.

I was short. I wasn't good-looking. I didn't have nice clothes, I didn't have new sneakers. I was a mama's boy—and my haircuts were pretty damn bad. These were facts: Anyone could see them. There was no point in hiding any of it or pretending otherwise. So I made the decision to be comfortable with it.

As the little guy, you have a choice to make if you want to be popular: You can be the tough guy and overcompensate for your mini-me self or you can be the funny guy and accept your size. An added incentive for choosing the latter is that it's hard for someone to punch you while they're laughing.

I chose to be the funny guy. Having nothing to prove is the most freeing thing in the world. Rather than constantly defending your ego, you can have a sense of humor about your shortcomings.

I was able to make this choice because of my ability to shoulder-shrug things. Because shoulder-shrugging is different than not caring: It's having perspective. It's looking at a bigger picture instead of being reactive. By having that outlook, I was eventually able to understand that if someone was making fun of my height or clothing, they weren't making fun of who I was.

Was what they were saying true? Yes.

Did it make me inadequate as a human being? No.

Did it really matter then? Hell no.

And with that realization, I could laugh at myself too.

Most of the star athletes in school had no personality. Hanging out with them wasn't a good time. Because I didn't take myself and life so seriously, girls started to hang around me more. And that's when I realized: The fun guy always wins.

This is because no matter where you are or what you're doing, if you're with the fun guy, you're gonna have a good time. You could be sitting in an empty room watching television with the fun guy, and it could be one of the best nights of your life. You could go out for a cup of coffee with the fun guy and end up laughing more in one hour than you have all year. Even if you're doing your laundry with the fun guy, you're gonna have a great time because he knows the secret to life.

You want to know what that secret is? It's two words: *Have fun.*

You can close this book now. Thank you for reading. Good night.

Or you can wait a little to find out how I lost my virginity, because otherwise a couple of weeks from now, there may be a knock on your door, and a man in a suit may be standing there and saying: "For one million dollars, tell me how Kevin Hart lost his virginity"—and you will not know the answer.

It would be a shame to lose that much money just because you decided not to finish a book.

Besides, I lost my virginity twice.

Her name was Angie. We didn't go to the same school, but she lived in the neighborhood. One day we were in the backyard at Ms. Davis's house, and we got to messing around. It was cold outside, and we were both wearing coats. She told me to lie down, and I lowered my pants a little so she could sit on me.

"Is it in?" she asked.

I had no idea whether it was in or what it was supposed to feel like. It was cold, and we were wearing tons of clothes, and I couldn't feel a thing. "I don't know. Is it?"

"I think so," she replied.

"Okay."

We sat there for a few minutes without moving. Then she stood up, and it was over.

I looked down and thought, *Well, my dick is kinda wet, and I didn't pee on myself, so something must have happened. I guess I got my dick wet.*

I stood up and asked, "Are we friends?"

"Yeah, we friends."

Afterward, I was totally confused. *Did we just have sex? Is that what sex is like? I must have missed something because it wasn't all that great.*

I saw Angie two weeks later, and we did it in the backyard with our coats on again. This time, I made sure it went in. I must have felt it twenty times just to confirm this fact. I even moved around, because friends said that's what you were supposed to do, and maybe it didn't count if you weren't moving around.

The first time, I couldn't tell whether we did it or not. This time, I was certain we did it. So I double lost my virginity. I *had* to lose it twice, just to make sure.

Not long after that, word about her being with different guys got out in the neighborhood, and people started to say mean stuff about Angie. She always liked me because I never spoke about our business or said anything hurtful about her.

People do a lot of things to make life hard for themselves, but one of the stupidest is guys who desperately want sex talking shit about the women most likely to give it to them.

Not long afterward, I discovered that a couple of girls in school actually liked me, which of course always makes more girls like you because it puts you in the category of Guys It's Okay to Like. Next, I found out that I was one of the guys who girls were passing notes about and talking in the bathroom about.

It took me a while to comprehend that even though I wasn't tall or good-looking, women were still attracted to me. And that little boost of confidence actually made me get better looking. I held my head up a little higher; pushed my chest out a little more; became a little less anxious and a little more self-assured.

Fortunately, around the same time all this was happening, my mom made a big change in my life. Because I had been respectful and obedient with the small windows of freedom she'd given me, she decided that, at age sixteen, I didn't need a babysitter anymore. I no longer had to go to old Ms. Davis's house after school. I could come home on my own. Sometimes, I'd have three hours alone at home, and this allowed me to invite company over after school and get myself situated to do the do.

My move was to sit on the bed with a girl and say, "Let me give you a massage." If I felt she wasn't ready yet, we'd watch a movie, which I hoped not to finish. I was consistent. It was the same moves every time.

However, it wasn't just about the sex. I usually liked her and hung out with her afterward and kept seeing her. If it ended, it was always because she got tired of me and wanted to move on. I was never the type of guy who got angry or upset about a breakup. *This is all part of the plan*, I'd think. *Let's see what happens next.*

21

A HART FAMILY REUNION

While my brother was in the Army in Oklahoma, something went wrong. During a drill, artillery fire accidentally overshot a target and hit a formation of soldiers. Three people were killed and twenty-three were injured.

That was the moment when I learned that love is stronger than anger, that family is stronger than stubbornness. Because my family came back together. My mom saw the article about it, and, for the first time since he left, picked up the phone and called my brother.

They didn't speak a lot after that, but when my brother called to tell her that she was about to become a grandmother, their relationship fully resumed. My brother had met a single mother in Hawaii and grown close to both her and her daughter. He'd become a father of sorts to the daughter, and had gotten her mother pregnant and was about to marry her.

He flew us out there for the birth of his daughter. It had been just me and my mom for so long, the two of us against the world, and now here we were, the five of us (including my brother's new wife and stepdaughter) celebrating the arrival of a sixth. After hanging out with my brother as he showed me around Oahu and took me to basketball games, plus becoming an uncle all of a sudden, I felt like my small world had expanded a little.

Eventually, my brother moved back to Philly with his wife, daughter, and stepdaughter. He had left a juvenile delinquent and returned a responsible man. The military and fatherhood had changed him. He got an apartment, found work cutting hair, and started saving to open his own barbershop. In the meantime, he found our dad and started working to build a relationship with him. He'd known our father in the good days, before the crack, when Dad was buying presents with money he'd legitimately worked for. To him, Dad was Superman, until he found his kryptonite.

When my brother saved enough money, he rented a storefront and started setting up his barbershop. My dad needed money, and he'd been a carpenter and electrician before, so Kenneth hired him to do the electrical work and remove one of the walls.

I'd drop by on weekends and see my brother and father working together. My brother was grateful for all the help Dad was providing, but more importantly, he was excited to be close to him again. The family was coming back together. My dad looked ragged and weak, but the work seemed to be making an honest man out of him. As a bonus for me, once my brother started serving customers, I wouldn't have to get haircuts from my mom anymore.

Then, three days before my brother's barbershop was set to open, I stopped by—and it looked like I'd gone back in time by a month. The place was empty. My brother was pacing back and forth, out-of-his-mind hysterical. "Dad had to fucking do this," he fumed. "He had to!"

"Do what?"

As I looked around, it dawned on me. My brother didn't have to say anything else. My dad had stolen everything, from the smallest set of clippers to the biggest floor hairdryers. Everything.

We knew it was him because he hadn't shown up to work that day and wasn't answering his phone. He'd disappeared.

"I know where to find him," Kenneth said. There was an area known as the Badlands where junkies and crackheads went to score and get high.

We ran around the corner to get into my brother's car. It was a Pontiac, but my brother called it "the Ac" because he wanted everyone to think it was an Acura.

However, the Ac was gone. Dad had stolen the car too.

We asked some of the employees hanging around the shop to give us a ride to the Badlands, but we got the same reaction from everyone: "I'm not fucking going down there, man. Spoon *crazy*."

Finally, a friend of my brother's named Phil agreed to drive us. We got into his car and sped to Second Street. The whole time, my brother was freaking out. One minute he'd be convincing himself it wasn't Dad, that maybe we were wrong and jumping to conclusions. The next minute, he was fuming: "I give him a chance, I give him a job, and he steals *everything* from me. How could he do this?"

"What are you gonna do when you find him?" I asked. I was worried about both of them.

"Look, it's just about getting confirmation that it's really him, finding the stuff, and getting it back."

We drove around the area until my brother spotted the Ac parked on a side street, with two people in the backseat. I'll never forget the pain that shot through my brother's face in that moment. Some part of him—that little boy who'd looked up to his dad—died.

My brother got out of the car and walked up to the Ac. My dad was in the backseat with a woman, and they were high as fuck.

Kenneth was crushed on a deep soul level. "What the hell?" he exclaimed through the window.

My dad opened the door, told the woman, "Stay right here, bitch," and then turned to my brother. We wondered if he was going to beg for forgiveness or deny everything. He did neither.

"It's about time you showed the fuck up," he said, as if he were angry at my brother.

This time, it was my brother's turn to say, "What?!"

"This raggedy-ass car of yours done ran out of gas." He then jumped out of the car, slammed the keys down on the roof, and started to walk away.

"Where's all my stuff?" my brother called after him, in disbelief.

"I ain't got your stuff," Dad replied, without turning back. "Your stuff's gone."

And he kept on walking.

My brother was hurt, he was angry, he was ashamed. But he wasn't crazy, so he didn't go after Dad. As he told me later, "He's the same motherfucker who sicced a dog on me over a basketball game, so I had no doubt he'd stab me over this situation."

As we sat in the car afterward in shock, my brother saw someone running across the street with a blow dryer from the shop.

My brother had a hard time accepting what had happened to him. Like my mom, he had learned to hold grudges, and it was years before he was willing to let go of that anger and speak to Dad again. That was understandable: It was one thing for my dad to "allegedly" steal from Mom, who was struggling to make ends meet and take care of their youngest son, but this wasn't just money he took from his son, this was his son's *dream*.

That's the power of addiction. It is stronger than family, honor, and morality.

Dad disappeared after that, and my brother managed to get back on his feet despite the betrayal. He called in every favor he'd ever been owed, got his employees to agree to defer pay, borrowed money, and got his barbershop open a couple of weeks later.

Meanwhile, I was a senior in high school, and I thought I was outgrowing the need for parenting. I felt like I was getting strong and confident enough to carry the world on my shoulders.

Unfortunately, the world turned out to be a little heavier than I thought.

22

INSIDE THE MIND OF A SUPER-GENIUS

A
B
A
C
A
D

That was my plan, because everyone knows that repeating this pattern of answers will hack any multiple-choice test.

This test happened to be the SAT.

It was pretty important. It was going to determine my future, so I didn't want to take any chances. That's why I didn't study. I was going to ace this test with cleverness: stay one step ahead, take the shortcut to success. Hard work was for basketball. In academics, less was best.

Besides, I had more important things to do: The SAT was happening at eleven in the morning, and my friends from swim team were going to Six Flags amusement park at noon. It was a three-hour test, so I had to somehow finish it in less than an hour if I wanted to ride the Batman roller coaster.

I wasn't concerned with college anyway. Turning eighteen, graduating, and being free—those were the things that concerned me. I could have gone to UPenn on a scholarship—my mom was now a computer analyst with her own office there—but I told her I wasn't interested.

"I ain't going there. I'll be eighteen. I can do what I want, like you said!"

"It's an Ivy League school. You can go there and get hired for any job you want afterward."

"I get it, but I don't even know if college is for me, Mom."

The last thing I wanted was four more years of being under Mom's supervision at home *and* at school.

"So what are you gonna do, Kev?"

"Something else."

"Like what?"

"I'll figure it out on my own."

I didn't have the heart to say it, but in that very conversation I had fulfilled my childhood dream: to be able to finally tell Mom "I'm grown; I ain't doing that." Those six words were the sum total of my ambition. If there was anything she wanted me to do after graduation, it wasn't going to happen, simply because she wanted me to do it.

So I sat in the testing room of George Washington High School in Philadelphia with my trusty #2 pencil and I whipped through that test. I only opened the booklet for show.

Twenty minutes after the test began, I stood up, handed in my answer sheet, and walked out of that room, to the amazement of my classmates.

In fact, I didn't just walk. I strutted. I felt good about it. At Six Flags, I bragged to my friends about how good I did on that test. They were serious about getting into good colleges and had already taken the SAT, so they were excited for me.

When I returned home, my mom asked me how I did. "Great!" I told her. "I know it."

"That's good," she said, and meant it.

It turned out that I nailed it: 790 verbal and 780 math. I was going to Harvard!

Actually, that's not what happened. If you believe that, then you probably have a gambling problem. My odds of doing well on that test with that stupid system were abysmal.

I got something like 400 in verbal and 350 in math. That's not much better than what someone gets for just putting their name on the paper.

My mom was disgusted with me. "You said you got this, but you didn't even try!" she scolded. "You know how hard I work to get you the best life and the best opportunities. And you're taking them for granted! I'm disappointed in you. You're better than this."

Her reaction hurt me more than the test results. She'd sacrificed so much for me, and I'd repaid her with apathy, cockiness, and ingratitude. There was no way to think or talk or joke myself out of this. I'd fucked up.

As the months passed, I looked around and so many kids my age, especially on the swim team, were celebrating their success. They'd gotten combined scores as high as 1500. They were stoked that their top-choice colleges would be getting these test results.

Me: What do you mean your colleges are getting these scores?

Teammates: The colleges we applied to—they get the scores directly.

Me: You applied to colleges?

Teammates: Yeah, months ago. Didn't you apply anywhere?

Me: Shit, I didn't know the deadline already passed. You think I shoulda done it?

Teammates: Don't worry about it.

Me: Why, can't I late apply or something?

Teammates: No, but it doesn't matter. With your scores, no one's gonna accept you anyway.

As graduation drew closer, and my teammates started getting college acceptance letters, I felt lower and lower. When family members asked what my plan was for after graduation, I couldn't answer them. My entire plan had been just to be free of my mother's rules.

I had no plans beyond that. I hadn't sent out a single college application. I bullshitted my way through the SAT. I'd never really considered the future.

Now I didn't have one.

The lesson that I drew from this at the time was that I should have tried harder. I should have taken school more seriously; I should have had a plan like everyone else. I still feel that way. But there's an additional lesson that I get from it now: It's never too late to start caring.

My future was out there. It was just waiting for me to find it. And the challenge was not to give up on myself just because it seemed like everyone else was pulling ahead of me—and leaving me further and further behind in the months that followed. That's the test that each of us faces in life:

Can you fail and still be strong?

Can you not fit in and still accept yourself?

Can you lose everything and still keep searching?

Can you be in the dark and still believe in the light?

Because no matter how low you go and how lost you feel, there is always tomorrow. And tomorrow just may be the day when you get lifted up and find your way.

There is just one thing that tomorrow demands of you to make this happen: that you never stop believing in your power to create a better day. This way, when your best possible future comes looking for you—almost always at a time and in a place you least expect it—you will be able to recognize its face and respond to its call.

I know this to be true, because although I never saw it coming—even when it came—it's exactly what happened to me.

Life Lessons

FROM WORK

*People with calluses work hard, but some people
with soft hands work even harder because
they got themselves to a level where they can
take care of their hands.*

Employee of the Month

This certificate is presented to:

Kevin Hart

For their outstanding performance during the month of:

April

Presented by:

Overachieving again

23

THE GREATEST ATTENDER
OF ALL TIME

You never know your level of underachieving until you see what overachieving looks like.

When you're a teenager, the best place to see this is at graduation, when the same name is announced over and over:

And the valedictorian is . . . Doug Wallace. And the most valuable player is . . . Doug Wallace. And the most likely to succeed is . . . Doug Wallace.

Each time, everyone in the audience, especially Mr. and Mrs. Wallace, thinks, *Goddamn, that Doug, he's gonna make something of himself!*

This was my experience sitting at our swim team graduation banquet. Though there were other underachievers like myself in school, the kids on swim team were superstars. Some were getting full-ride scholarships and going to places like Spelman College, the University of Maryland, even Harvard; others were planning to train for the Olympics. There were so many overachievers around me, and they were getting up and receiving plaques, trophies, and awards to consistent applause. The hard work I'd seen them put in was paying off.

But every dog has his day, and mine came when I finally got my award that night. It was the honor I deserved: for best attendance. My mom had been so strict that she never let me miss a day of practice.

I think it was called the Participant Award, and it wasn't even a trophy. It was a certificate. Everyone knew it was the lamest award of the night.

When they called out "Kevin Hart" from the stage, there was a sympathetic smattering of applause. I stepped up to the podium and placed one hand on the microphone. Every other kid who'd spoken had written his speech on a piece of paper or an index card. Now I was on stage—for the first time in my life—with no paper, no index card, no preparation, and no clue what to say.

"Hello—I'm Nancy's son," I began, "though a lot of y'all know me as 'the cheater.'"

The room burst into laughter. Everyone there knew, and had probably made fun of, that photo on the pool building's wall of me adjusting my goggles.

"But I would like to say for the record tonight that I never cheated. Otherwise, how would it be possible for me to go to more swim practices than anyone else here, yet not get a single award for my swimming?"

I heard people laughing, clapping their hands, slapping their knees.

"Best Participant? That's like getting an award for being the team's Best Kevin. It's not an accomplishment or a talent; it's something that my mom decided. She should be up here getting this award. Mom, come on up! I hope this was worth all those whuppings."

It felt as if something unlocked in me. I'd known that I was the fun guy who helped people lighten up and feel good. But I'd never known it was possible to do the same thing outside of a conversation and light up a whole room.

On some level, my smart-assery on stage was also fueled by my disappointment in myself, and I was trying to make the best out of a bad thing. So I just kept going. I started doing an impression of Coach Ellis, then the other coaches, then the most loved swimmers on the team.

Most of all, I made fun of myself—for being on that team for nearly ten years and getting the most pathetic award of the night, which I said I knew for a fact they gave me out of pity. After all, if they really liked me, they wouldn't have cropped me out of all the team photos. The best and the brightest had free-ride scholarships to the best universities, I went on, and all I had was a damn Best Participant certificate. "That's not even gonna get me a job at the Shell station."

I looked at my mom. She was shaking her head in shame. Yet I kept going—for a full fifteen minutes. I didn't know I was doing stand-up, but in retrospect, it was my first comedy set. And it killed. Even though I wasn't the star of the team, I was the star of the banquet.

Afterward, people kept coming up to the table where I was sitting with my mom, saying, "Great speech," and "Nance, that boy's funny," and "You got a real comedian on your hands."

Only when I look back on this now does it seem significant.

It was the only comedy show of mine that my mother ever attended. "It actually was a good speech," she admitted when the ceremony ended. But I didn't feel good. I was walking out of a room full of winners with a goddamn perfect attendance certificate in my hands.

That night felt like a farewell to my childhood. After nearly a decade, it was the end of swim team and the end of most of those friendships. I wouldn't be going to practice the next day or competing in a swim meet the next weekend. It was over.

I used to resent being forced to spend so much time swimming, but when I was hugging people goodbye that night, I was practically crying. I didn't understand that what I'd done that night could be a career. I just thought I had made a funny speech that compensated for the fact that, unlike everyone else there, I was going nowhere in life.

24

ANOTHER DAY IN THE LIFE OF A HERO

Graduating high school was one of the most schizophrenic days of my life.

"I'm fucking *free!*" I danced through the hallways. "Fuck school. Fuck swimming. Fuck everybody. Mom, kiss my ass, I ain't doing none of your shit no more!"

But when I left that building for the last time, reality dawned on me again and I thought, *Wait a minute. Where do I go? I still don't have a plan. And the SATs? I should have tried. Hold on a minute, you're all going away? And you all got a plan? Every single one of you?*

I woke up the next day with nothing to do and nowhere to go. All the structure and control that I hated so much was gone. I had total freedom—and it was terrifying. It felt like a giant sinkhole had opened beneath me and I was falling in. Everything had been for free, and I'd taken it all for granted and blown it off.

I spent the next few days lying around the house, watching television, hanging out with friends, and trying to think of a direction for my life. One afternoon, my mom came home from work and said that we needed to have a talk.

It turned out there was a plan, but it was something I'd forgotten. My mom said she was going to keep her end of a bargain we made a few years ago. All I remembered about the deal was that when I turned eighteen, I would be free. But there was another piece to it. "I'm not going to pay for you to live under my roof, and come and go as you please, and do nothing with your life," she lectured. "Like I said, you're going to find a college."

With her help, I registered for summer school at Community College of Philadelphia and picked my classes. Then I hastily put together a plan: get my scholastics together, take the SAT again, and go to Temple or another big college to play basketball. It felt like going backward, but it was a life lesson and a chance to start over.

Then she delivered the worst news of all: I'd need to get a job too.

There was only one job I was qualified for: lifeguarding. I went back to visit my swim team coaches, who had a list of the community pools in need of lifeguards. When they handed me the printout, there was only one pool on it: Belfield, which was more like a wet jail cell than a swimming pool.

It wasn't much of a job, since I was only working two or three days a week, but it was just enough to keep my mom happy. On my first day of work, I saw what looked like half the neighborhood crammed into a tiny pool. It was more people than should reasonably be in a pool, and definitely more than a young, inexperienced lifeguard could control.

On my second day, the pool was even more crowded, and I saw a little boy playing in the middle of everyone. He seemed excited, like he was having a good time in the midst of the chaos. As I sat there watching, one of the senior lifeguards jumped in the water, grabbed him, and brought him out onto the deck.

I jumped off my chair and ran to him as the other lifeguard was turning him over. The boy was on his back now and coughing. I stood there stupidly, trying to figure out if he was breathing or if I needed to give him CPR. Then I realized that if he was coughing, he must be breathing.

"Hart, you didn't see that?" the senior lifeguard shouted at me.

"Nope. No, I did not. I thought he was playing. I had no idea that he was serious."

People, before you judge, you need to know that it's not always possible to tell the difference between someone who's playing and someone who's panicking. They're both usually yelling. They're both waving their hands. They're both splashing around. And if they're surrounded by fifty other kids who are also yelling and waving their hands, it's like some *Where's Waldo?* shit, except harder because everyone's wearing swimsuits.

My point is: If you're planning to drown, tell somebody first.

My other point is: There were fifty motherfuckers standing around that kid, and they didn't notice either.

My real point is: I got fired.

The call the next morning went exactly like this: "No need to come to work. We don't think it's safe for you to be here." By that, they meant safe for *me*, not for the swimmers. Motherfuckers at that pool were mad.

Fortunately, basketball tryouts were coming up at community college, and that was what I really cared about. Maybe my playing could make up for my poor academics and I could go from here to the Temple Owls to the 76ers or something. That struck me as a good plan. And it would be easy to shine because the community college didn't have a big team: They probably played like three other schools.

So I showed up at tryouts, feeling overqualified.

And . . . I didn't make the team. *I didn't make the fucking team.* I didn't make this small-time community college basketball team.

It had never occurred to me that when I stopped growing during school, and everyone else kept growing, my basketball career was no longer on a growth trajectory either. My totally impractical and pretty vague but only plan for my life went up in smoke that day.

Meanwhile, classes were going horribly. In math, the teacher handed out a pop quiz. I was in no way or shape prepared for it. I thought you just had to study for the regular tests. The quiz may have been his way of checking to see how much we already knew, but whatever the case, I failed it. Probably got the lowest score in the class.

After I failed that test, didn't make the basketball team, and got fired from my first job, the terror really sank in. Up to that moment, I'd just made a mistake by not trying and not having a direction. Now I was putting in effort and planning for the future, and I still failed. This meant the problem wasn't my thinking: The problem was me. I wasn't good enough.

And on top of everything, I'd been going through a five-month dry spell.

25

CROSSING THE DESERT. OR IS IT THE DESSERT? I'LL JUST PUT BOTH IN HERE, SO I'M SAFE.

I applied myself to the one thing I could succeed in that summer: taking advantage of my mom's more relaxed regime. My friend Spank had been inviting me to a club called Dances, and finally, I was able to go with him.

I'd known Spank since high school, because he used to play basketball in our neighborhood. He was another friend with a plan. He was attending Temple University, but he'd stop by the community college to meet me all the time because he thought the community college had a better male-to-female ratio.

We started going to Dances and trying to meet girls; if nothing worked out, we'd end up at a twenty-four-hour McDonald's nearby. I spent a lot of nights at McDonald's. I was on a drought that felt like it would never end. No matter who I talked to in the club, she had no interest in me. It's one of the worst feelings in the world when you start to believe that the person you see in the mirror every day may not be attractive to anyone except your mama.

I couldn't afford to buy the designer clothes other guys were wearing, so I didn't even have a fighting chance. The best I could muster was a baggy food-stained sweater and baggier jeans, with dirt so deeply embedded in the denim that no detergent was strong enough to remove it.

Spank, on the other hand, was a big guy with a booming voice, a colossal personality, and enough money to buy himself a Guess denim jacket and matching jeans. He'd get on the dance floor, and women surrounded him. I'd try to dance my way in there, half swallowed up by my dirty clothes, and the next thing I knew, girls would be asking each other, "Y'all tired?"

I had the desert dick of a lifetime.

Until one night, I met someone who didn't excuse herself to go to the bathroom or run off to her friends after twenty seconds of talking to me. She was packed into a tight dress that showed off everything, but she was fun and loudmouthed like one of the guys. We laughed and snapped on each other the whole night, until finally she said, "We should hang out."

I'd been on such a losing streak that if she hadn't made the first move, I probably wouldn't have suggested it myself. "Where do you work?" I asked.

"I'm in school."

The next day, I ran into her at community college. We hung out in the cafeteria, laughing for hours. She was as witty as me, but much prettier. Soon, we were hanging out between classes, going to the movies, eating dessert at Dave & Buster's, and doing the corny shit you do when you're too scared to make a move because you don't want to lose the only female in your life with whom you have a chance.

"How long you gonna be her best friend?" Spank would ask me.

"I'm just taking it slow. I don't want to ruin it."

"Well, you better hurry before you get so thirsty you die of dehydration."

———

I was now in my third week of community college, and I just couldn't bring myself to crack open a textbook and care about these random subjects that had little to do with the real world. I felt like school, and this way of learning—cramming random knowledge into my head and then trying to retain it long enough to pass a test or two about it—wasn't for me.

Like most things I'd done in my life up to that point, I didn't think much about the decision that came next. Better to be happy, I figured, than successful or rich.

The next day, I left the house with my book bag just like every other day. But instead of going to school, I went to a clothing shop called Net and filled out a job application. Then I applied to work at a Ross Dress for Less store. I didn't tell my mom about my change of heart; I couldn't bear to see the disappointment in her eyes.

I had no work experience outside of those two disastrous days of lifeguarding, so I figured it would be a while before I got hired somewhere. But at my third stop, a City Sports on Walnut Street, I got lucky.

The manager was a woman named Brooke, and she asked why I wanted to work there. I knew that the words I spoke didn't matter. She was judging something deeper—my personality, my values, my character. Like anyone in her position, she was looking for someone who'd make her job easier, someone who was committed to the work and not just going to disappear into school in the fall. So I poured on the charming manipulation. "School isn't on the horizon for me, Brooke," I told her—with a laugh in my voice, but all the while thinking about how my mother would reach for the closest Hot Wheels track to whup me with if she heard that. "So I'm looking for a job where I can be for a while."

It worked, because she soon told me, "With your personality, I think you'd be a good fit in the sneaker department here." Then she gave me a pamphlet. "Memorize this," she instructed as I left. "You have a week to study it, and then you start training. You need to know these sneakers inside and out, because our customers expect us to be experts."

"Yeah, yeah, I got it, thank you, thank you. You won't regret this."

It was a miracle. Not only did I find a job quickly, but that store and the people there ended up changing my life. I might not be doing what I am today if I hadn't walked into that particular place on that particular street with the exact combination of people who worked there.

I was on such a high that night, I finally ended the drought: I slept with the girl I'd met at Dances. It was worth the wait. We'd spent so much time talking and getting to know each other that it wasn't just sex by that point. It felt like love, which was a scary thing.

Her name was Torrei. We would have an on-and-off, up-and-down, round-and-round relationship together for the next twelve years. And well before the end of this story, you're going to be scratching your head just like our friends and families did, wondering how—and more importantly, *why*—we put up with each other for that long. That first love casts a spell that's hard to break.

A few days after I was hired at City Sports, I broke the news to my mom. I knew her well enough to add just the right amount of optimism to the conversation.

"I told you, you're not gonna do nothing," she said, predictably, after I informed her that I was leaving community college.

That enabled me to respond: "I'm not doing nothing. I got a job. They hired me at City Sports."

She hesitated, trying to figure out how to get me back into school, and I continued. "I need more time to figure out what I really want to do, but in the meantime, I'll work."

I watched her chew this over in the steel teeth of her mind, until at last she spat out the one word I was hoping to hear: "Fine."

26

WARNING: THIS CHAPTER CONTAINS A TWELVE-LETTER WORD, SO YOU MAY ALSO NEED TO BE A GENIUS TO UNDERSTAND IT

A week later, I reported for work. "Did you study the pamphlet?" Brooke asked.

Once again, my aversion to studying had bitten me in the ass. "Inside and out," I replied. That was true: I'd spent a lot of time studying the *outside* of it, then put it *inside* a drawer.

After a short on-the-job training period, I received my first test: I was on the floor, and a customer was asking for a good running shoe. I had no fucking idea.

I looked around and grabbed a nice-looking sneaker.

He seemed surprised. "Really? That one?"

I committed. "It gives you great forefront protection and ankle support. You're gonna get a lot of mileage out of this one."

He picked it up and examined it.

"And it's built with Thinsulate for comfort, so it won't feel bulky on you."

I had no idea what I was saying, but I kept going—until, to my complete shock, he tried it on, thanked me, and bought a pair.

After that, I was on a roll. The next customer played tennis. "Oh, okay,

I got something for you. These are some of my best tennis sneakers. I like them because they're more flexible for those short sprints."

I just talked out of my ass, and people bought it. At the end of the day, they were happy customers, and that's what it was all about.

I didn't need to study that pamphlet. I didn't need to study anything again. I could bullshit and personality my way through all the footwear here.

Personality, man. It'll save your life.

After a few weeks of this, I started to think, *Damn, I'm actually pretty good at shoe sales. I could really shine in this space.* Then I thought, *How much better would I be if I actually took the time to learn about the sneakers, the verbiage, and how to spit the shoe talk?* That night, I surprised myself by opening my drawer, pulling out the pamphlet, and studying it.

One week later: "Sweetie, first of all, what do you do? Yeah, let me see your feet. Oh my God, amazing arches, with normal pronation—you're a lucky woman. And the good thing about that is you're protecting yourself from future shin splints. Let me get a shoe for you. It's got a nice EVA midsole for a softer run, plus a padded sock liner for extra comfort. With those beautiful feet of yours, it'll be like walking on air."

I thought I had done well when I was making it up. But now that I was starting to understand the merchandise and learn the differences between supinate and overpronate, compression molding and injection molding, ethylene-vinyl acetate and polyurethane foam, I was unstoppable.

It turned out that personality *plus* knowledge equaled success.

The store paid us hourly and only gave us a commission after we surpassed a certain number of sales. When I finally got that first commission check, I was hooked. I kept asking for more hours at the store. I was willing to work as much as they were willing to let me and to cover anyone's shift. I wanted to see how big I could get those checks to grow.

Thanks to my mom's training in keeping busy, working double shifts came naturally to me, even with the forty-minute commute each way. And this was better than all my past activities: Not only did I get a check for it, but the better I got at it, the more I was paid. It was instant gratification.

One of my supervisors was a woman named Alice. She was in her late twenties, with a close-cropped haircut like mine, and always dressed casually in sweatpants, a T-shirt, and whatever new sneaker was out that season.

She was the first out-of-the-closet lesbian I'd known, and one of the coolest people I'd ever met. During the quiet night shifts, we'd sit together and she'd break down the way the world worked. I'd listen eagerly as she told me, in her easygoing way, about rent and bills, politics and culture, and other things I'd never learned in school.

She was also the first older woman I'd met who, like me, was a people person. She loved meeting everyone, and everyone loved meeting her. It wasn't an act either. She had an accept-me-for-who-I-am-or-don't-accept-me-at-all personality. And I thought, *You're so dope. The fact that this is who you are, and you embrace it without tiptoeing around it—I love it.*

I realized through her that we move through life, especially in our first twenty-five years, as sponges, slowly soaking up information from different people, environments, and experiences—and this becomes *us.* Some people fill up early and get stuck in their ways, and others keep absorbing their whole lives. From Alice, I soaked up the idea that I can be me and be loved regardless of what others may say or think.

Not going to college, not taking the safe route, and not doing the by-the-book thing was tough. I doubted myself a lot, especially when I saw so many friends from high school and swim team moving into adulthood in a traditional way. But here was Alice: She hadn't gone to college or followed a traditional path either, yet she'd become a store manager and was working her way up to the corporate level. She was smart, confident, and happy just as she was, and she never complained or envied anyone. She had her life together. I was in awe of her, and it helped me see that even though I was different from the high-achievers on swim team, I could make something of myself as well.

As the weeks continued to pass, the enjoyment I experienced from letting my personality shine and convincing people to buy sneakers intensified. City

Sports became my world. After work, I'd hang out with Alice, her girl-friend, a security guard named James, a manager named Jay, Jay's girl-friend, and half a dozen other store employees. They became a second family. Most of them were older than me, and I started to mature just through being with them and trying to keep up with their conversations. It was my first time in the adult world, and I was hearing about real problems with real consequences:

"My check for this week hasn't cleared yet, and I can't pay my bills."

"I hear you. I don't know if I'm going to be able to keep living in my place. The landlord is trying to evict me."

"Well, look, let me check my balance and see if I can help you, but then you gotta pay it back by the end of the month because I got a car payment to make."

I just sat there listening, thinking, *Damn, I'm living at home with Mom, using my paycheck to buy the latest pair of Jordans. I need to grow up.*

When I came home after work most nights, my mom would grill me like a police detective. She was sure I was on a street corner somewhere selling drugs. Otherwise, it didn't make sense to her that I was working so hard without any lectures or discipline from her.

Eventually, she decided to come to City Sports and find out what was really going on. She walked through the entire store, examining every-thing. She watched me work and deal with customers. She even spoke with my coworkers. She would have made a great parole officer.

When I got home that night, she barraged me with more questions: "What are you getting paid? How much of that is commission? How often do you get a check? Are you looking to get promoted there or to work somewhere else?" And then came the real question, the one behind them all: "What are your plans for your life?"

I took a deep breath and told her that I was ready to take the next step: "I want to save up enough money to find my own place. This way, you won't have to take care of me anymore."

I waited for her reaction. She thought about it for a moment and then said, approvingly, "At least you're starting to think ahead."

27

ALL HAIL GENERAL HART

There was a Nike rep who used to come by the store with the latest sneakers and apparel. He was sharp, and his sales skills put me to shame. All I had was personality and entry-level knowledge, but he had the hookup, he had true expertise and authority, and he had a rare attribute that's hard to learn: taste.

Whenever he came to the store, he made sure all our Nike products were placed and displayed to the company's liking. If they weren't, he'd rearrange them himself and explain why this way was better. Then he'd tell us about the products we were going to get in the next shipment, what was cool about each new item, and why we should be excited about them.

I never knew that this could be a career: just traveling to different stores and representing cool shit. He had what seemed like a high-level position with a prestigious brand, and he was apparently trusted to hustle alone, without a manager or supervisor breathing down his neck.

One night, after his third visit to the store while I was there, I came home and told my mom: "I got it figured out—I have a real plan now. I want to work for Nike, Mom!"

I told her my dream: to gain more knowledge about the sneaker business, climb the ladder at City Sports, and then transition to Nike and become their rep. My mind was made up. That was my life goal.

I started doing triple shifts whenever I could. I worked holidays, my birthday, all the time. It wasn't just about money anymore; I had a dream fueling me. Nothing mattered but work. I wanted to be employee of the month. I wanted to make manager. I wanted to go to corporate. I wanted to do whatever it took to get to Nike. I saw my future in front of me and was running to greet it, with a nice EVA midsole and a padded sock liner to prevent shin splints.

I became known as the guy in the store with all the energy. I learned where everything was in the storage room and I'd leap down the stairs to get sneakers for someone to try on, then sprint back with their size before they knew what hit them. During the lunch rush, the manager loved having me on the floor, because I'd be helping half a dozen customers at the same time.

Soon, customers were stopping by the department just to see me. If they were having a tough time at work, I tried to lift them up and make their visit to the store a highlight of their day. I discovered that I had a talent for remembering faces and names. And by recognizing and acknowledging people, I started getting regulars: "Hey, Ross, good to see you, man!" "Did your kids like them sneakers, Abby?" "You ready for a new pair of gym shoes, Mrs. Daly?"

However, even a people person doesn't like *everyone*. So I learned the flip side of customer service: meeting people who aren't so friendly, but still smiling and being cool with them. There were the grumpy middle-aged men who sent me up and down the stairs twelve times for different sneakers and sizes, then didn't buy anything. There were the careless teenagers who put on a pair of sneakers, walked all over the store with them, creased them up, and then left them scattered on the floor in another department.

This taught me a level of patience that I hadn't yet learned. When my patience was stretched too thin, I'd go down to the storeroom and talk shit about customers with my coworkers.

"That motherfucker's had me running down here fifteen times for sneakers, and he's not planning to buy nothing."

"Who, Green Shirt?"

"Yeah, Green Shirt! You know he does that all the time. I hate it when he comes in here."

"You know who's worse? Tortoise Glasses."

"He back?"

"Yeah. I'm not taking him. One of y'all take him. He gets me mad, and I'll end up saying something I'll regret."

One afternoon, Brandon, one of the managers, called me into his office. I didn't know if he was going to cuss me out for talking smack about customers or praise me for all the hard work I'd been doing.

"I wanted to talk to you," he began very earnestly, "and say that your drive and work ethic are not going unseen around here." I breathed a visible sigh of relief. "We see what you're doing and we really, really like it. And we want to give you a small raise and move you up a little bit on the chart."

I couldn't believe it. I was climbing the ladder!

"We'd like to make you floor general and give you a seventy-five-cent raise."

"I'll make you proud as floor general, sir."

I was beyond excited. I was going places. I was successful out here in the real world, more successful than I'd ever been in classrooms and pools.

I left his office and marched back to the sneaker section:

Me: Hey, guys, look, y'all know I'm the floor general now.

Colleagues: What?

Me: Didn't they tell you guys? Yeah, they're gonna give me the shirt tomorrow.

Colleagues: Floor *general*?

Me: Y'all know what that means, so let's make sure all these displays are straightened up here.

Colleagues: All right, they're straight, Kev.

Me: Good—good job. You guys are doing really nice work. I'll put that in my report.

I had no idea what a floor general was. It was probably some bullshit title to motivate employees; for all I knew, they gave it to a different employee each month. But, man, it had the word "general" in it and it sure felt good. When I started walking around in a shirt with "FL General" written on the back, while everyone else had shirts that just said "City Sports," it went straight to my head.

As soon as a customer crossed the threshold of the department, I'd march right up and introduce myself: "How you doing? I'm Kevin Hart. I'm the floor general here, you know. So if you need anything, come to me. If somebody else isn't taking care of you, I'll take care of you in the best way possible."

I understood then why people who are given a title start acting high and mighty and think they're better than everyone who doesn't have that title. A title carries authority. A uniform carries authority. Even a security guard putting on a badge and utility belt and heavy flashlight starts to think, *All right, they gotta listen to me at this mall, because I look like I'm in charge.*

Though I probably became insufferable for a little while, the authority also helped me grow. I wanted to live up to that title and the store's trust in me, and I became more professional and responsible than I'd ever been. I took the position so seriously that when my friend Spank visited me, I refused to give him an employee discount because it was against store regulations. He never returned.

After I saved a few hundred dollars, I started looking for an apartment, but I couldn't afford both the deposit and the first month's rent.

I knew a crazy motherfucker from my neighborhood named Zachary, who had originally introduced me to Spank. I always thought Zachary was bowlegged, because he'd walk like he was squeezing a bowling ball between his thighs.

One day, I asked him if he was born like that. "Born with a big package," he responded.

"What?"

"Yeah, it's like the male equivalent of a chick with her back arched and her tits thrust out. She wasn't born that way. She learned to walk that way to send a signal, know what I mean?"

"You gotta be kidding me."

"Girls love this bow-legged shit."

I asked if he wanted to get a place together, because living with him would be the opposite of living with my mom. However, Zachary and his big package were living with a girlfriend for free, so he introduced me to a buddy of his named Paul who was looking for a place. I convinced Paul that it would be a good idea to get an apartment together, and we found a two-bedroom spot above a barbershop. The rent was four hundred dollars a month, which we split. I'll never forget the address, because it was my liberation: 22 Westmoreland Street.

I no longer had to get permission from my mom or answer a million questions when there was something I wanted to do. I could go wherever I wanted and stay out all night and answer to no one. Most importantly, I got my own room with a door I could close for privacy.

Meanwhile, the fact that Mom was all alone at home became more and more upsetting to my brother. He didn't like that she was on her own in a dangerous neighborhood, especially considering she'd already been robbed—even if that robber happened to be our dad.

"Listen, I didn't go to the military just to come home and end up going to jail," he told my mom when we were at the house visiting. "If someone came in here and cooked and robbed you, fine. But people know you're alone now, and what if someone walks in here and knocks you upside your head? Then we're going to have a problem because I'm going to go find him and take care of him."

But my mom refused to move. Eventually, my brother got fed up with her stubbornness and pulled me aside.

Kenneth: Look here, man. She's getting old. She don't know what's right for her anymore. This is what we're gonna do. We are going to go there when she's at work, and we're going to move all her shit to my house. I got an extra bed she can use.

Me: So let me get this straight. You're upset that Mom got robbed while she was at work. So while she's at work, you're going to come in and take her stuff and put it somewhere else.

Kenneth: Yeah, exactly.

Me: So you're gonna rob her?

Kenneth: No, man, that's not what I'm doing at all.

Me: Then what's the difference?

Kenneth: I'm not stealing it. I'm moving it to *my* house.

Me: So if I walk into someone's house while they're out, take their stuff, and move it to my house, it's not stealing?

Kenneth: Never mind.

Me: Okay.

Even though I was out of the house, I was still a mama's boy. I told her what Kenneth was up to, and she told him not to even think about it.

"What the fuck is wrong with you, man?" my brother yelled at me.

"She's our mom. It should be her choice whether she moves or not."

I didn't like the idea of my mom, who was so strong and independent, becoming a guest in my brother's place and dependent on him like that. It didn't seem right for her. I also didn't want to lose my childhood home and all the memories that were stuck in my head as firmly as the roaches on the duct tape by the sink.

Eventually, Kenneth moved all Mom's shit anyway and she ended up living with him. She wasn't too happy about it. So I consoled her the best I could: "Mom, this was all Kenneth's idea."

Our family had changed again. I was independent, Kenneth was the man of the house, and Mom was the kid. Growing up is a strange thing.

28

I WAS GONNA CALL THIS ONE "MY GENIUS FINALLY GETS RECOGNIZED," BUT THE CHAPTER BEFORE LAST HAD THE WORD "GENIUS" IN IT AND THERE ARE ONLY SO MANY CHAPTERS YOU CAN NAME "GENIUS" IN A BOOK. THAT'S ONE OF THE MANY BURDENS OF BEING A GENIUS.

I eventually became so comfortable at City Sports, I started letting all the strange parts of my personality loose. You get a lot of weird parts to your personality when you spend half your adolescence in an imaginary fort in an old lady's basement.

I'd ask my coworkers, "You want me to be a completely different character for the next two people?"

"Sure, Kev, be Urkel or something."

"Okay, but y'all can't laugh. You gotta let me talk the way I'm talking and go the way I'm going. Don't even smile, cause that's gonna make me laugh."

I'd sell shoes as different television characters or using a silly voice. When that got too easy, I'd try selling a Timberland boot to someone looking for running shoes, or we'd have contests to see how many times we could make a customer say "What?" Even at work, it was still about being the fun guy.

One day, during the after-work rush, we were playing my favorite game: slipping in cuss words without customers noticing. Alice was working that day, and Michelle, one of the oldest employees in the store, was keeping count.

Me: You know, this is a great shoe, but I would say you need to probably go get a dick or something first.

Customer: I'm sorry, what?

Michelle (*quietly, in background*): One.

Me: I said this is a great shoe, because it's got a great polyurethane
fucksole. But you should try it on to make sure it farts first.

Michelle: Two, three.

I won that round with four curses to a single customer. Then we got
bored and played the "What?" game.

"I really think this is a good shoe for you," I told a businessman, then
started mumbling, "And you know what, at the end of the day, you'll probably fall or something if you don't get 'em."

"Excuse me? I didn't catch that."

I cursed under my breath, because it didn't count if someone didn't
actually say the word "what."

As the stream of customers thinned out and the end of the day approached, I was leaning on a countertop where we sold watches, heart-rate
monitors, and other electronics, recapping the highlights of the day with
Alice and Michelle. We were all laughing about it so much that Alice was
wiping tears out of her eyes.

"You're fucking hilarious. You should do stand-up comedy," she said.

"Really?"

"You're probably one of the funniest guys I've ever seen come through
here, Kevin," Michelle answered. She was even more enthusiastic. "No one's
even close. You should think about doing comedy for real as a second job."

"Where would I even do comedy at?"

"There's a comedy club near here. I've been there."

"What do you gotta do there?"

"People get on stage and they tell jokes. It's cool. You have to try it."

That's when I said the word that changed my life: "Okay."

It was as nonchalant as every other "okay" I'd uttered. I basically
shoulder-shrugged my way into comedy.

"You gonna do it for real?" Alice asked. She couldn't believe I'd agreed
so easily.

"Yeah, I'mma do it."

"I know you'll be good," Michelle said confidently.

On the bus home that night, reality sank in. *Who do I have to speak to so I can perform there? What if they say* no? *What the hell am I gonna talk about? How much time do they give me? How much does it pay?* I basically became my mom.

When I told my friends about it, their reaction was the exact opposite of everyone's at work.

"What?!" Zachary asked. "You gonna do *what*, man?"

"Stand-up comedy, at this place near work."

"Why you gonna do that? I don't know about that, man."

Spank wasn't any more encouraging. "Those people at work don't know you, man. They think you're funny because you talk too much and you get silly with it. But on stage, that's gonna be pesty to people. They're gonna tell you just like we do: 'Yo, shut up, Kev!'"

"Really?"

"I'm playing with you, man, but really, you need more confidence before you try to go up on stage."

Your friends may love you, but the problem is that they love you as you are. You play a role in their lives that they've gotten used to, so they don't always want you to change. Most of them think their job is to keep you humble and in your place.

As for the person you're dating, he or she may support you or not. It depends on a few variables: how good the relationship is, how old the relationship is, how your last plan turned out, and whether this change will bring you closer to or further away from that person. Fortunately, my relationship with Torrei was new and I had a good track record with her, so she was supportive. "I think you're funny. You can do this." Those few words meant a lot.

I had never thought that being the fun guy could be a legitimate career. I was always being told to get serious about my life. Sure, I'd seen Eddie Murphy cracking people up, but he was Eddie Murphy. I was Kevin Hart, a sneaker salesman struggling to pay the rent and hoping one day to get hired by Nike.

The next day, Alice and Michelle told the other employees that I was going to try stand-up comedy, and they all came up to tell me I'd be great. Their confidence was probably what ended up motivating me to go through with the idea.

I called the comedy club, the Laff House, and asked if they had spots for new comedians. The woman who answered said they had an "amateur night" every Thursday where anyone could perform: sign-up was at seven in the evening, the show started at eight.

I asked how much it paid. She said it didn't pay anything.

29

RISE OF THE BASTARD

"**W**hat's your name gonna be, Kev?"

I was confused by my friend Raheem's question. I'd been trying out some jokes on him, my roommate Paul, Zachary, and Spank in the car to warm up for amateur night at Laff House. But they were barely laughing—and when they did, it seemed to be out of politeness. I was starting to have some serious doubts.

"What do you mean?" I asked for clarification.

"Your comedy name. Everybody got a comedy name: You got Cedric the Entertainer, Earthquake, Sinbad. So what's yours?"

"I don't know."

"You mean to tell me you be thinking up all these jokes and you haven't thought of a name for yourself?"

"I guess so."

"The Bastard."

"What?"

"Yeah, your name should be the Bastard."

"Why?"

"Cause your dad ain't never around."

Unlike my jokes, Raheem's got a laugh. Maybe he knew what he was talking about. "Y'all think that name's funny?" I asked.

"That's funny as hell," Paul said. "When people hear that, they'll go crazy."

Raheem turned down the stereo, then announced, "Philly, make some noise for Lil' Kev the Bastard!" and cranked the volume. Everyone in the car started whooping.

"All right, if y'all say it's funny, I'mma go with that."

In retrospect, I wish I'd put a little more thought into it. A stage name is like a relationship: easy to get into, but hard to get out of.

In the days that followed, I tested out jokes on my coworkers and customers. I practiced every night on my roommate. Everything became a joke or a potential joke. If I burnt food I was cooking, I'd say, "Yo, I just burnt the food. Uh, I got food burn. I shoulda put suntan lotion on."

Paul would smile politely, and I'd ask, "That was a funny joke, right? You think that's a funny joke?"

My pocket was full of paper scraps with joke ideas I'd written on them. If I ran into a friend, I'd pull out a scrap and say, "Tell me if you think this is funny."

Fortunately, my friends continued to "encourage" me:

Paul: I don't think that's funny, man.

Spank: That ain't gonna work, Kev.

Zachary: You sure you wanna do this, man?

Even Kenneth: Hey, you're my little brother and I love you. So whatever you do, I'm gonna back you. But I don't know, man. I just don't think this is your thing.

When the day of the show came around, I had so much nervous energy, I couldn't sell a thing at work. All my friends thought I was fun to hang out with, but none of them seemed to like my material. My other worry was that each amateur was allowed only five minutes to perform. The night before, however, I'd practiced in the mirror and timed my routine to seven minutes and some change. And I couldn't get it any shorter.

Please don't let this go badly, I kept praying. *Please, God, let me be funny. That's all I ask for.*

I was so inexperienced, I worried that if I sucked, people would throw tomatoes at me. That's actually what I thought happened at comedy clubs. It never occurred to me to go to the Laff House or check out another comedy show first.

Some friends were planning to drop by only to see me fail, so they could fuck with me about it later. My brother was coming with his buddies—dudes who knew me when I was four years old. They were all expecting to watch something horrific.

Of course, they had every right to set the bar low. The last, and only, time I'd been on stage before was at my swim team's graduation banquet. If this were a musical talent show, I could play some shitty song and everyone would politely clap afterward. They could even yell and scream like I was a star. But this was comedy, and laughter can't be faked. I would know instantly whether I really was funny, like Alice and Michelle said, or whether I was a joke, like my friends thought.

My enemy that night would be silence.

I had to do everything in my power to get that room going, to shine on stage or die trying, and, most importantly, to prove my friends and brother wrong.

Sometimes, other people's doubt can be the best motivation there is to succeed.

Life Lessons
FROM PASSION

*Putting all your eggs in one basket will lead to
the birth of chickens that you will have to eat.
What I'm trying to say by this is love what you do,
which of course means... What are we talking
about again? This writing stuff is tough
sometimes. Just read the section.*

With Torrei

30

THERE'S A FIRST TIME
FOR EVERYTHING EXCEPT
THE THINGS YOU'LL NEVER DO

I rushed into the employee locker room, changed into my nicest pair of pants and a button-down shirt, and ran to the Laff House. When I entered, I saw a few people signing up on a list. They didn't look like comics, I thought. Then I realized that I didn't really know what comics looked like. They probably didn't all wear red leather jumpsuits.

I took a deep breath and tried to steady myself. *Okay, this is it, Kev.*

I signed up; I was the fifth name on the list. The other comics had notebooks and were going over their material, writing things down. They all looked like regulars, and they didn't pay any attention to me. They were too worried about their own performances to make a new guy feel comfortable.

I took out my notes and started working on my set, frantically trying to remove material to get it down to five minutes. For a moment, I felt like one of the regular comics. Soon, an absurdly tall dude with a shaven head, a mustache that already made him look funny, and an oversized blue button-down shirt walked in. "Hey, everybody, let me get y'all attention," he said in a deep voice. "I'm the host, TuRae Gordon. Let me see the list."

He grabbed it and scanned it. He seemed to know every name there except one.

"Kev Hart, aka Lil' Kev the Bastard—who's that?"

"That's me."

He then said the three words that will turn any new performer's jitters into a panic attack: "You're on first."

Shit. I wanted to ask him if he could put someone else first, but I didn't know how things worked. I didn't want to upset him or seem unprofessional—even though it was a night dedicated to unprofessionals.

So I had to cowboy up. "You got it!"

"Here's how it works: I'm gonna go on stage and call each comic's name. When I say your name, you better be by the side of that stage waiting. Come up during the applause, and you got five minutes to do your set. At four minutes and thirty seconds, a red light will go on. You won't miss it cause it'll be shining right in your eyes. Make sure you get off that stage at five minutes so I don't have to go up there and yank you off. That's it."

Here's what I didn't know back then: Amateur nights and open mics aren't really a way for clubs to look for new talent; they're a way to make extra money. Instead of waiting until people are done with dinner and ready to go to a comedy show with professional headliners, the club can open a few hours early, invite the wannabes to perform, and either charge them to get on stage or require that they bring a certain number of friends, who each have to pay a cover charge and drink minimum.

When the show started, there were ten coworkers there to support me, ten friends there to make fun of me, ten strangers there who couldn't give a shit about me, and ten other comics there who were just thinking about their own sets.

TuRae came on stage and warmed up the audience. I looked around and saw my friends cracking up and enjoying themselves. I began to worry that everyone would stop laughing and just stare silently at me when I walked on stage next.

My throat went dry, and sweat trickled down my forehead as TuRae got ready to introduce me. "Keep in mind you've seen none of these comedians anywhere. With that being said, let's get the show started with our first amateur coming to the stage: Ladies and gentlemen, Lil' Kev the Bastard!"

I ran in place a little and shook my body to snap out of the fear and get into the moment. I repeated to myself: *Energy, energy, energy.* That's what I thought comedy was all about. Then I ran on stage and exploded in a hot mess of overenthusiasm.

"Wassup, wassup, wassup!" I yelled into the void.

The lights on stage were brighter than I'd imagined. It was hard to see individual faces in the audience. But I could feel them staring at me, waiting to laugh. I needed to make them crack up . . . somehow. "Yeah, yeah, wassup!" I also needed to stop saying "wassup." Everyone knows what's up: This here comic is about to get tomatoes thrown at him.

I gotta move on. "You know the bus man?" Silence. "You ever see that guy?" Silence. *Kev, you gotta stop asking questions.* "What's up with that guy?" *Shit, that's a question.*

The more nervous I got, the quicker I spoke. "That guy like a pervert. Man be grabbing everybody, putting his dick on everybody that walks by. Ungh, ungh, ungh. Yeah, man smelling seats and stuff cause some lady with a fat ass just sat on 'em."

Suddenly, I heard it: a laugh. No—a few laughs. Lights were in my eyes and laughter was in my ears and the cold steel of the microphone stand was in my hands. And it felt good. Better than sex.

Well, *almost* as good as sex.

It was the feeling of acceptance, of success, of your friends enjoying your company, of a three-point shot, of your mom telling you she's proud of you.

Riding the high of that feeling, I soared with confidence and flew through the rest of my set.

"Then, you know, there's that person on the bus that stinks, and when they get up, for some reason you worry that maybe it's you that smells. So you smell the seat just to make sure it was them—and then all of a sudden you realize, *you* the pervert that be sniffing seats."

More laughter, even louder than before. *I got this.*

I went into a joke that I thought at the time was Eddie Murphy–level material. It was about getting robbed by a midget. The punchline was: "He didn't even have a gun. He just kept head-butting me." Again, the laughter came.

Before I knew it, I was done. It felt good to have just said my last joke and made it through this trial-by-laughter successfully. There was just one small problem: I was still standing on stage, and the red light hadn't gone on yet. I was so nervous I'd raced through five minutes of material in like three minutes. It was like having sex, then patting yourself on the back for your great performance while she's still lying there unsatisfied.

"Man, I'm so glad to be here!" I stalled.

I had to use up my time somehow. Everyone was staring at me, waiting to see what was next. The anticipatory anxiety before my set had been tough, but it was nothing compared to the awkward silence on stage. Everyone could see me struggling. I felt frozen in place. I tried to remember the material I'd removed. "Okay, uh, another thing . . . " I was going to have to slow down the couple of jokes I had left to make it to five minutes.

Suddenly, from the darkness of the audience, one of my brother's friends yelled, "Yeah, Kev, yeah!" A few other people joined in, and I thought, *Yeah, Kev, you can do this.*

I reinserted a joke I had cut about people getting tattoos with Chinese writing. "You don't really know what it means. All you know is what they tell you, and they tell you that it means all of this crazy spiritual stuff. But you're probably walking around with the Chinese words for 'salt,' 'pepper,' and 'ketchup' on your back."

Another peal of laughter and clapping got me back into a flow. Going slower was awkward, but the laughs actually got bigger. I'd already learned my first lesson in performing: Slow it way the fuck down, because stage fright is an accelerator pedal. A couple of jokes later, the red light finally came on. "Okay, guys, I gotta get off," I told them. "They're giving me the signal."

The room erupted with applause, whistling, screaming. It was probably just my friends being my friends, but it felt good. As I walked off stage, exhilarated and relieved, TuRae clapped me on the back and said, "Good set. Good job, man." I basked in those words.

I grabbed a seat next to Spank, and he gave me the nicest compliment in the history of our friendship: "Yo, man, that wasn't as bad as I thought it would be."

It took just five minutes for me to fall in love with stand-up comedy. Everything was a high: the stage, the lights, the microphone, the nervousness, the host announcing my name, the sound system blasting my voice, the faces staring up at me, the experience of sharing the weirdest parts of my mind, the laughter, and the applause.

I felt like I could do this again. I wanted to do this again. I wanted to do this all the time.

31

WHAT PERFECT PEOPLE DO

At work the next day, Alice came up to me: "You were so good! I told you that you could do it."

I was still high from the night before, so I didn't hesitate when she asked afterward, "You gonna do it again?"

"Yeah, I'mma do it again!"

I returned to the club the following week, and I was much better. This time, I was familiar with the club, the host, the audience, and how the whole open-mic thing worked. My brother's friends didn't show up, but a few of my friends from work did. There were only about twenty people in the audience, but they were all laughing.

As he was closing the show, TuRae made an announcement that got my attention. "We're going to raise the stakes a bit." I listened closely; even then, I liked my stakes high. "Next week, we're changing things up for amateur night. It's going to become a competition: Blazin' Thursday! The contest will be judged not by me, but by you, the audience. Whoever gets the most applause wins the night—and a cash prize of seventy-five dollars! So, for you performers, make sure to bring your friends so you get that money."

Though I didn't know it at the time, with twenty people a night, TuRae's amateur night wasn't making the Laff House much additional money before its regular show. The real purpose of the contest was to motivate us to bring more friends to the club on Thursdays in hopes of winning.

As I got ready to leave that night, TuRae sauntered over. It seemed like he wanted to speak directly to me, which was exciting because he'd barely acknowledged me before, outside of introducing me. "Come to amateur night," he said. "You'll be great. I'm telling you, you'll kill it."

To this day, I still don't know whether he said that to everyone or not, but he was the first comedian to believe in me—or at least act like he believed in me. If it was a hustle, it worked. I told everyone who came the first two nights about the competition and asked them to come next Thursday with as many friends as they could round up. The other comedians did the same thing: That night, there were almost a hundred people in the audience. And unfortunately, because I was still the new guy, I was up first again.

I'd moved some jokes around so the set started out rough. The room was quiet, and it felt like people were laughing to break the awkwardness. But when I hit them with the midget joke, and those hundred people went from silence to laughter and hollering, any thought I still had of being a Nike rep was gone. I wanted to be on stage. It was competitive, like a sport, and I could do what I did best: be the fun, loud guy.

At the end of the night, TuRae brought the comics back to the stage. I was sure I'd lost. A few of the other comedians were really funny, and I was so inexperienced.

TuRae began the judging by holding his hand over the head of one of the comedians, and a light round of applause ensued. He moved on to the second comic, and the room erupted. Then me, and the room exploded again, but it didn't seem as loud. I felt certain the guy before me had won, and I resolved to come back and keep trying.

When TuRae got to the end of the line, however, he kept me and the guy next to me on stage and did a final clap-off. Not only did all my friends applaud, but other people's friends applauded for me too. These were people I'd never met before in my life, and they were rooting for me to win. I looked around the club and tried to take it in.

A moment later, TuRae announced, "Congratulations to this Thursday's winner, Lil' Kev the Bastard!"

I pumped my fist into the air and did a victory lap around the stage. It was the third time I'd ever performed, and I'd beat out all the veterans. Maybe I did have a talent for this—or at least a lot of loud friends.

That day, I became a professional comic. I was amazed that I'd gotten paid to do something I genuinely enjoyed. I couldn't stop talking about it on the train ride home.

Me: Damn, I won. Like, *I won*. That's crazy. I can't believe I won.

Spank: Yeah, Kev, you won.

Me: And I just started doing this! How'd I win so fast? I gotta think of some more jokes. Hey, though, you think I was really that good?

Spank: Yeah, you was all right.

Me: You think I won cause I was the best there, or just cause y'all were really loud?

Spank: Cause we felt sorry for you.

Me: No, come on, for real. This is important.

Spank: Come on, Kev, stop talking about it already.

I was obsessed. All week I worked on new jokes to add to my set—most of it hacky, obvious stuff, like about the differences between the way white and black people dance.

The amateur competition kept me and the other comics working hard and bringing our friends. I reached out to practically everyone I knew in high school. I even had my customers coming in. It was like a friends arms race among the amateurs.

My performance at the second contest was stronger, and I won again. At the third contest, I was no longer first on stage; I was in the middle of the lineup. When TuRae announced me, he said, "This guy here has been tearing up the amateur scene. He's won two back-to-back Blazin' Thursdays!" When I walked on stage, people in the audience were no longer bracing themselves to feel sorry for me but getting hyped for a good time.

After my third win, I stopped doing triple shifts at work and started taking comedy more seriously. I went to the club on nights when I wasn't working to watch professional comics. The first thing I noticed was that they didn't just think about their jokes; appearance was also important to them. Like Eddie Murphy, they had a look they'd crafted for the stage.

As I sat there in the club night after night, I thought about who I was and what kind of image I should be creating. Should I buy a suit, a leather jacket, a sports jersey? Each of those items conveys a specific personality. Which should mine be?

After winning my fourth contest, I spent the money I'd accumulated on a safe look that I thought would appeal to everyone: thick Banana Republic dress slacks, black dress shoes, a stiff dress shirt, and a J.Crew sweater. I thought I looked like a professional comic, but in retrospect, I looked more like a deacon's son. Of course, how you *feel* you look is more important than how you actually look anyway, because it's all about your attitude. And I was Lil' Kev the Bastard—I was *all* attitude.

On the fifth week of the competition, TuRae scheduled me in the headlining slot as the last comic of the night. When he introduced me, he seemed as excited as I was: "Yo, it's been four weeks in a row. Somebody's gotta stop him, man! Is this gonna be the week?"

I felt like I was a big deal now, and I grabbed the mic with confidence. I was getting comfortable with my set, so instead of just trying to remember my material, I was able to think about pausing, pacing, facial expressions, and being more animated with my body. Most exciting of all, because I was a familiar face, I started making friends with other amateur comics and feeling like part of the scene instead of an outsider. Acceptance is a drug as powerful as crack.

By that time, the crowd had leveled off at about eighty people, but they were all ordering drinks and spending money. After I won again that night, TuRae sat down next to me and said, "Hey, I'm going to Virginia tomorrow. I got a show up there. You wanna roll?"

Instantly, the world got a lot bigger than the Laff House. I hadn't even considered the fact that there were other comedy clubs to perform at. I could be doing this every night! However . . .

"I can't," I told him reluctantly. "I gotta go to work."

"All right, I feel you."

He walked away from the table and I sat there alone, watching the blue back of his shirt recede into the club, feeling like I'd just blown a big opportunity to make something of myself.

32

K HART QUITS HIS DAY JOB AND NEVER LOOKS BACK. (ACTUALLY, HE KIND OF GOES BACK, BUT THAT'S IN CHAPTER 98.)

After I won my sixth contest in a row, TuRae approached me again. "Hey, I got a gig way out in West Chester, Pennsylvania, if you wanna come with me this week."

"Man, I still got this job, you know."

"I know."

You can say no to someone once, and they may ask again. You can even say no twice and get another shot. But three nos and you're definitely out.

I was one no away from being out. The job I'd loved so much was suddenly a prison. There was a whole world of comedy clubs out there I was missing out on. If there were other amateur contests like this one, I could make a good living doing this. But even if there weren't, I could still make my rent and food on seventy-five dollars a week. I was so confident, the possibility that I'd lose a contest didn't even occur to me.

Here are some of the things people might say to you when you decide to pursue your dream:

"I know you're excited about this right now, but you can't make a living at it."

"Are you sure this is what you want to do? Take some time and really think about it."

"Don't quit your day job." "Stop dreaming." "Be realistic." "There's no money in it." "It's not a smart choice." "There's too much competition." "You're not good enough."

Many people will tell you to ignore these doubters. Others will tell you to listen and then prove them wrong, which worked for me in those first shows. But I'm going to recommend something better that I learned much later: Don't invite them into the conversation. You already know what you want to dedicate yourself to, so you don't need to ask for their approval. There's no need to seek *external* approval when you already have *internal* approval.

That's why, even though I had sought everyone's advice about performing at that first open mic, I didn't ask anyone about quitting City Sports to become a stand-up comedian. I just did it. It was all or nothing: I was ready to give this my all, and I didn't want anyone saying anything to me otherwise. I was going to be a professional comedy amateur.

Even though I'd made up my mind, there were a few people I had to share that information with, people who made me nervous as hell: the managers at City Sports and my mom.

When I gave my two weeks' notice at City Sports, the manager, Brandon—who'd been to the club to see me perform—couldn't believe what I was saying.

Manager: Kevin, are you serious right now? You want to be a comedian?

Me: Yeah, that's exactly what I want to be.

Manager: A *comedian*, Kevin? What's going on? You have a career here. You're good at it. There's room to grow. You could get to corporate and be making seventy-five thousand dollars a year, and you're just going to throw it away because you won amateur night at some comedy club?

Me: Pretty much.

Manager: I'm worried you're letting this go to your head. You know, you're headstrong; that's your problem.

I didn't say "okay" this time. I said:

Me: I know what I want to do with my life. I quit.

Less than two months before, these same people had been encouraging me to try comedy because I was so funny. Today, they were telling me to stop doing it. They believed in me then; now, suddenly, they didn't believe in me?

I couldn't understand it at the time, but later I thought about it. The problem is, many people want you to do things, up to the point where they lose control of you. As long as they're still your boss or mentor or partner or good friend, it's fine. But if it starts pulling you away from them or making you more successful than them or keeping you too busy to see them as much, then your dream can become their threat.

I knew who my real friends at the job were, people like Alice, because when I told them what I was doing, they supported me. "Keep going," she said. "You're gonna make it. Go be a star."

After I gave my notice, doubt crept in: It wasn't going to be easy to live off my winnings from amateur nights, especially since TuRae would probably want to let someone else win or another comedian might show up with louder friends than mine.

Unfortunately, I didn't have to worry about this problem for long.

When I went to the club to perform that next Thursday, they told me that the amateur competition had been canceled because it still wasn't bringing in enough money for the club.

My entire life plan was made and destroyed in the space of a week.

What was I supposed to do now?

33

A LICENSE TO KILL

I still needed to break the news to my mom.

First I bombed the SATs. Then I dropped out of community college. Now I'd left my job, abandoned my plan of becoming a Nike rep, and switched to comedy, which wasn't even going to pay the rent anymore. She'd sacrificed so much for me, and I was about to disappoint her yet again.

"I don't want to go back to City Sports," I explained nervously. "I really want to give this a chance."

I studied her for a reaction. She didn't look angry. She didn't reach for a Hot Wheels track. She didn't change her expression at all. She thought about it for a few seconds, then responded: "I believe in supporting anything you tell me you want to do with your life."

My eyes got watery as she spoke those words. But then her expression changed, and the mom-hammer came down: "But you've got one year to be productive and figure out how to take care of yourself this way. And if you can't, you're going back to school."

Some people hate deadlines, but deadlines are motivation to get things done. My mom's support, along with that deadline, made me more determined to find another way to make a living with laughter. A few days later, my mom handed me a check for the next month's rent. She wanted just one thing in exchange for her support: She handed me a Bible and asked that I read it, since I wasn't going to church with her anymore.

I stopped by the Laff House that night and told TuRae that I'd left my job, had no income anymore, and didn't know what to do.

"It's not just the money," I explained. "I need to perform more so I can get better."

"That's good that you want to do that. The best way to become better is through stage time."

"How do you get that?"

"You can roll with me for a little while and see how it works."

It was his third offer, and this time I was able to say yes.

Besides talent and timing, success is also about work and relationships. Rolling with TuRae was the first comedy relationship I built, and he quickly became a mentor.

When TuRae said "stage time," I imagined we'd be driving to comedy clubs all over the East Coast. But he was inventing his own spots in Philadelphia, so some of those stages were just the corner hamburger restaurant or a small student center. TuRae had become the comedy king of Philadelphia by doing this. He was always looking out for new places to start a comedy night.

The first room he took me to was a bowling alley, and he put me on first. No one was paying attention. At the end of a joke, instead of hearing laughter, I'd hear: *Crack!* "STRIKE!"

"Whenever you can get ahold of a microphone and be around people, it's an opportunity to hone your act," TuRae told me that night, after I expressed my disappointment. "So never turn down those moments."

———

For months, no one on the scene knew my name. They'd just say to TuRae, "Hey, who's the new guy with you?" And TuRae would respond, "He's actually funny. I'm showing him around the scene."

After I performed in the smaller rooms for a couple of weeks, TuRae let me do a guest spot on a weekend show at the Laff House. A guest spot was just five minutes of stage time to add variety and keep the audience warm between more polished comedians, but to me it was a big deal. Surprisingly, it was easier than an open mic. The house was packed with an audience paying to have a good time; none of them were friends with the comedians. And only the best comedians were performing. The room was buzzing with energy, and the audience was warmed up and ready to laugh. I went on stage that night and killed like I'd never killed before.

My mom had tried to keep me away from the violence of the streets, but here I was trying to *kill on stage, destroy the room, murder the audience, crack people up,* and *bust guts open.* To this day, I still don't know why comedy is described in such violent terms. Even if you don't do well on stage, it's not called *failing* or *sucking.* It's called *bombing.*

I'm surprised the government's wiretapping programs haven't sent a lot of innocent comedians to Guantánamo:

"You going to the club?"
"Yeah, I'm gonna kill there."
"I'll probably bomb."

Whenever I wasn't on stage, I was working on my Lil' Kev the Bastard persona, trying to create the best, most fun, most high-energy five minutes that I could possibly perform.

I found that if I amplified the character of Lil' Kev, anything he said could be funny. I'd say, "You ever take a bite out of a potato for no reason? Then you look up and go, 'What happened to that potato?'" Everyone would laugh because my eyes would be bugged out and my voice high-pitched. I'd dance for no reason at all, yell at the DJ, or say whatever nonsense came to my mind.

As I grew more comfortable with the character, people on the scene started to notice. "Man, the new guy's getting good. This kid got potential."

They weren't saying this because I was a great comedian, or even a good one. They were saying it because I was persistent, and that persistence was starting to show up in small improvements. When you're trying to make it, you're not judged necessarily by your talent but by your potential. And that potential is all about your willingness to listen, learn, and improve.

The best gigs that TuRae booked were college shows. They each paid a few hundred dollars, and as he noticed me improving, he began letting me open for him. I was too new and raw to be doing those spots, but getting thrown into the deep end forced me to raise my game and get better. He'd slide me twenty-five dollars a day for traveling with him, purely out of kindness. That was his money, and no one was at those shows to see me.

At one of those shows, there was a student from the college on the bill named Na'im Lynn. I was performing at his college, and he was also doing a set. I don't remember the comedy, just his beady eyes, which were always peering up at me even though I was smaller than him, and his quiet seriousness, like he was studying everything in life for a big exam. He knew my roommate, and we'd met a few times before, so we started hanging out afterward. It was good to finally have a friend in my circle who was also new to the comedy scene.

There was just one big obstacle standing in my way: money.

34

OILING UP

"Mom, where's the rent at?"

I was a month behind on rent and the next check was due the following day. My mom had promised to support me, but she wasn't holding up her end of the deal.

"Are you reading your Bible?"

"Mom, I don't have time to talk about that. I'm late to meet TuRae. I need the rent money."

"Are you reading your Bible?"

I didn't want to lie to her, so I told the truth. "No, I'm not, okay?"

"When you read your Bible, then we'll talk about rent."

I stormed out of the house, angry that she was trying to blackmail me. I hated studying, and the Bible was straight-up work. "Thou hast also taken thy fair jewels of my gold and of my silver, which I had given thee, and madest to thyself images of men, and didst commit whoredom with them." What exactly is going on there?

Two months of rent—four hundred dollars—was too much money to borrow from my friends, so it looked like I'd have to work a day job again. It was the last thing I wanted to do when I was starting to make a dent in the comedy scene, but my back was against the wall.

I couldn't go to my brother for help, because he was struggling with the barbershop. The building had a glass storefront, so that people passing by could see everyone working inside—and every now and then, he would glimpse Dad's face pressed against the glass, staring. But as soon as my brother spotted him, Dad would disappear into the street. That's pretty much all we saw of our dad for years.

I couldn't go to Torrei for a loan because we'd gotten into an argument after I went to a party one night and didn't answer her calls. So we temporarily broke up because I felt like I was losing my freedom. In that period, I started seeing someone else very casually, and one day she came up with an idea.

Me: My mom's playing around with this rent money. I gotta do something.

Her: You know what? You should dance.

Me: What?

Her: You small. You got a nice-sized package. You should dance. They'll love you.

Me: You mean *strip*?

Her: Yeah, why not? I got a few girlfriends who dance and clean up. You'll kill the game.

Me: Yo, I probably would do okay, huh?

Her: I'll help get you right.

The next day, I was hanging out with my friend Zachary and I asked him what he thought about the whole thing.

Zachary was always down for pretty much anything, so naturally he responded, "Let's do it."

"You don't wanna talk about it?"

"Naw, man. We should do it."

"Well, let's talk to this chick and get the breakdown."

I called her later that day, and she laid out the plan: "All I need is an hour of your time every day for a week, and I'll get you guys comfortable with it. Then y'all can go out there and make a lot of money."

"Okay, why not?" I was desperate. And TuRae did say that the way to get better at comedy was through more stage time.

She took Zachary and me shopping, and with my last dollars I bought a bow tie, a G-string, and some Johnson & Johnson baby oil. Zachary bought something equally ridiculous. We got back to my house and class began.

The first lesson was about choosing a song. I picked Ginuwine's "Pony." I think Zachary went with Usher's "You Make Me Wanna . . ."

Lesson two was about choreographing a dance routine. I started working on some moves, while Zachary just stood there.

"What's your move?" she asked him.

"I only wanna do bow-legged stuff."

She gave him a funny look.

"You know you been looking," he shot back, completely serious.

Lesson three: Oiling up.

We went to the bathroom, doused ourselves in baby oil, and changed into our stripper outfits. When we emerged, we looked more like victims of a fraternity prank than hot strippers, plus we'd gotten oil stains all over our bow ties.

"You sure this is how it works?" I asked.

She looked around the house for something. "This right here can be the girl." She placed a wooden stool in the middle of the room.

Then she put on "Pony." I started gyrating my body and running my hands over my chest to the song.

"It's cool, Zachary, you can dance too," she encouraged him.

He joined me in the middle of the living room. The lights were blazing, Ginuwine was pumping, and we were glistening.

Zachary got to the stool first and started humping it, while I stood behind him, shirt off and oiled up, trying to do the R. Kelly move where he bends all the way backward until he looks like a table with two legs. It doesn't look sexy now, and it probably didn't at the time, especially cause I didn't have half his flexibility.

When Zachary finished doing the chair and I finished doing the table, we looked up and saw my brother, my roommate, Spank, Na'im, and my upstairs neighbor staring at us. The music was so loud we hadn't heard them enter. And now, with one exception, they were doubled over, breathless with laughter. That exception was my brother, who was pissed off: "What the fuck is going on in here?" He always felt protective of me. Throughout my life, he was constantly trying to help me become what he considered a man, and I let him down on that front pretty regularly.

"What does it look like?" I yelled back, in my G-string and nothing else. "We're working."

"Working at what?"

"Laugh all you want, but you'd do it too if you knew how much money strippers made."

"You think anyone's gonna pay to see that shit? Man, the only thing I'd pay for is the therapy to get that fucking image out of my head."

That was the end of my stripper days.

35

SALVATION

After I was two months late with rent, the landlord put an eviction notice on our door. I visited my mom, begging: "Mom, I just got an eviction notice. I need to pay the rent. I'm serious."

"Have you read the Bible?"

This time I lied. When your survival is at stake, morality is the first thing to go out the window. "Yes."

"Don't lie to me, Kevin. Talk to me after you've read your Bible."

She must have had a sixth sense. "Mom, whatever, I don't want to talk about Scripture. Forget it." I slammed the door shut. I was so angry that she'd bailed on her part of the bargain.

But of course, she hadn't. It was me who'd broken my word.

I got home and figured I'd open the Bible and pray for guidance. Maybe Mom knew something I didn't.

I pulled it out of a drawer and opened it for the first time since she'd given it to me. A stack of rent checks, all signed and dated for the first of each month for the whole year, fell out.

She'd kept her promise after all. I felt so low and ungrateful. She was a tough woman and always true to her word.

I'd never expected to fall on such hard times. Once I finally found my passion and made a plan, I thought I was set. That's how it works, right? You make a plan, work hard to execute it, and then succeed.

But I've learned that I'm not the only person in the world who's making plans. Everyone is reaching for what they believe is a better future, and not all of those futures are in alignment. Some people's plans conflict directly with the plans of others: In a basketball game, both teams are planning to win, but only one is going to succeed.

Now add to this mess of plans the forces that are beyond our control. There is so much that is greater than us, whatever you believe. So while we get to choose the roads we take, we don't get to know where they lead. Acceptance, then, is knowing that when your plan fails, or your road dead ends, it means a bigger plan is at work. And I'd rather be part of a big plan than a small one.

So I cracked that Bible open and read the entire books of Genesis and Exodus on the spot. Then I called my mom and apologized with all my heart.

"Mom, I'm so sorry. I just began reading the Bible, and I found my salvation."

"That Bible will serve you better than those checks," she replied. "You're going to need to stay faithful if you want to succeed on your journey."

My mom had a funny way of doing things, and even in my darkest days, she was able to turn the hard times into a lesson or cast a positive light on them. Even when things got negative in her own life, she stood tall as a model of optimism and resiliency.

Out of respect for her, I started reading Scripture every day for years after that.

And pretty soon, a miracle happened.

Life Lessons FROM APPRENTICESHIP

You need a teacher, because those who can't do, teach.
So if you wanna learn something, go to someone
who can't do it. Dammit, I think
I wrote this one wrong.

At the Laff House

36

I'M RUNNING OUT OF CHAPTER TITLES. HOW MANY MORE OF THESE ARE THERE?

Dad: Kev, you like getting your dick sucked, don't you?

Me: Uh, yes . . .

Dad: Well, have you ever had your dick sucked on crack?

Me: I can't say that I have, Dad.

Dad: Well, that's how it happened. I was fucking around with this chick after your mom and I split up, and she told me to try it. She was right: It was the best dick-sucking I ever got. I did it again and again, until I realized it wasn't her that was so good. It was the crack.

Me: Okay, Dad.

My father was back in my life. It was the last thing I'd expected. We were sitting in the kitchen of my mom's house, having his version of a heart-to-heart talk.

He said that with those magic rocks, he'd gained the power to sleep with women who were way out of his league.

He said, they would do *anything* for crack.

He said, all he was trying to do was get his dick sucked more, but he got hooked.

Evidently, in a crevice of my dad's brain that wasn't clouded by crack smoke, he had a conscience. A few weeks after he stole my brother's car and barbershop supplies, he asked for help from a local priest who'd been trying to get him to quit drugs. Since then, he'd been in and out of rehab.

I'd been working hard in the interim to get my brother to forgive him, track him down, and see if we could help him. Eventually, we found him: at a rehab program in Mount Airy. We visited him there and told him that whatever he needed to stay committed to the process, we were ready to do. And now he was back.

As we sat in the kitchen where he'd once lived and cooked grits, Dad opened up for the first time that I could remember. I listened to every word closely, piecing together the puzzle of my father.

When he said, "Y'all got no idea what it's like to get all tricked up with crack and be treating all these people in the crack house to everything you got and then they won't buy you a damn twenty-five-cent bag of potato chips," I tried to understand.

When he said, "I thought I could turn it off and on like a faucet. Then I discovered the faucet was broke, you understand? But now I'm done with that shit and I got a clear head and I don't miss it," I believed him.

And when he said, "Do you wanna hang out or something?" I knew that we were going to have a relationship again.

Though my brother still understandably held a grudge, I didn't. The man had made an effort to clean himself up and face his family. He was still my dad and the crazy-ass person I loved.

With my brother and father back in town, I had something like a family again. I could pick up the phone and call or see them anytime. Dad was sober. Mom was happy. Kenneth owned a business. And I had a direction in life. Things were looking up for your humble narrator—and they were about to get even better.

37

FIVE CHAPTER TITLES AGO, I REFERRED TO MYSELF IN THE THIRD PERSON. DOES THAT MAKE ME SEEM EGOTISTICAL?

For a solid year, I slugged it out in the clubs and bars, hamburger restaurants and fish-fry places, bowling alleys and community centers. I didn't just rely on TuRae for work. Every time I met a comedian, I'd ask if I could open for them. I was never afraid to approach them with my hand out; the worst thing they could say was "No." And if they did, then I'd stop by their shows and support them anyway. Often they'd come around and that *no* would turn into a *yes*.

I went from making no money a week to fifty dollars to seventy to, finally, ninety. Once I hit that number, I felt good: I was earning more than I'd budgeted when I left City Sports, enough to pay my rent after my mom's checks ran out.

This was possible because of a plus-sized, foulmouthed character named Big Jay Oakerson that I'd become friends with. He lived in New Jersey and had something that I sorely lacked: a car. So every time I got booked as a headliner, I'd make sure to get Jay a guest spot too so I'd have a ride. Being able to accept more gigs meant being able to accept more money.

Big Jay was the only white comedian I saw at that time doing black rooms and getting love—at least most of the time. I once saw a dude tell him, "Shut up, white boy," with such hatred that Jay just said, "Good night," and walked right off stage.

We were finishing a show in South Philly one night when TuRae told us the news: *Def Comedy Jam*, which was the biggest thing in our world at the time, was hosting a competition—and they were going to do it at the Laff House. Bob Sumner, who created the show with Russell Simmons, was going to be there judging the comedians. He was known as "the star maker," so every comic in the city signed up: me, TuRae, Big Jay, Tommy Too Smoov,

Michael Shawn, Jamal Doman, Denny Live, and Michael Blackson, the African King of Comedy.

The prize was five hundred dollars and a personalized *Def Comedy Jam* championship jacket. But more important than the jacket or the bragging rights that went with it, the winner got an opening slot on the actual tour when it came through Philadelphia. This was a chance to perform on stage with Earthquake, D. L. Hughley, A. J. Johnson from *Friday*, and other national headliners.

Before the competition, the other comics were intensely focused. They had headphones on and notepads out and were busy warming up as if it were the Super Bowl of comedy.

What worried me most of all was that this was a real contest. I couldn't just bring my loud-ass friends. *Def Jam* had its own judges who would determine the three finalists—and then the one winner.

I was on fourth. When the stakes are higher than what you're used to, there's one rule: *Go with what you know—don't change it up.* Because when you start performing new stuff instead of polished stuff, you're more likely to bomb. I did my tight five minutes, and I destroyed.

The three finalists were me, TuRae, and Tommy Too Smoov. Word got around, and two weeks later, we performed for a packed house. That night, I was chosen as the *Def Comedy Jam* competition winner.

My brother was there. My friends from City Sports were there. My buddies from the neighborhood were there. Torrei, who I was dating again, was there. Even my dad was there, though he slept through my set. Afterward, he gave me the kind of encouragement that only a father can: "Ah, I don't think it was that good."

"I saw you sleeping during the set!"

"If it was better, it would have kept me awake, wouldn't it?"

Despite Dad's words, that day was the first time my brother said he was proud of me. When it comes to family and friends, either they believe in you right away, before you've ever done anything, or they're your toughest critics and the last ones to offer praise. Those words from my brother further sky-rocketed my mood that day, that week, that month.

The only person who didn't see me win was my mom. Because she was turning her life over to God more and more each year, she didn't want to hear me using obscenities and talking about sexual or violent situations. And she definitely didn't want to go to a place where people drank alcohol. However, I wasn't upset about it. It's a true act of love to believe in someone and support them wholeheartedly, even though you don't morally or ethically agree with them.

At the end of the night I was given the championship jacket, but it was Bernie Mac–sized. I was practically swimming in it, so they promised to get one custom-made with my name on it.

For weeks, I waited for that jacket to arrive in the mail, and it never came. In the meantime, I wore the oversized jacket every day. People accused me of lying about winning the contest and stealing someone else's coat. But because it had *"Def Comedy Jam* Winner" emblazoned on the back and I knew that winner was me, no drug could have gotten me higher and no intervention could have brought me down.

Until I met Keith Robinson.

38

OR IS IT MORE EGOTISTICAL THAT FIVE CHAPTERS LATER, I'M STILL WORRYING ABOUT HOW IT MADE ME LOOK?

I wasn't "the new guy" in Philadelphia anymore. Everyone knew my name. Comedians who'd never spoken to me before would come up and say, "Congratulations, man." People who had never seen me perform were saying I was funny, just because that's what everyone else was saying. And I was taking every show I could hustle, because I needed all the stage time I could get to prepare for when the *Def Comedy Jam* tour came to town.

I took so many shows that I started making more money. So when Paul lost his job and tried to steal from Torrei's purse to pay the rent, I decided it was time to start living alone. I carefully prepared a budget, and determined that if I continued to work this hard, I could afford four hundred dollars for rent plus another one hundred dollars for utilities and other expenses.

On a Saturday night a few weeks before the *Def Jam* show, I stopped by the Laff House, where a local comedian named Keith Robinson was headlining. Although I'd never met Keith, he'd been around for a while and was one of the most respected performers in the local scene. He'd acted in a TV movie with Don Cheadle. I think he even performed on *Star Search* back when I was in elementary school.

I strutted up to him at the beginning of the night, wearing my *Def Jam* jacket, and asked him for a guest spot, which I was sure he would give me because of the aforementioned jacket.

"Can I have a spot tonight?"

"What's your name, young fella?" he responded, in what had to be the most grating voice to ever rub my ear.

"Lil' Kev the Bastard," I told him proudly.

"The Bastard?" He screwed up his face. "That's fucking horrible."

"Tell me how you really feel." I smiled, assuming he was joking.

"Fucking horrible," he repeated. He wasn't joking. "What's your *name*, stupid?"

"Kevin." Pause, no response. "Kevin Hart."

"Much better. I wanna see what you got, young fella. Yeah, you can get a guest spot."

There were several other comedians there jockeying for stage time, but he shut them down and said, "I'm only giving this kid here a spot."

I was in great form from all the practicing I'd been doing, so I went on stage and *boom, boom, boom*, I hit them with every joke I had. It was Saturday night, and the place was thick with laughter.

After the set, I asked Keith, "What did you think?" I was certain I'd impressed him with my young, raw talent, and waited for the praise to roll in.

"It was awful."

"Awful?" In all this time, no one had said anything that direct and harsh to me—especially not an older, established comedian.

"You're not talking about shit," he continued. "I'm not getting to know who you are."

"What do you mean? You just *saw* me. Everyone was laughing."

"So what? People will laugh at anything. You're doing 'black crowd tricks,' son. Comedy is about experimentation. You're rehashing corny bits that have already been done and will always work. It's TV dinner comedy: prepackaged." His words hurt, but I tried not to show it. "Stop catering to the audience and start working on being a comedian, young fella."

I tried to respond, but I couldn't get any words out. I'd just beat out all the other comedians in Philly. I had to at least have *something* going for me.

"Now, I definitely saw some pizzazz," Keith went on. "I saw a solid stage presence and a lot of energy. But none of that set was about you. So it means nothing."

There's only so much abuse a person can take. Who was this guy to come out of nowhere and tell me to change my whole act?

"You tell 'em your real name." He slapped me hard on the back. "It'll take you further and it'll sharpen you up. Stay and watch my set."

I stuck around and saw Keith perform. His entire routine was about him: his life, his point of view, his family. He told jokes about his mom and his brother, sharing insights about them that were so specific, they had to be true. Unlike me, he was very relaxed on stage and wasn't afraid to take long pauses and let things settle. He didn't seem to be putting on a persona so much as sharing his own personality at its best. He was right: Compared to him, I looked like an amateur who was trying too hard.

I decided that night to try letting go of my comedy name. When there are no consequences to taking someone's advice, then there's no reason not to test it out and see if it works.

In the days that followed, I told hosts to introduce me as "Kevin Hart." And I discovered that while Keith's advice worked for him, it didn't work for me. I had no swag as Kevin Hart. I wasn't interesting as Kevin Hart. I wasn't funny as Kevin Hart.

Just imagine: You're on a date. You're at a comedy club. You're both a little nervous and hoping to have a special night together, a night to remember. You've never heard of the performers, but your friend promised you that this club was a good time.

Someone comes out and says: "I'm Kevin Hart. What's up?"

Someone else comes out and says: "I'm Lil' Kev the Bastard. What's up?"

Which one is going to get you more hyped, have you smiling at your date with that look in your eyes that says, "See, I told you this place was fun"?

From the start, Lil' Kev the Bastard is funnier. He has attitude. He has presence. He's memorable. He's original. He doesn't give a fuck. You are ready to laugh at this little bastard.

When I was Kevin Hart, none of the bits that I did as Lil' Kev the Bastard were funny. Kevin Hart was dull compared to crazy-ass, loud-mouthed, unpredictable Lil' Kev the Bastard.

I was nothing without the name, and with the *Def Jam* show coming up in just a week, I needed to follow my own advice and not change up an act at the last minute. I didn't want to bomb in front of thousands of people, so I ended the experiment and dropped Keith's advice.

"So you're back to Lil' Kev the Bastard?" TuRae asked when I told him to announce me by my stage name at the next show.

"Yeah, I tried what Keith said cause he was so cocky about it. But that 'Kevin Hart' shit just doesn't work for me."

"Cause you would know, right?" He rolled his eyes. "You've been doing comedy longer than anyone here, so you're the expert now?"

"I gotta be doing something right. I won the *Def Jam* competition."

"That's because you're new and young. You don't know who you want to be yet."

I tried not to listen to his words. It was like dropping poison into my ears right before the biggest show of my life. Maybe they were jealous that the new kid was eclipsing them.

I'm embarrassed I thought that, but those first wins can go to your head. More importantly, I couldn't afford to have any self-doubt and fuck my game up before the show. So I hid behind overconfidence and arrogance.

On the big night, I got a ride to the Liacouras Center with Torrei. *Def Jam* said they didn't have enough extra tickets for me to give to friends, but they had my name on the backstage list plus one, which was even cooler. I'd spent what remained of my savings on a rayon shirt, dress pants, and black patent-leather shoes, so I was feeling on top of the world.

When we arrived, I saw security guards outside with walkie-talkies and tons of people rushing around backstage. It wasn't just a show; it was a well-oiled machine run by what must have been a hundred people. At every other show I'd been to, the comedians had almost no support. Maybe there'd be a host, who was usually also doing sound and lighting, and sometimes a separate DJ. But at the Liacouras Center, I couldn't even imagine what jobs all those people could possibly be doing.

I walked through the corridor looking at the names posted on the doors: D. L. Hughley, Earthquake, A. J. Johnson. But there was no door for Lil' Kev the Bastard. In fact, everyone was ignoring me. Torrei and I just wandered around lost backstage.

I started to get nervous. Did they know that I was supposed to open the show? What if they'd forgotten?

I finally found Bob Sumner in an office, where he was talking with three other people. He greeted me without enthusiasm, then introduced me to someone he identified as a production manager and told me to stay close to him. Torrei and I followed the production manager around, still ignored and feeling like we were in the way, until finally we arrived at a little area just to the side of the stage.

"All right, it's showtime," the production manager said.

I stood there, waiting to be announced.

"I said it's showtime," he repeated.

All the house lights were on. People were still arriving, getting drinks in the lobby, and finding their seats. The host hadn't even come on stage to announce the show.

I was totally confused. "What? Isn't someone supposed to announce me or something?"

"Just get out there and do your five minutes."

Okay, no one was announcing me. At best, I was warming up the audience for the show's host. At worst, the contest was just a promotional stunt to boost ticket sales, and now they were stuck with an amateur comedian who they had to put on stage without ruining the show. I hoped they'd at least turned the sound system on for me.

All the confidence I'd gained from winning the competition drained out of me, leaving a trail of sweat from the backstage area to the center of the stage.

"Hey, everyone," I began. So many people in the audience were talking to each other and making noise that I couldn't hear the sound of my own voice in the arena. I felt tiny and invisible.

I pushed forward with my set and worked my heart out, doing all the material that had gotten me there. Some folks were looking at the stage, but in the same way people at movie theaters look at the advertisements before the show. I could count on my hands the number of people who laughed that night.

"Thank you, Philly," I ended. "I love you, Philadelphia."

I heard a smattering of polite applause as I walked to the wings of the stage, dejected. No one said a word except Torrei, who gave me a pity pat. Everyone else was running around getting ready for the *actual* show to start. I felt like I would have gotten more laughs if I'd just stood on a car in the parking lot and done my set.

My big moment was over. As much as I wanted to go home and hide from the world, I didn't want the moment to end; I didn't know if I'd ever be back there again. So I asked the production manager if we could stay and see the rest of the show.

I stood on the side of the stage and watched each comic kill on a level I'd never witnessed before. They were so tight, authentic, and comfortable that even when they paused to breathe, they had the audience screaming with laughter. I'd never seen, up close and in person, comedy at that level of mastery and control before. Even Torrei was dying with laughter. I looked at her doubled up and thought, sadly, *She doesn't even laugh like that at me.*

In that moment, I understood that I had been given the slot I deserved. I wasn't good enough yet. In the small bubble of the Laff House and the Philly comedy scene, maybe I stood out. But it was like standing out in a high school play. It wasn't the real world of entertainment. The stage I was on at these tiny clubs was the size of a subcompact parking space. This was a real venue, with a stage the size of a barn. I was a long way from being able to perform on this scale and at this level of professionalism, even as an opening act.

As humbled as I was, I knew one thing: I needed to somehow get from *here* to *there*.

I wanted to be as funny, natural, and polished as the headlining comedians there. I wanted to be as successful as them. I wanted to be playing on stages that big every night. I wanted to make as much money as they were probably making. And . . . I wanted to make my girlfriend laugh that hard.

Watching the *Def Jam* show from behind the scenes filled me with an ambition that I'd never felt before. It raised the ceiling on what I thought was possible and where this all could lead. As we walked out, I thought, *I gotta get it together so I can be here one day.*

For the first time, I didn't just have a path I was excited to be on. I had a destination.

39

STAYING TRUE TO MY FAN BASE

Now what?

After experiencing the scale and energy of the *Def Comedy Jam* tour, it was hard going back to the same clubs, bars, and random Philadelphia spots. It started to feel like the top rung in town was a weekend headlining slot at the

Laff House, but that wouldn't get me to the place Earthquake and D. L. Hughley were at. I couldn't understand how I was supposed to reach that level, or how anyone did. Was I supposed to just keep performing until the next contest came to town?

I was only twenty, and it felt like I was already peaking. I needed to figure out the next step.

"What did I tell you, stupid?"

That was when Keith Robinson came back into my life. I'd have recognized that voice anywhere. I'd just stepped off stage at the Laff House, closing with the usual "I'm Lil' Kev the Bastard. Thank you, and good night!"

"Stop telling people you're Lil' Kev the Bastard!" A nasal voice drilled into my skull.

I told him that I'd taken his advice, but it wasn't working for me. Audiences didn't find Kevin Hart nearly as funny as Lil' Kev the Bastard.

"Sit down." He gestured. I sat down obediently. "Let me ask you a question: How many people do you think are gonna remember Lil' Kev the Bastard?"

"Shit, my whole fan base, man!" My fan base was like twenty-seven people.

"Okay, then tell me some comedians with nicknames who are stars."

"Earthquake, Cedric the Entertainer, Sinbad—"

"I said *stars*. People that are worldwide. People that are globally known household names for telling jokes. Name just four people."

I thought of the legends: Eddie Murphy, Bill Cosby, Richard Pryor, George Carlin. None had stage names. "I don't know," I stammered.

"That's my point. That name may work for you in the short term, but you're cutting off an entire group of people that may not get Lil' Kev the Bastard. If you wanted to be a wrestler or a rapper, Lil' Kev the Bastard would be fine. However, you want to have a relationship with the audience, and the name you were born with is going to have more depth and authenticity than a character you made up."

"Yeah," I sighed. On an intuitive level, I knew that he was right. But I didn't want to start all over as Kevin Hart and throw away the work I'd done so far.

"I can see the doubt in your eyes." Keith grew more impassioned, leaning in a little too close. "Stop being a dummy. Your job as a person with talent is to make yourself interesting *after* the audience hears your name. Define the person who was just introduced."

"How do you do that?"

"It's simple, stupid. You *be yourself*. When they say *Kevin Hart*, your first words should be 'Hey, what's going on? My name is Kevin Hart. I'm happy to be here.'"

It felt like he'd just told me to pull down my pants and take a crap on stage. In fact, taking an on-stage shit would have made more sense to me. At least that was interesting and memorable. Starting out by greeting the audience like I was at a job interview made absolutely no sense. But I was willing to try it again.

"Oh, man. I can do that, I guess."

"It's a long journey to finding yourself. Just go on that journey. It's worth it."

He advised me to stick around and watch him perform again. I paid attention as he did exactly what he'd suggested I do, and I noticed that because of it he was coming across more like the stars I'd seen at the *Def Jam* show than like me or Tommy Too Smoov with our gimmicks. And that's when I got it: I could be funny for ten minutes at my best. Same with most of the other new guys on the scene. But when Keith started talking, you felt like you could listen to him for hours. He wasn't delivering material or playing characters. He was just being himself—it was a radical concept.

After his set, he hung around talking to audience members and other comedians, then returned to the table where I was sitting. He slapped my head, then spoke the words that would change my life:

"If you're really serious about this, you gotta get out of here. Philadelphia isn't the place that's gonna make you better. You gotta get to New York. It's the comedy capital of the world. Your game has to seriously rise up to make it there."

My eyes widened and my heart raced. "Man, I'd love to. How do I do that?"

He wrote down his phone number on a napkin, handed it me, and said, "If you're serious about going to New York, you call me and I'll take you there."

I couldn't believe this guy was inviting me to New York out of the blue. Either this was an opportunity to move toward the goal I'd set at the *Def Jam* show or a total scam. He could be a pervert, trying to get me alone on an isolated road. With his pulled-up-too-high dress slacks and creepy goatee, he kind of did look like a guy who hung around playgrounds pretending to read the newspaper.

I had to make a choice: Risk getting in the car with a stranger, or risk missing what could be the biggest opportunity of my career. There was only one path I could reasonably take. It wasn't the one my mother would have approved of.

40

LIL' KEV VS. BIG KEV

I called Keith the next day and told him I was ready to go to New York.

"You got a car?" he asked.

"No, but my friend does."

"Meet me tomorrow at four at the 7-Eleven on City Line Avenue. Bring the car."

I hung up and called Big Jay Oakerson: "Yo, we gotta go to New York! I just met this guy. He's saying that's where we need to be. He said to call him when I'm serious and I just called him."

Jay agreed to come with, since it would be an opportunity for him as well. The next day, he picked me up and we drove to City Line Avenue.

Keith parked his car in a lot there and jumped into Jay's car. As we drove to New York, Keith broke down the scene for us: "We're going to the city where all the best comics are. This is the big league. The goal is to make everyone think you live there. You have to be the first one in and you gotta be the last one out. Got it, dummies?"

When we arrived, he directed us to a place called the New York Comedy Club in Gramercy Park. He ran inside while we found parking, then we met him at the club and watched his set. As soon as he finished, he had us drive him to the Boston Comedy Club in Greenwich Village and we did the same thing. Next, we drove him to the Gotham Comedy Club in Chelsea to watch him do the same jokes all over again.

"What about us?" I finally broke down and asked after the Gotham show. "Are we getting up anywhere?"

"Y'all need to see what this is first," he responded.

And here's what that was: more comedy clubs than I could ever imagine in a city, more talented comedians than I'd ever seen in a night, a seemingly endless supply of audience members, and a total lack of parking spaces.

We must have chauffeured Keith to seven comedy clubs that night, and we spent most of the time searching for parking. When he finally finished around one in the morning, he took us to a brick-walled basement club called the Comedy Cellar. The show had ended for the night, and upstairs there were a few lingering customers and a table full of loud comedians, who greeted Keith as he entered. I recognized some of them from television: Patrice O'Neal, Rich Vos, Jim Norton, Bill Burr.

Keith led us to an empty table. "Y'all hungry?" he offered. "Order some food. I'm gonna take care of you."

He then stood up and headed to the long, dirty, drink-filled table full of loud comics.

"Can we sit with you?" I asked.

"No, that's *The Table*. It's for real comedians. Y'all ain't qualified to sit there."

He walked off, leaving Big Jay and me by ourselves.

"What the fuck is this, man?" Jay griped. "This is a waste of time. He didn't even let us get on stage."

I tried to be positive about it, but after sitting there for another ninety minutes while Keith completely ignored us, I had to agree: "We took him everywhere he wanted to go. Now he's pretending like we don't even exist?"

Around three in the morning, Keith decided to notice us again. "Come on, y'all," he said. "Let's go."

We didn't say a word as we shuffled back to the car. "What did you dummies see tonight?" Keith, in high spirits, asked as we began the long drive home. We said nothing. "What did y'all see? Did anything pop out to ya?"

"Man, we saw you perform seven times, and you ain't even talk to us," I finally said.

"I saw a lot of taxis trying to hit my fucking car," Big Jay grumbled.

"That's all you saw? Open your eyes, dummies. What you saw was a comedian get on stage seven different times and work on his material seven different ways. You saw a community of comedians. And you saw how many comedy clubs?"

"A lot," I replied. "But why couldn't we go on stage?"

"It's not about you getting on stage, stupid. It's about you seeing what's out there. This is the world where you need to be if you wanna make it. I could easily get you guys into these clubs, but I'm not using my good name to help nobody that's not serious and not making this a number one priority."

"We're serious. We just think we should have had the chance to get up."

"Shut up about the get up. Get serious about *learning*. They spit on me for years before I could even think of getting up somewhere."

I relented. "Okay, okay. We're serious about learning."

"Then keep rolling with me, and everything will fall into place."

"All right."

Jay agreed: "All right."

Then Keith fell asleep and didn't wake until we pulled up next to his car.

We drove Keith to and from New York four different times in the next week.

The following week, it was another four days.

Each trip was the same: We watched him perform in some half a dozen clubs, sat around like sullen children while he talked to famous people at the Comedy Cellar, then drove him back to Philadelphia while he slept in the backseat. It was some Mr. Miyagi shit.

When Keith finally deigned to introduce us to his friends in the scene, it was solely to tease me about my stage name and make the point that Lil' Kev the Bastard wouldn't fit in at The Table with people like Patrice O'Neal, Jim Norton, and Bill Burr.

On the long ride home that night, instead of crashing out, Keith spent the whole time talking to me. He said the reason he'd offered to take me to New York was because he'd seen me bombing on material that I wasn't sure about. The fact that I was testing myself and trying out new material let him know that I had potential—if only I would get rid of what he called the hacky, pandering garbage.

"The main thing is to come from the heart," he went on. "Say something that matters, rather than stuff you think the crowd wants to hear, and you won't go wrong—even if it doesn't go over well. All that matters is *you*."

"But what should I do to make that stuff funny without pandering?"

"Just tell the truth, then work your way to funny from there. When you let them in on what's really going on with you, you'll automatically find the jokes in your life."

"What's an example of someone who does that?"

"Look at Richard Pryor. That's why he's still unanimously the number one comic. Sometimes life is brutal, and he isn't afraid to come out with his truth and say it. And when he changes his mind about things, he isn't afraid to tell people he doesn't feel the same way anymore. Just speak what you know, dummy. I lived in the projects back in 1980, but they're not the same now. So I don't speak about them and pretend like I know what it's like to grow up there today."

My heels were still dug in a little, so I told him some of the things I was worried about: losing momentum, not being memorable, not being funny.

"I get it," he replied. "If you have pretty girls in the audience, you don't want to bomb in front of them. And a black crowd will give you a nice boo-ing. But you have to look at the bigger picture, which is growth. I've been through all the stuff you're going through and had the same worries, so trust me when I tell you that you're going to get worse at first and then you're going to get better. *Much* better."

On my free nights, I tried taking his advice: I started performing as Kevin Hart again. And I struggled every time.

"What's up, y'all?" I'd begin. "I'm Kevin Hart."

The audience would stare at me blankly. It felt like I was forcing myself to be *normal*. I'd gotten so used to being a clown on stage that I didn't know how to be myself. I wasn't connecting with anyone in the audience. And being exhausted from all those late nights in New York didn't help.

I asked TuRae for advice. "You're still trying too hard," he said. "Just talk how you talk. Can't nobody steal that. Be Kevin, and whatever you think is funny is just gonna have to be funny."

I felt like I was at war with myself.

Lil' Kev: Don't listen to these dudes. They're trying to fuck up your game.

Kevin: But remember the graduation dinner? That was me just being me, and everyone loved it.

Lil' Kev: Those fools were your teammates. They knew you. At these here clubs, nobody knows you. You gotta explode and grab 'em by the throat and keep 'em laughing.

Kevin: What about City Sports? I had new customers cracking up and loving me there every day without even trying.

Lil' Kev: Look how far we've come together. If it ain't broke, don't fix it. You're not enough on your own. You need me.

Kevin: Wait, man, what's the point of even doing this if I can't be me? What I should do is stop using you like a crutch and trust that I'm like-able and funny just as I am, whether I'm talking to one person or a hundred.

After that conversation with myself, I exhaled, and fifty pounds of pressure seemed to lift off me. It was like an epiphany or an exorcism or a punch in the back of my damn head.

I knew then that Lil' Kev the Bastard was dead.

The problem is that Kevin Hart still needed to come to life. I'll never forget the day that happened and I learned to be myself on stage. Because my life depended on it.

41

NOT AFRAID TO BE AFRAID

It was a Tuesday, which was always a dead night at the Laff House, but it was a chance to get some stage time in and make a little money during a day off from New York. The audience was usually a smattering of comedians and their friends, with TuRae claiming the night as host.

I arrived with Spank and Na'im, and sat in the back with the regular comedians—Buckwild, Shawn Clayton, and Tommy Too Smoov. The room was nearly empty otherwise, except for a small group of rowdy guys sitting at the center table in the front of the house, yelling at TuRae as he was trying to host.

"Yo, man, I know those guys." Spank nudged me. "Bad dudes. From the Richard Allen projects."

TuRae did his best to keep it together on stage, but he was clearly rattled. "All right man, look, you know, we gonna get this show started and have a good time. Who's ready to have a good time?"

"Yo, shut the fuck up and bring the next nigga on!" one of the guys in front yelled.

I looked longingly at the exit and tried to think of plausible excuses I could make to leave, or at least not perform. I didn't know how to handle them, because they were at a level far beyond heckling. They weren't there to laugh but to start something that neither I nor anyone else there could finish.

Shawn Clayton went on first, and they went after him instantly. "You're a weak-ass nigga," one of the guys yelled.

"Yeah, I *am* a weak-ass nigga," Shawn replied. "I know that cause I used to run from all y'all."

They laughed, but I looked up at Shawn and he wasn't laughing. My hands began trembling, and before I could stop it, my next thought was: *Mom, help me.* I'd never before, as an adult, been so scared that I wanted to run to my mama.

"Fuck this. I'm going up there," Buckwild said bravely after Shawn's set ended. I felt like those might be his last words. On stage, he had a fast-talking, rough-voiced street persona, complete with cheap gold-colored jewelry. I think his confidence that night came from the mistaken belief that he had street cred and would be able to relate to these guys on their level.

"You know, y'all niggas in here trying to stunt on me, you better back off, cause we all trying to get money in here, know what I'm saying?" he began. Then he threw in his catchphrase, which never failed to crack up Philly audiences: "Dick suck everything."

Next thing he knew, the toughest-looking killer in the group stood up, said, "Get outta here," and threw his drink in Buck's face, drenching him with alcohol and ice cubes.

"Did they just do what I think they just did?" I stuttered to Spank.

"Oh, they done did what you think they just did, and they 'bout to do more."

I couldn't believe what had just happened. The stage was a sacred barrier, and just in case someone did get rowdy, there was a security guard in the club, Brother Carlton. Where the fuck was he?

Buckwild took off his glasses, then brought them to his shirt and started cleaning them slowly, as if in a daze. I'd never seen Buck do anything slowly in my life. When he was done, he mumbled *salaam alaikum* into the microphone. He kept repeating it like it was a magic spell to cast peace over the club. "I'm saying *salaam alaikum*, brothers."

He put his glasses back on and made one last attempt to pacify them, mentioning the neighborhood he was from. Their response: "We know where you at. We know your block. Get on out of here, motherfucker."

And that motherfucker got on out of there. He was done.

TuRae scrambled back to the stage and worked up all his confidence to tell them, "Y'all gotta calm down and let these here comics perform." They proceeded to tell TuRae that they knew who he was and exactly where he lived too.

Brother Carlton leapt into action. He was twenty minutes late in leaping, but at least he was gonna finally take care of this and get them out of there. He walked to the front table, bent down, and started talking to the guys in a low whisper. Every now and then, he'd clap one of them on the back and say, "That's all I'm saying, all right? Come on, man, y'all know how it is."

Even from the back of the room, I knew what was going on: He was *pretending* like he was doing something. He wasn't saying shit, other than talking to them like they were his friends. Nobody was gonna get kicked out of that place tonight except the comics.

Eventually, Brother Carlton straightened up, walked away, and waved. "Go ahead, TuRae. We good."

I shook my head in despair. I was up after the next comic, and everyone in the room knew that all Brother Carlton had done was give these guys a free pass to do whatever the fuck they wanted to the remaining performers.

The next victim was one of the best in the city: Tommy Too Smoov. He was a true professional, famous for playing different characters on stage, and I knew he'd stick to his set. As he began his first impression, however, the guys in the front came up with another move I'd never seen in a comedy club before.

"You ain't funny," one of them snarled. "You broke as hell." All of a sudden, *whap*, dollar bills were flying everywhere on stage as the guys made it rain.

I looked around for Brother Carlton so I could tell him with my eyes: "I don't know what kind of talk you just had with those guys, but I don't think it worked."

However, I couldn't find Brother Carlton's eyes. All I saw was the door of the club closing really quickly. I think he figured, *If I'm not inside the club to see what's going on, then I'm not responsible for stopping what's going on.*

"All right, well, that's my time," Tommy was saying when I turned back around. He quickly gathered as many bills as he could and walked off stage. "Least I got paid for the night."

Ol' Kevin Hart was up next. As soon as TuRae announced me, I was grateful I'd killed off the name Lil' Kev the Bastard, because the heckles would have been merciless.

I wanted to pass. "That's all right, I'm good. Move on to the next performer." But my respect in this scene was important to me, so I trudged toward the stage like it was the electric chair. As I did, I tried to figure out what to do. I knew I couldn't perform my set because they'd keep interrupting it and making fun of the punchlines. These guys were here to laugh *at* us, not *with* us.

As I got on stage, I realized that there was only one thing I could possibly do to survive the situation—and that was to throw out everything I'd planned and talk about what was going on. I couldn't stop them or befriend them, like I'd seen others try and fail to do that night. The only thing I could do was what no one else had done: talk about what it felt like to go on stage and perform in front of them. Tell them the truth of my experience, because it was all I had.

"This has been weird all night, guys, okay?" I began. I felt like I was performing for my life. The stage is a vulnerable place. To people who like you, you're in the spotlight. To those who don't, you're at the center of a target.

I recalled the lesson I'd learned as the little guy in school: With humor and logic—or even better, humorous logic—you could disarm someone without fighting.

"Y'all threw drinks on one dude," I continued. "Y'all threw money on somebody else. That one guy admitted he was a bitch. I'm sitting in the back praying for help from my mama. This can't keep going on and on. For one thing, there's probably a stripper out there who really could have used those dollar bills to pay her rent. So why don't we break the chain right here?"

It was the first time I was glad to hear silence in a comedy club. They were listening to me, because I was speaking *to* them, not at them.

As I grew more comfortable, I began sprinkling in material from past sets that applied directly to the situation. "Everything I say up here tonight is a joke, okay? I don't need none of you guys coming up to me after the show, talking about, 'So who's the funny one now?'"

Suddenly, I heard quiet, begrudging laughter, the kind that happens when someone keeps their mouth closed and the chuckle escapes through their nose in a little puff of air. It was the smallest laugh I ever got, but it was the biggest relief. In that moment, something broke open inside me, and a wave of calm washed through my body. I became comfortable within my fear. I realized that what these guys had been picking up on the whole time was people trying too hard. It was exactly what Keith and TuRae had told me I needed to stop doing. And because these guys were predators—trained to sniff out and pounce on the slightest vulnerability—they were more attuned to weakness than even the most discerning comedy crowd. I was surviving this only because, for the first time in my short comedy career, I wasn't trying. I was just *being*.

The rest of the set flew by. Everything came out of my mouth effortlessly: "I don't like to fight; I get scared real fast. Don't you guys be making no sudden movements. In fact, put your hands on the table so I can see 'em."

It may not have been the funniest set I'd ever done but it was one of the best so far, because I wasn't just playing the role of a scared guy on stage—I *was* a scared guy on stage. I was telling them that they'd won, because that was the only way for me to win too. I did get heckled a few times, but I was the only comic who got off that stage without being humiliated.

It is through our most extreme experiences that the biggest growth happens—if we survive them. That night, I learned how to be vulnerable on stage.

42

LIFE OF A BALLER

Kevin Hart, however, had money problems, as usual.

Not only was going back and forth to New York with Keith calling me stupid the whole time starting to wear thin, but I wasn't making money on those nights. Some weeks, we drove to the city five times.

I told Keith that I was performing under my own name and getting better, but I needed more stage time. Still, he wouldn't let Jay and me get on stage in Manhattan. This meant that I had from one to three free days a week to perform in Philly, and always on off-nights, which wasn't enough to earn rent money.

I understood then why TuRae never wanted to go to New York with me: He had a good setup at home. He had rooms all over the Philly area that brought him good, consistent money. He didn't want to give all that away, because someone would instantly take his place, and he seemed happy where he was. I guess that was the difference between me and many of the people I met over the course of my career: I always wanted to be bigger; I always wanted to do more; I always wanted to find the next step and the step after that. I didn't want to settle like I had in school and on swim team. This is as true today as it was then.

When that envelope with a rent bill for four hundred dollars was slipped under my door, I looked in my sock drawer and all I had was a hundred and fifty. I wasn't even close. I didn't have the heart to ask my mom for money again, but between help from Torrei, who'd recently been hired to work for Adelphia cable, and my brother, I managed to make the month's rent.

When I paid, I told my landlord that I was working hard to make it as a comedian and had gotten a big opportunity to start going to New York. "Look, I assure you that once I get a rhythm going, I'll figure out how to be on time with the rent every month."

Fortunately, the landlord was understanding, and said he'd give me a little leeway while I got things together.

After our next trip to New York, I talked to Big Jay about it as he drove me back to my house. His solution: "Fuck this. Let's not go anymore."

"We don't have a choice," I protested. "If we go back to doing what we were doing before, nothing's going to change. This is at least a way out. Once we know some people in New York, maybe we can even get on stage without Keith."

"Good luck with that. I'm tired, and I'm out."

Jay wasn't being callous or cruel—he was taking care of himself. He was understandably fed up with spending what were sometimes twelve-hour days going back and forth to New York like an unpaid chauffeur.

But with Jay backing out, I now had two problems: no money and no way to get to New York. It is in these moments that you get nostalgic for a day job. At least there's a structure, set hours, a predictable paycheck, and a clear path.

The following afternoon, Keith called with the usual instructions: "Hey, meet me at City Line Avenue at three o'clock."

"Jay said he's not coming."

"Why not?"

"Cause he's not getting on stage. He said he wants to get on stage."

"Didn't I tell him to be patient and trust the process?"

"I guess he don't trust it."

"Do you trust it?"

I wasn't sure if I trusted it or not, but it was the only process I had. So I told him, "Yes."

"Then are you coming today or what?"

"I don't have a way up there."

"If this is something that you want, figure out a way to City Line Avenue. Find me there, and I'll take you the rest of the way."

"Okay. I may be a little late, on account of having to take the buses there and everything."

"I'm leaving at three. If you're at City Line Avenue on time, you can roll with me. If not, I don't know what to tell you, stupid. Bad time for games." Then he hung up.

I ain't going, I decided on the spot.

Then, on the next spot, I decided, *All right, fuck it; I'm going.*

I figured out the bus lines, and got to City Line Avenue shortly before three. Keith pulled up at three sharp, then walked around from the driver's seat to the passenger's seat. Evidently he still expected me to drive him.

"I'm glad you're serious," he said as he stretched out to sleep. "I want you to know that I wouldn't lie to you. You see the way everyone treats me up there? That's because I know what I'm talking about and I know what I'm doing. They trust me, and I'm going to prove that to you today."

At Catch a Rising Star, we saw Wanda Sykes perform. Afterward, Keith introduced me to her. "Wanda, tell dummy who got you up here."

"You did."

"How many times have I cussed you out, Wanda, for not doing what you were supposed to?"

"A lot of times."

"Did I ever once lie or mislead you?"

"No."

"Little dummy here got something, Wanda. But he stupid—he don't know how to use it. I'm trying to show him how to work it."

Wanda turned and spoke to me directly for the first time: "Well, shut up and listen, stupid. He knows what he's talking about."

As we made the usual circuit, Keith encouraged me to notice details that I'd previously overlooked. "You really are a dummy. You've been coming up here all these weeks and missing the whole point. All these people are coming up, and what? They got a piece of paper in their hand and they got a tape recorder on the stool."

"I noticed that. They're working to get better."

"No, young fella! These guys are working for the weekend. On Monday, Tuesday, and Wednesday, they're preparing for the big shows on Thursday, Friday, Saturday, and Sunday. That's where your packed houses are. Until then, everybody's trying to polish their set for the weekend. And they're trying to polish their weekend sets so they can get TV spots. And they're try-ing to kill their TV spots so they can get their own television show. If you stay ready, you don't ever have to worry about getting ready."

"I get it. I'm ready!"

"No, dummy. Remember that set Wanda did? Did you notice how she changed some stuff around at the next show at Carolines? That's the level of refinement you need to learn. She knew that if she moved that one line further back, it would get a bigger laugh. And it did. Next time you see her, I guarantee that she keeps it there and adds some more to it."

When we saw Wanda do another set at Dangerfield's and she did ex-actly what Keith had predicted, that's when it hit me like a lightning bolt: I was frustrated before at Keith for constantly telling me I wasn't ready when I believed I was. A firm "no" is the ugliest sound in the world, and it trig-gers a defensive response in the brain: "Naw, *you're* wrong!" But he was right: I wasn't ready. I still knew nothing about the *art* of comedy. The problem was not Keith's slowness. It was my impatience.

I recognized that I had a lot of work to do to get to that level. Instead of thinking about getting on stage in New York, I needed to think about re-moving, rewriting, reconstructing, shifting, and shaping every phrase in my set, examining every nuance from my tonality to my gestures. One of the comics who had this perfected was named JB Smoove. He was very animated, and before he even opened his mouth, audience members al-ready knew they were going to have a good time and bust up laughing. As I worked to sharpen my act at my Philly shows, I tried to focus on what was naturally funny about me.

Keith was relentlessly critical when I asked for feedback. The biggest lesson I learned from him was how to hear a "no" or a "stupid" or a "Get the fuck outta here with that" and to not take it personally, but instead see if there was a lesson behind it.

I don't know why Keith Robinson was the guy I shut up for and listened to. Maybe it's because he was the only person I'd met who was as strict, systematic, and demanding as my mom.

In life, some people can cut through the noise and get through to you in a way that others can't. If you're playing sports, one coach may not reach you, but another will. Or no coach may be able to get through to you, but a teammate will. When it comes to your future, your mother may be telling you exactly what you need to hear but putting it in a way that makes you disregard her. However, Calvin from two doors down the street says the same thing, and it comes off as so simple and helpful that you pay attention and take action.

Cultivating the ability to listen to advice I didn't want to hear, objectively evaluate it, and know when to implement it didn't come naturally to me. I had to learn it the hard way, from someone who was very difficult to listen to. It was one of the most valuable gifts Keith gave me.

43

A WELL-RESPECTED MAN

"**H**ey, little dummy thinks he should be on stage up here already."

It was the end of my first night in New York without Big Jay, and I was at the Comedy Cellar, standing awkwardly on the periphery of The Table. Keith was introducing me to a comedian I admired, someone who would become another tough mentor and eventually a good friend, an inspiration who was never too shy to say what was really on his mind: Patrice O'Neal.

"Oh, is that what you think?" Patrice snapped at me. "You got some jokes? Let me hear one of your jokes."

"Why do people get on—"

"Shut up. I don't wanna hear your jokes for real; it was a figure of speech. Jesus, Keith, he *is* dumb."

I winced at his words. "Shut up and take it." Keith nudged me. "This is what we do."

"Tell him to go back home," Patrice went on. "I can tell he's not funny. Look at that stupid face. He looks like he's about to cry or something."

I stood there, reeling, then decided not to take Keith's advice. I didn't have to take it, not when I could throw it back. "I ain't stupid; you stupid." I thrust a finger in his face. "Look at your teeth. You look like you should be in a rodeo or something."

"Ha, New Guy attacked back!" another comedian at The Table yelled.

Soon, everyone was yelling and talking over each other and snapping on each other. I had no idea what was going on, except that they didn't seem so intimidating anymore. This wasn't the grown-ups' table. It was the kids' table.

"Should we let Dumb Kev sit at The Table with us?" Keith asked the group.

"Naw, keep him at the loser table," Patrice said. "I don't wanna sit near him. I don't want to see that ugly face. He looks like he smells. Keep him over there."

"Little dummy, sit at that table," Keith ordered.

I looked at the table where Big Jay and I had sat and thought about the prospect of eating there alone, like a lost puppy, for two hours while these guys were having the time of their lives. Then I decided: "I'm gonna sit right here with y'all. Who are y'all to tell me where I can and can't sit? Patrice, you shut your fat ass up. You wanna talk about smells? You got rolls of fat so big you gotta use deodorant underneath 'em."

"Ah-ha, Patrice is fat!" another comedian yelled. "Patrice smells."

If this was just about being in grade school again, I could handle that.

I sat at The Table and crossed my arms over my chest. I wasn't going anywhere ever again. However, whenever I tried to join in the conversation, they still shut me down:

Patrice: I still need a tag for that joke.
Me: What about—
Patrice: Shut up!
Keith: You're too green. You don't deserve to be part of these conversations yet.
Me: Better to be green than old and rusty.
Everyone: SHUT UP!

I'd made progress, finally. I may have been the greenest comic at The Table, but at least I had a new aspiration: to become an equal to everyone there.

Jay never came back to New York with us, but I kept taking the buses to City Line Avenue and driving Keith to New York. Under his tutelage, I began studying the comedians there at an even finer level of detail. I started regularly taping my own shows in Philadelphia and reviewing the performances afterward for the same subtleties. As the weeks passed, Keith went from introducing me to comedians to introducing me to comedy club owners to helping me prepare for auditions.

"How you gonna get out of this maze if you don't know that you're in a maze?" he kept saying.

The first audition he helped me land was at the Boston Comedy Club, which had an urban night on Sundays. I easily passed—not because I was so good but because I was so ready. I'd been to the club dozens of times. I knew the audience. I knew the comedians. I knew the waitresses, the bookers, the tables, the lights, and every single drink on the menu. I was so comfortable there that it was impossible to fail.

Standing on stage at the Boston Comedy Club at that urban showcase felt like a major milestone: I was performing in New York City!

Keith was right to make me wait so long to perform. You only get one chance to make a first impression—and it turned out to be a good one, because they asked me back the next week.

I often speak about the value of hard work, but hard work is not enough. I've seen many people sabotage their career before it's even started by refusing to do anything unless they're compensated or rewarded directly for it. Or they become bitter, expecting that they'll be rewarded in exchange for just working hard.

One of the key factors for success—beyond work, talent, timing, relationships, and all the other qualities I've mentioned—is the glue that holds all of these together: *commitment.*

What is commitment? Here's what it means to me: keeping the promises you make to yourself and to others. I promised my mother I'd figure out a way to survive in comedy. I promised myself I'd find a road out of Philadelphia and on to bigger opportunities. I promised Keith I'd trust him and stick with the process.

All three of these promises turned out to be much harder, and take much longer to keep, than I'd expected. I still wasn't surviving on my own. I still wasn't getting big opportunities. I still wasn't done with Keith's mentorship. I was still spending more than thirty hours a week getting to and from and around New York just for that five minutes on stage on Sundays. Though my sleep, time, finances, relationship, and even my patience and self-esteem were negatively impacted and I wanted to quit many times, I remained committed.

That's the biggest difference between the amateur and the professional, between the wannabe and the star, between the dabbler and the expert. The unsuccessful get halfway to the finish line, then turn around. The successful get halfway, then keep going. Both run the same distance, but only one makes it to the finish line.

To win the race, then, having talent, speed, and endurance help, but those things are nothing without commitment. To commit successfully, you don't have to always believe in yourself—because, let's face it, we all have our doubts at times. But you do have to believe in something higher than yourself: your purpose. If you believe in your purpose, you can survive the most challenging times, because God or destiny or your will—or whatever you prefer to believe in—is on your side. If you know it's your purpose to win the race, then you're not going to turn around, because there is no other option but to win.

And for me, there was no other option besides succeeding in New York.

The other comedians would say, "Get Kev out of here." They'd tell me to "beat it." They'd tell me I was a "hack" and that I was "never gonna make it" and that I should "crawl back home." But I'd never leave, and I'd never keep my mouth shut. I was relentless. Even Keith said he'd never seen anyone with this level of focus and drive, which is why *he* stayed committed to *me*.

I wanted in and I would not stop, no matter how much the older comedians tried to discourage me. I went back and forth to New York for years—studying their style, studying their poise, studying comics from a generation back, and studying myself—until, eventually, I became one of them.

Life Lessons
FROM THE GRIND

Without the grind, there is no reward. Think about it:
What kind of sex have you ever had that hasn't
started with a nice grind? I'll wait.

On the outside of the Comedy Cellar table with Jim Norton,
Dave Chappelle, and Keith Robinson

44

WHY YOU SHOULD NEVER LEND ME ANYTHING THAT BREAKS WHEN IT HITS A HIGHWAY MEDIAN

Eventually, I landed auditions at two more clubs, Stand Up NY and Gotham Comedy Club. I passed them both and was soon performing in New York more regularly, although I wasn't going up until one in the morning sometimes, to play what they called "food spots." What this meant was that instead of getting cash for performing, I got a hamburger and a Coke.

Because I now sometimes had gigs in New York when Keith didn't, I begged Torrei to let me borrow her 1995 Maxima so I could get up there on my own. However, more food spots in New York meant fewer paying gigs in Philly, and unfortunately my landlord wouldn't accept "food rent."

Meanwhile, my relationship with Torrei was deteriorating. The more she did to help me with my rent and transportation, the less I was around. And the less I was around, the more her family and friends tried to convince her that I was a loser who was using her and giving her nothing in return. It was a fair argument, though in our minds we were making sacrifices for a better tomorrow. When we fought, however, she'd throw her friends' criticisms in my face.

Admittedly, I was guilty of the same thing she was doing, because friends were putting ideas in my head about the relationship too. During one of our drives to New York, Keith gave me a lecture about priorities. He said that years ago, before he started going to New York regularly, he was in the mall with his girlfriend and rented a movie to watch. They came home, flipped on the television, and happened to see his friend Robin Harris doing comedy.

"Why aren't *you* on television?" Keith's girlfriend asked.

He thought about her question for a moment, then answered honestly: "Because I'm sitting here with you."

His point was that I shouldn't let my relationship get in the way of putting in the extraordinary amount of time and dedication it takes to make it. Being a comedian was like joining the army, he explained: You had to leave home and form a new family with your fellow soldiers.

The difference, though, is that soldiers make one choice—to enlist—and then leave home for a certain number of years. Comedy is a choice that must be made every day, and it can feel to your partner like you're choosing the clubs over them. So it put a serious strain on my relationship when I'd come back from New York at four or five in the morning, then sleep until two the next day and catch the afternoon bus back to Manhattan.

One night, it was snowing pretty hard, and I was racing to New York in Torrei's Maxima, worried that I was going to be late to my show. I didn't want to miss a spot, because I might not get another one.

In the midst of the storm, as I was exiting the highway, the Maxima's wheels hit a patch of ice, and the car spun out and crashed into a concrete barrier. I wasn't injured, but pieces of the car were all over the ramp.

The worst damage came later, when I told Torrei about the accident. Not only was she pissed at me, but her parents were too. They yelled at me for fifteen minutes, telling me I was a loser and a dropout and the worst thing that had ever happened to their daughter's life. Torrei and I got in a huge blowout afterward, which only served to prove them right.

"You got my family believing that I'm dumb," she said.

"You're going to New York every day and you still got nothing to show for it," she said.

"I gotta take the car to work, so now you're hurting my career too," she said.

I didn't have a leg to stand on. I just put my head down and took it. The next morning, I brought her car to a body shop and gathered every cent I had—and a lot of cents I didn't have—to pay for the repairs.

45

WHAT HAPPENS HERE DOESN'T NORMALLY HAPPEN TO WINNERS, WHICH IN A SENSE MEANS I WON

I was so broke after covering Torrei's car repairs that I had to pawn my stuff to make rent money. Sadly, I had nothing of value to pawn except my CD and DVD collections, for which I received eighty dollars. It was movieless nights for a while after that.

I was still struggling in New York, but Keith continued to warm up to me. "You're doing better, Kevin," he said after one of my sets at Stand Up NY. "The material isn't personal enough yet, but it's getting stronger. I think you're ready to audition for Lucien."

Lucien Hold was a legend, the owner and booker of the Comic Strip on the Upper East Side. Every great comedian from Chris Rock to Jerry Seinfeld had gone through this same audition with him on the road to making it. For Eddie Murphy, passing his audition with Lucien was the first big break in his career.

When I arrived a couple of weeks later for my audition, the host told me how the process worked: I'd perform on stage for Lucien and the audience. Afterward, Lucien would call me into the back room, share his thoughts on the set, then let me know whether I'd passed or failed.

Fortunately, I had an unbelievable set that night. I was on fire, the audience exploded, the room was destroyed. Any other violent comedy metaphors you can imagine, they happened. (For an art form that's about making people happy, comedy really does have a lot of unhappy imagery about things people don't want in their lives. No one ever says, "I tickled the audience" or "I made the building turn to gold.")

Afterward, Lucien called me into the back room. He had a pencil mustache, a thin frame, and pale skin, as if he lived in the club and never saw sunlight. I joined him, excited to get feedback from the legend himself.

He sat me down, adjusted his shirt, and spoke: "Kevin, I watched you, and I don't think this is for you."

I could barely get the next words out: "W-w-what do you mean?"

"I don't think stand-up comedy is for you. I didn't get it. The jokes didn't resonate for me." I stared at him, dumbfounded. "I've been watching comedy for some time. I've seen the best of the best. I've seen them all, and I don't see *it* in you."

I stuttered something incomprehensible. How could it be that the audience was laughing so much if I wasn't any good? It didn't seem possible, unless I was somehow misperceiving things from the stage.

"I'm just being honest and straight up rather than holding things back," he continued. "I don't want you to waste your time. Maybe you should start looking into other things, finding different interests that suit you better. I think it would be very valuable to you at this point."

In that moment, I felt my heart drop out of my chest, splat onto the seat, and slide onto the floor under Lucien's feet as he stomped on it. His words cut deeper than any insult I'd experienced before. If he'd been racist, at least I could have understood where the hate was coming from. It wouldn't have been personal to me as an individual, but about something I couldn't control. But this was specifically about my talent, or lack thereof.

My whole comedy life passed before my eyes: the first open mic, winning Blazin' Thursdays, quitting my job, telling Mom my life plan, traveling around Philly with TuRae, Keith telling me to change my name, and all the long drives to New York.

Was all that just a waste of time? I was so confused. Everyone else seemed to be giving me a positive response. Maybe I had overestimated my talent once again. If comedy wasn't in my future, then I had no future. There was nothing else I wanted to do. I couldn't go back to selling sneakers.

On the other hand, what kind of person has the audacity to tell someone to give up their dream? Maybe I just wasn't the type of comic that he liked. Maybe he was having a bad day. He could have just said, "You're not right for this club," instead of saying, "Give it up forever."

I didn't get angry at him. I didn't tell him he was wrong or cuss him out or defend myself. I just said, "Okay, thank you."

Then I shook his hand and left. I took the subway to the Comedy Cellar, found Keith, and told him what had happened.

Keith: Fuck Lucien. So what?

Me: I don't know. It was harsh. Hurt a little.

Keith: Get thicker skin.

Me: Uhh . . .

Keith: What are you gonna do, bitch about it?

Me: No, I just thought we could talk about it.

Keith: Shut up, stop being a bitch. Get your dumb ass up.

Me: Okay.

Keith: Don't you have a spot tonight? Go get on stage. I'll see you later.

Me: I just need to get back out there, right? Don't give up and all that. End on a high.

Keith: Stop blubbering about it, dummy, and go do it.

I walked to the Boston Comedy Club, got on stage, and . . . bombed. It felt like I'd been kicked in the back of the head by ten kids, then shit on by a flock of birds. I couldn't have felt any more humiliated as I drove Keith back to Philly that night.

"Look," Keith explained. "You have people who understand what you're doing right away, and you got people who won't get it until everyone else does. That's just the way it is. To succeed, you have to see how good you're capable of becoming before anybody else sees it. I'm one of those people that see it, and that's all you need: just a couple people backing you who believe in you."

He spoke almost the whole ride home, lifting me up. He told me that when he auditioned at the Comic Strip, even though he passed, Lucien told him there were too many black people in comedy and no one was looking for more. And when Sam Kinison auditioned there, Lucien told him there were too many white people in comedy and his act was never going to work. Kinison went on to become one of the most famous comedians of the eighties.

"It ain't gonna happen overnight," Keith went on. "It takes time. So until it happens, don't fucking bitch about it. Be a man. Have a man's intuition about taking care of business and go do what you're supposed to do, which is work on your shit."

"Goddammit, you're right," I finally said.

If it weren't for the talk I had with Keith in the car that night, I don't know what I would have done. I might have given up, at least for a little while. But instead, I kept going back to New York and working harder. I was eventually booked at every other club in the city, but I never went back to the Comic Strip.

46

THE STRUGGLE IS EVEN MORE REAL WHEN PEOPLE ARE LAUGHING AT YOU

In the wake of Lucien's rejection, I became a little more sensitive to criticism. When the guys at the Comedy Cellar called me a "hack" and "slow" every day, it started getting to me.

It took me a while to remember that it was a compliment to be harassed by the comics I respected. They wouldn't be doing it if they didn't see potential in me. Keith wouldn't be spending all this time with me if he didn't feel the same. I just needed to get better—and get better faster.

Determined to prove Lucien wrong and to shut the other comics up, I became stronger and more dogged. The guys at the Comedy Cellar started calling me "Mission Man," because I worked like I was on a mission. Once Estee Adoram, the booker at the Comedy Cellar, took a liking to me and began putting me on stage there regularly, I felt redeemed, like the hard work was paying off.

Since showing off, bragging, or egotistical behavior of any kind was mercilessly savaged at The Table, I kept my excitement in check, even when I was proud of myself for a new booking or a good show. Instead, I'd cut myself down before they could get to me or just roll good-naturedly with the punches.

Some people make fun of you because it makes them feel better about themselves. Others make fun of you to make you a better person. These comedians all belonged to the latter category. Eventually, they set up something called *hack court*: They'd put someone's joke on trial, and if it was found guilty of hackery, they'd all work to hack-proof it.

The comedians there felt like they were doing important work, and the more they drank, the more passionate they became. They were the Drunk Knights of the Dirty Table, and their quest was not just to improve each other's material but to elevate the art form of comedy.

Buried, occasionally, among a thousand snaps was a genuine compliment. One night Jerry Seinfeld sauntered into the room, and Colin Quinn said: "Hey, come here, Jerry. Meet Kevin Hart. The son of a bitch is funny." I coasted on that for the next six months.

When Chris Rock walked in one night and Tracy Morgan dropped by the next, I was introduced as a guy "with a lot of potential." These compliment islands made the ocean of invective easier to take, because I knew that at heart, they saw me as one of their own. I'd been accepted onto the comedy Division 1 team—maybe as a benchwarmer, but at least I had a shot at playing.

But then, in the midst of feeling good about myself and my future, I fell asleep at the wheel of a new Jeep that Torrei had just leased with help from her parents. I smashed it up good too.

After I managed to pay for the repairs and asked to use it again, Torrei lectured me. "You keep falling asleep and wrecking my cars. It's about time you got your own car." She stepped closer to me and thrust her face into mine. "Oh, that's right, you can't afford it. You're saying that we gotta figure this out or figure that out before we move in together, meanwhile your rent isn't paid on time and this bill's late and that one's overdue. What the fuck is going on? How is it possible for you to go back and forth so much and not bring any money back? Who are you with up there?"

Her logic was as follows: *If Kevin is going to New York every night to work and coming home at the crack of dawn with no money, is Kevin really working? Probably not. He's seeing someone else up there.*

And in a sense, I was: New York was my mistress. But I wasn't sleeping with anyone up there. I didn't have time to.

"Hey, I'm with you, and only you, one hundred percent," I reassured her. "But this is my life. Either you're on board with it or you're not, but I gotta do this stuff if I want to make it."

The more I tried to explain the situation to her, the less she understood. I had to leave for New York soon, with or without her car. So eventually I just said, "I gotta go. So if you still feel like you don't trust me, then come with me tonight and see what it's all about."

That was what you call a bad decision. In my mind, I thought she'd see for herself that I was moving forward in my career. She'd see me getting recognized at the big comedy clubs. She'd see me being accepted by successful comedians. She'd see me making a name for myself in the city of "If I can make it there, I'll make it anywhere."

But I didn't consider the fact that I wasn't performing on that particular night; I was only networking and promoting my upcoming shows. So from Torrei's perspective, the fact that everyone knew me at the clubs just meant I was a club rat. The fact that I was sitting at a table getting drunk with a bunch of comedians just meant I was an alcoholic. It looked like I was having a good time partying in New York, like I was choosing to go out with the guys every night rather than be with her.

On the way home, she was annoyed. "You call that *the struggle*?" She scowled. "Looked like a good time to me."

"You should have come up on a day when I was performing," I tried to explain. "What you saw was me building relationships, me getting people to come to my shows, me doing what I have to do to get into these comedy clubs."

"That's bullshit. You're all sitting there drinking and laughing all night, and you didn't get on stage one time. At least at home, you're performing and working and making money. I don't know what you think you're doing there, but I know what you're not doing there: putting time into our relationship."

And that was that. She never let me use her car again.

47

WHEN THE GOING GETS TOUGH, THE TOUGH GET GOING. (WHICH MAKES ME WONDER WHETHER TOUGH PEOPLE SHOULD LEAVE OR STAY WHEN THINGS GET HARD. I DID BOTH, SO EITHER WAY I'M TOUGH.)

In the past, when I wasn't able to use Torrei's car, it wasn't too big a deal. I could take the bus to City Line Avenue and then ride with Keith. Sometimes he'd even pick me up.

But now that I had my own shows, there were nights when Keith wasn't going to New York and I had to make it up there on my own.

The Amtrak train was too expensive, so I had to catch the Greyhound or Peter Pan bus, which could take as long as five hours round-trip. It would have been easy to just not go to New York when I didn't have a ride, but I refused to get lackadaisical. I had no room to be comfortable or slack off; I felt an obligation to Keith because he'd invested so much time in me. I'd seen Big Jay and other people drop off, and I didn't want that to happen to me.

Just like in Philadelphia, I found the underground rooms and urban nights in New York. I started doing it all. But now my goal wasn't for people to laugh, like it had been when I started comedy, but for them to understand who they were laughing at. I was still working toward conveying more authenticity and relatability on stage.

Some black comics at the time were picky about the rooms they played. "Naw, I ain't goin' for that white shit."

A lot of white comics were the same: "I'm not messing with that black shit."

And a lot of people of all colors would say: "I'm making money over here. I'm not going over there to perform for food. Hell no! I'm above that."

Because my goal was to appeal to everyone so I could sell out big venues like the *Def Comedy Jam* tour did, I played the rooms that were frowned upon by other comics. My job was to make all kinds of people laugh, so anyplace where there were *people* was my home.

My thought was: *New York is so big, and there are so many places to perform spread out across the city and beyond, why not just do them all?* I never turned down anything. Sometimes I got sent away. Sometimes I got burnt. Sometimes I traveled seven hours to do a college show where no one laughed and I wasn't paid. But not once could anyone say that I didn't try.

The comics who made it from that time were the ones who felt the same way and thought: *I'm not above this place or these people. No one is. I'm here to get on stage—any stage.* If you grind without that mentality, then you're wasting your time.

Over time, because I never said no, the bookers took a liking to me. Most exciting of all, Estee at the Comedy Cellar let me host on a peak night. I tried hard not to let these small steps go to my head, because I saw other comedians mistaking success at a local club for fame. They'd confuse familiarity—like the waitresses and valets knowing who they were—for popularity. If they went just across the river to another borough, they'd be in trouble.

Slowly I started getting paid in something besides food for most of my New York shows, though the money wasn't as good as it had been in Philadelphia. At some shows, I'd make as little as five dollars; other spots paid twenty-five dollars; and on a good night with multiple sets, I'd end up with seventy-five bucks in my pocket. The end game was to add up what I was making that month and make sure I could pay my rent, utilities, transportation, and food.

———

Eventually, I got a big break financially, and it came from a Philly comic, Buckwild. He was stepping down as host of a Saturday night show just off the strip in Atlantic City and offered me the opportunity to take over. It paid one hundred and seventy-five dollars each week, which would allow me to cover my expenses every month and have money to spare. It was my first chance to run a room and book the talent. So I was excited to help out newer comedians, just as TuRae and Keith had done for me. So many guys I looked up to, like Donnell Rawlings and Rob Stapleton, were running rooms in the underground comedy scene, and that had given them the flexibility to perform anywhere.

The opportunity seemed like a dream come true—until I arrived and saw pretty quickly why Buckwild had quit. The club was called Sweet Cheeks. As I should have extrapolated from the name, it was a male revue. Some nights, however, to bring in more customers, the owners would turn it into what they called a nightclub but in reality was a hood bar.

When I arrived that first night, the place was thugged the fuck out with dudes partying, fighting, playing pool, and preparing to destroy comedians. My introduction was the DJ announcing over the sound system: "That's enough. Time for us to start the comedy show."

Then the music stopped, and I was expected to somehow get everyone's attention and respect.

All I said was "Hi, I'm Kevin Hart," and the yelling began.

"Stand up, Kevin!"

"Go home, Kevin!"

"Fuck you, Kevin!"

My heart froze. This was a whole club full of guys like the Richard Allen hecklers. I wasn't going to be able to get a single joke out. So I just introduced the next comic and cleared off the stage. He tried to push through his planned material, despite the heckling, and got destroyed by the audience. He didn't even finish his set.

I forced a smile onto my face, walked back out, and tried to do something like the speech I'd given the Richard Allen thugs acknowledging the truth of the situation. I thought that would go over well. But less than a minute into it, a voice boomed through the room: "Naw, man, enough!" I looked to my right to see a bald, bearded giant holding a hot buffalo wing. He took a bite out of it, I guess so he wouldn't waste it all, then threw it at me and sat down. It hit me all saucy on the side of the face. I could feel it bounce off my cheek, leaving a burning red mark of chickeny shame.

I was furious.

"Stand back up!" I yelled at him. "You think just because I'm here telling jokes, I'm not a man? I'm a man first."

"You not a man, you a chicken," someone called out.

"This is stupid!" I yelled stupidly. "Us people got to stick together."

I walked off stage and didn't even introduce the next comic. He just went on himself, petrified. I was so mad at myself as I sat there watching him get obliterated. I couldn't believe I had lost my cool and composure.

I didn't want to go back the next week and face that crowd again, but I remembered that the point of doing an underground club was to learn to survive in any situation. And if I could survive this, then I could definitely survive anything.

Now that I knew what I was getting into, I had time to plan for it. An audience this crazy didn't have the patience for jokes. It wasn't about doing a tight five here; it was about survival. And that was familiar to me, because it was exactly what we did at The Table. I just had to pretend like I was at the Comedy Cellar, and be aware that the Sweet Cheeks regulars were testing me. If I could talk shit back to them and hold my own without buckling, then they'd accept me. It was a familiar game, but a hundred against one.

Once you know the rules of the game, you can play it. If you don't know the rules, you'll always lose.

My friend Na'im was trying to make inroads in New York, and he had a car, so I "Keithed" him and asked him to drive me to Sweet Cheeks for my next performance. I did a few early shows in New York, then we drove to Atlantic City. On the way, Na'im asked me what I thought of his act. "It was funny," I said, parroting Keith. "You just gotta make your stuff more personal, more about you. Let people know who Na'im is."

We arrived at Sweet Cheeks, and I met with the other comics. As a host, I had a responsibility to let them know how the room worked, which was more like a cage match than a comedy club. "Look, just go up there," I explained. "All I need is for you to do your time. Good or bad, it don't matter. Just hang in there, whatever happens, and get your money. If you do that, I can keep this room full and you can keep coming down."

When the comedy show began, I was ready. As soon as the first thug's mouth opened, I went after him before he could finish what he was saying: "Man, shut up with that goddamn half-a-mile-big head of yours!"

The relieving sound of laughter and "damns" filled the room, and I knew I could handle this. By the end of the night, I started to enjoy the verbal knife fight, even when I got out-shouted or out-insulted. It felt like I was in my element. In one way or another, whether it was with school bullies, other comics, or at the swim team banquet, I'd been doing this my whole life.

Eventually, Sweet Cheeks got so packed, I had enough leverage to switch the night to Wednesdays, so I could perform the big weekend shows in New York. I was also able to get more money to bring in comedians I liked. I'd pay them as much as $250, making sure to always let them know that they were getting that much to make up for the horrible experience they were going to have there.

I can count on one hand the people who had successful sets in that room. There wasn't a night that went by without a lot of booing. However, just like at

The Table, I hung in there and kept talking back, until the regulars came to accept me and even respect me.

Performing today is easy in comparison with shows like Sweet Cheeks, where the audience didn't give a shit about me, where a bad joke would get me booed off stage (and sometimes even a good joke), and where I had to win over an audience that was there with the sole intention to humiliate me.

The entertainer who chooses the easy road, lined with cheering fans offering flowers and likes, won't survive when the terrain gets challenging. The entertainer who chooses the hard road, lined with jeering haters throwing chicken wings, not only learns to survive any terrain, but to run even the easy road better than the competition.

48

WHEN OPPORTUNITY KNOCKS, OPEN THE DOOR, HEAR IT OUT, THEN SLAM THE DOOR IN ITS FACE IF YOU DON'T LIKE WHAT IT HAS TO SAY

Here's the thing about performing live: If you do it enough, the right person will see you.

One night at the Boston Comedy Club, a big executive on the scene named Barry Katz saw my set and said he wanted to meet with me.

When I reconnected with Keith later that night, I asked him what he thought.

"Barry *Katz*?"

"Yeah, he wants to meet with me."

"He's one of the biggest comedy managers in New York. He's got Dave Chappelle, Jay Mohr, Jim Breuer. You name the big guys, Barry Katz has 'em."

I took the meeting. It was my first, and it started off great: I just sat there while he blew smoke up my ass.

"Buddy, I think you're hysterical," he said. "You're funny. You got it. I wanna manage you."

This was it, I thought—the comedy industry had finally noticed the new guy and recognized his potential. It was the next step on the road to comedy stardom. "All right," I told him. "What do we do?"

"Just keep doing what you're doing, and I'll take care of the rest. Think of it like a bucket of shit: I'll take it and throw it against the wall and see what sticks."

I was young. I was inexperienced. And I definitely wasn't the smartest guy in any room. But I knew what shit was, and here was a man who wanted to manage me comparing my career—the one I'd begged my mom for money to help support and sacrificed all my time with my girlfriend for and spent probably a thousand hours going back and forth to New York for—to a bucket of shit.

I left the meeting with a smile plastered on my face, then immediately spoke to Keith.

"Man, that's no good," he responded. He thought about it for a moment, then continued, "So I say: Fuck Barry. You don't have the time for anybody who doesn't see what you have the potential to be. Don't do anything with him."

I'd never turned down an opportunity before. In fact, the reason I'd done so much was precisely because I was waiting for a single opportunity like this one, and I didn't know when it was going to happen again. But I had to follow my gut, even if Barry had—and continues to have—a great reputation.

Saying no to the biggest comedy manager in New York was one of the hardest things I had to do in my career. On paper, it seemed like the worst decision I could make. But from it, I learned that trusting your gut in situations where your logic contradicts you is terrifying—especially the first time you do it—but it's always the right move.

I returned to the New York circuit and became Multiple-Set Kev. Some nights, I performed as many as five shows. I had to get a subway pass so I could haul ass from one gig to the next.

And then, one night, I got a second chance. This time, I was at the Comedy Cellar, and Dave Attell caught my set. Attell was one of the funniest performers on the circuit; every local comic looked up to him.

"Hey, dude, I think you're extremely funny," he said to me after my spot. "Do you have a manager?"

"No, I don't."

"I want my manager to come see you."

Attell's manager, a big, friendly dude who looked like a cross between a jock who'd smoked too much weed and an extra from *Planet of the Apes*, came the next week. He introduced himself as Dave Becky, said he loved my set, and set up a meeting at the place he worked, 3 Arts Entertainment. He wasn't as hot of a manager as Katz, but he was up-and-coming and well respected. I was relieved that I hadn't shut all the doors to my future by saying no to Katz.

I came home excited about this second chance and asked Torrei if I could, just this once, borrow her car. I even promised to come home early, since I didn't have any shows that night.

Her response: "Whatever. You're not gonna see no bitch in my Jeep. You get up there on your own."

The meeting was at four in the afternoon, but I was so worried about being late or something going wrong on the way that I planned to leave that morning at ten. My friends were baffled that I was taking this meeting so seriously.

Zachary: What's it for, a job?
Me: No, it's just a meeting. I'mma see what happens.
Zachary: Sounds like a waste of time.
Me: This could be big. You never know.

Zachary: What if they cancel that shit? Do it another day when you have to be in town anyway.

Zachary always wanted to schedule life at his convenience, and consequently he had a reputation as someone who was irresponsible and whose word couldn't be trusted. I was learning to treat everything as if it were a high priority, because that next meeting or show or dinner just might be the one where you get what you've been looking for. It just takes one person to say one thing, and your whole life can change. If success happens in part by chance, then the more you expose yourself to it, the luckier you will be. I worked hard in order to get lucky.

And I was lucky the day I went to that meeting. I'd never been in a place like Dave Becky's office before. It felt like something out of a movie. We met in a big glass conference room in a big glass building, at a big glass table surrounded by plush armchairs. It looked like the kind of place where the decisions that run the world get made.

Dave, who always dressed like he was coming back from the beach, introduced me to a guy in a suit who seemed to be about my age and who never spoke, even when I shook his hand. As they both sat down, almost in unison, across the table from me, I felt both intimidated and excited. It's funny to remember how awed by this I was, because I've compared notes since with other comedians and no one has said they were impressed by a conference room. "What happens in here?" I kept asking. "Who else comes through here? *Who?* Wow. So what's a 3 Arts?"

I kind of knew what a manager was, and that this was someone who was supposed to get me more gigs and more money, but I had no idea what a management company was or what they did. My mind was reeling with questions: *Am I starting to make it now? Is this how all the big stuff starts happening? What's the catch?*

Fortunately, Dave didn't call what I was doing *shit*. He called it *craft*. One of the great things about working with someone young is that they're not jaded, bitter, or cynical. Dave said some of the same things Barry did, but in words I could hear. He explained that my goal right now should be to keep working on my craft, and he would look for opportunities and bring them to me.

"I don't know what you've experienced in the past," he continued. "With me, there's no paperwork. There's no contract. There's nothing binding you to me. We just shake hands. If you believe in the things I'm saying, let me show you what I can do. If, later on, you don't feel like I'm doing enough for you or it's not working out between us, you're entitled to leave. It's that simple."

It made sense, and I couldn't see a downside. I didn't even have to pay him: He just took a percentage of my pay for the work that he brought in. "Okay," I told him. "I don't have a manager, so now I guess I have a manager."

He smiled and we shook hands. "What are the next steps?" I asked.

"Just keep getting stronger in comedy. The best way to get the right people's attention is to hone your craft. Your stand-up is going to open up all the doors you need."

I walked out of his office into the busy, nobody-saying-hello, strangers-won't-even-give-you-directions streets of New York, and it felt weird. I was a professional comedian with a big-time manager now. I had thought I would feel different somehow. But it was more like losing your virginity: Everyone says it's such a big deal and it will make you a man, but afterward, you're still *you*. You look the same, you talk the same, you have the same amount of money in the bank . . . Or maybe you pick leaves out of your hair, hope Ms. Davis didn't see you, and go back to your mom's house. Either way, nothing's different.

I decided to stay in New York that evening. I walked around the city until the comedy clubs opened. Then I went to the shows, sat in the back, talked to the other comics, and caught the last bus home. I kept waiting for lightning to strike me or a marching band to start playing, but nothing happened.

The only thing that changed after the meeting was that every week or two, Dave would call to check in and ask how things were going. It was nice to have someone whose job it was to care.

So I kept hustling and booking those rooms.

"Do you have any spots?"

"Can I do your room?"

"How do I get an audition?"

"Can I start a night here?"

More often than not, I eventually got those spots, those rooms, those auditions, and those nights, until I was going to New York every day. I was successful not because I was the most talented person they'd seen and not even because I was the most persistent person they'd seen; I have no doubt that there were people more talented, more persistent, and harder working than me. But there was one other thing that gave me the winning edge, and will always give you the winning edge: being likeable.

No person succeeds alone. Success is a community effort. The more relationships you have, the better you'll be able to survive, thrive, and grow. A lot of times, I've seen people booked for parts on TV shows and films who weren't the best actors, but everyone liked them, was treated well by them, and knew they'd enjoy having them on set.

I pride myself on being a good guy. There's no bullshit with me. When negative shit comes my way, I try to bat it back with positivity. I haven't always succeeded, but I've eventually learned from my mistakes. It's not a technique I use: It's the way I was raised. My mother worked hard to make sure I had a good heart, that I wasn't an animal, that I didn't treat other people like objects. No one is above anybody and no one is below anybody, she taught, so if you're treating people in any other way, you are out of line with reality.

In always respecting and acknowledging people as equals going through their own struggles, whether their status in the room was higher or lower than mine, I noticed a side effect: Eventually, I wasn't grinding alone anymore. Comedians, bookers, bartenders, and waiters started telling me about openings and opportunities.

In most action movies, one person rises out of a humble beginning to discover that they have been chosen by destiny to save the world. But that's not how it works in real life. You rise out of your humble beginning to become part of a community, and it is only together and as equals that we will save the world.

Life Lessons
FROM TRANSITION

The toughest transition is the transition to understanding that being yourself is all you need to be.

With Dave Becky

49

IN WHICH I DISCOVER THAT I'M NOT ACTUALLY AS GOOD AS I THOUGHT, WHICH THEN PUTS ME ON THE PATH TO BECOMING AS GOOD AS I THOUGHT

It was the biggest comedy festival on the planet: Just for Laughs in Montreal.

The entire comedy industry would be there: not just promoters and bookers but television network executives and film casting agents. Just being on the bill was enough to generate buzz in the business, but a great performance could make a comedian's career, even get them their own TV pilot.

Scouts for the festival saw me perform in New York and offered me a slot on their New Faces showcase. I called Dave and breathlessly told him the big news. I'd never even been out of the country before.

His response: "You're not ready."

"Huh?"

"You're not ready. We're gonna pass this up."

"What? No, man. This is the biggest shit ever. Dude, what are you talking about?"

"Come in, and we can talk about it."

I decided to ask Keith for his opinion. If he agreed with Dave, then maybe I'd actually have to pass on this.

He didn't agree. "Stupid, that's the biggest show out there. That's where you get a deal. That's where they give you some money. He said what?"

"He wants me to turn it down."

Keith couldn't wrap his head around it. "Look, stupid, I think you should definitely do it. But the comedians who work with Dave Becky all say he knows what he's doing. So you gotta make your own call on this."

I had no other opportunities in my career at the moment besides this festival performance, so I stormed into Dave's office, ready to make my case.

He sat me down and calmly explained that I was still too green. "You only get one shot at these festivals to make your presence known," he elaborated. "They want to put you in the New Faces showcase, so all the studios, all the agencies, all the casting agents, *everybody* is going to see you. And the first time they see you, they need to be blown away. Take a year and work on your material to make sure you stand out from the pack. Then, when you go next year, they'll be fighting over you."

I stood staring at him with my jaw open, processing his words. They stung a lot. I wanted to say that with him or without him, I was going. But he was highly respected, and I'd gotten this far by listening to the advice of people like him, even when I didn't agree with their logic.

"Are you sure?" I asked.

"A year will go by like that." He snapped his fingers.

"Okay." It was one of the toughest *okays* I'd ever spoken.

Then I thought: *Shit—what if they don't invite me back next year?*

It was a good thing I waited, because later that week, I did a show at the Comedy Cellar with the material that had gotten me the Just for Laughs offer. I asked Keith to take a hard look at my set, and let me know what I needed to improve so I could stand out at Just for Laughs the following year. I still thought it was my best stuff—until I sat down next to Keith at The Table.

Keith: Good set, man.

Me: Thanks! I killed.

Keith: Yeah. Who was the midget robber you were talking about?

Me: I made it up.

Keith: Oh, okay. Hey, you know that whole bit about you and a dirty sock, and the dirty sock is talking? When did a dirty sock talk to you?

Me: You know that didn't happen. I made it up.

Keith: Oh, okay. And what about the black people with the Chinese tattoos? How many black people you know got a Chinese tattoo?

Me: Naw, I was just saying, like, you know how black people be gettin' 'em and they don't know what they say.

Keith: You made that up too?

Me: Yeah, it was just a funny thing.

Keith: Now, after all that stuff, what do I walk away saying about *you*? You're not a midget. You're not the voice of a dirty sock. You don't have a Chinese tattoo. I could go on and on. Who's performing?

Me: It's me. They're jokes I made up out of my head, so they show the way my mind works.

Keith: Oh, so you're the crazy comic? You're the comic who's got another world going on in his head. Okay, I get it.

I understood his point. Even though I'd changed my name and tightened my set and started writing from my own perspective, I was still *making up* jokes instead of sharing personal experiences. On the way home that night, I went through my set with Keith, and he demolished just about everything. It was my own private hack court.

It turned out I only had one bit that was actually about me. It was the joke I'd told the thugs from the Richard Allen projects: "I just wanna let you guys know that I'm not a fighter. I'm a bitch, okay? I don't want nobody coming up to me after the show, talking about 'Who's the funny one now?' "

Keith approved of that joke: "That's the only thing you have that's personal. Start there and build off that. What else? Why are you a bitch? What happened?"

"I don't know. Good question."

"Here's what you gotta do, dummy. Go home and think about the answer. Look at what's actually happening in your life, so you can talk about it on stage."

"There's nothing happening. I just travel back and forth to New York all the time."

"Man, you really are a big dummy. The answer is staring you right in the face."

50

YOU CAN SKIP THIS ONE

The next part of this story is hard to write, because I did have things happening in my life. I just didn't know how to talk about them.

Around this time, Torrei and I moved in together. With the money I was making at Sweet Cheeks, we were able to rent a house on Second Street in Philadelphia. In the filing cabinet of my life, I would put this decision in a thick folder labeled "Seemed Like a Good Idea at the Time." It was my first real relationship, and I was too young, dumb, and horny to take care of her emotional needs, communicate honestly, and repair the damage from the mistakes that had already accumulated.

Those mistakes came mostly from times when we argued so intensely that we broke up and messed around with other people—sometimes for sex, other times for retaliation. When we inevitably got back together, the knowledge—or sometimes just the suspicion—that one of us had been with someone else made the next fight that much worse. These fights usually took place under the influence of alcohol. Where drinking used to be a way to have fun together on my off nights, it soon became a match that was continually lighting our short fuses.

Once, during a period when Torrei moved back in with her parents, I had someone else at the house. Suddenly, I heard the sound of glass breaking outside. I ran into the street to find Torrei kicking the other woman's car in. By the time she finished, the fender was hanging off the front, the headlights were broken, and the hood was dented.

Torrei and I didn't talk for a while after that. Lust and habit eventually brought us back together, and before long we were fighting about why we left in the first place. We couldn't live with each other and we couldn't live without each other. We were in relationship limbo, caught between hope and hurt.

One night, while out drinking, we got into an argument about a guy she had seen during our most recent split. She then flipped it on me and got upset about the woman whose car she'd wrecked. The fight continued all the way back to the house, each word a weapon aimed at a specific wound. The more I slashed, the harder she slashed back, breaking skin and cutting deep.

"Fuck you and your comedy. You're not even funny."

"Are you listening to yourself right now? You fell in love with me cause you thought I was funny. Your head is so far up your ass that only shit comes out of your mouth anymore. I don't know why I stay with you."

"You're not gonna be successful. Everyone knows it but your dumb, broke ass."

What soon followed was one of the lowest points I ever hit, and it fills me with an amount of shame that's beyond words. When we are triggered at the place where our deepest wounds lie, we respond with what we know, and what I knew was what I'd seen my parents do when they were fighting. At one point, Torrei spit on me. I let loose a volley of curses at her, and she lunged at me.

Next thing I knew, I looked up and I had scratches all over my neck and head, and she had a red, swelling mark on her face.

The next day, we didn't talk to each other. I was so mad at myself for what I'd done. Eventually, one of us crawled back to the other to apologize, we had incredible sex, and then we acted as if everything was fine.

Another night, I passed out at home after a fight and woke up with the police handcuffing me. I was so drunk, I couldn't remember what had happened. I didn't have any marks on me, and neither did Torrei. As best I can tell, we got in a screaming match, and she decided to call the police because she thought it would hurt more than physical violence.

While I was sitting in jail, I realized that she was going to start doing this all the time. But there was a way to stop it. Next time we fought, if she laid hands on me, I could just as easily call the cops on *her*, and she'd get taken away.

The next time shit went down, she slapped me across the face.

"You going to jail for that!" I yelled as I ran to the phone. "*You* going to jail this time!"

I dialed 911. As soon as the cops arrived, I told them what had happened. "She hit me," I said, glaring at Torrei.

They looked at me like I was an idiot. "So where'd she lay her hands on you, sir?" one of them asked.

"She slapped me across the face. Right here. Take her away."

"Is there any blood or bruising, sir?"

"No. I called y'all as soon as it happened so y'all can get her up out of here."

"I'm sorry, sir, but there are no scratches, no wounds, no marks. There's nothing we can do here." He turned to Torrei. "Ma'am, are you okay?"

"Well, Officer—" she began.

"No, it's not about her! It's about *me*. I'm the one who called y'all."

"Sir, please—"

"This ain't fair! Y'all took me away last time, and she didn't have no marks."

If I'd ever had a chance of getting help or understanding from them, it was gone after that comment. They were ready to take me away again.

From then on, threatening to call the police, or sometimes actually calling them, became a regular feature of our arguments. One day I told Keith that I wasn't going to make it to City Line Avenue because Torrei and I were fighting. At this point, he knew how committed I was, so he offered to pick me up and get me out of there before it escalated into another police incident.

For all his tough love and shit talk, Keith has a great big heart and was a true father figure to me during this time. To this day, I continue to ask him for advice about everything. In many ways, I owe my career to him, beyond just the guidance and opportunities he gave me. If he hadn't been taking me to New York almost every day, I might have been in prison.

Recently, I learned that those rides to New York were just as powerful for him. His mom was sick, and calling me "dummy" for a few hours each day helped him survive that time. A good mentor learns as much from teaching as the apprentice does from learning.

Despite all the drama, Torrei and I couldn't seem to break up for good, because our ups were just as strong as our downs. In those times, we supported each other, laughed a lot, and fucked a lot. The one thing the good and bad times had in common was that they were passionate. We thought that sex and passion were the same as love and intimacy.

Our friends felt differently. To them, we were *that* couple. One night, I stopped by Na'im's place and asked if him and his girlfriend wanted to go on a double date to Red Lobster. Na'im said yes, then had a conversation with his girl in the other room that went like this:

Na'im's girlfriend: Why'd you say yes? You know what happened last time.

Na'im: I felt bad when he asked if we were avoiding them.

Na'im's girlfriend: We are—one of them always says something, and the other one says some shit back, and they end up ruining everyone's night. So buckle up.

Na'im: Well, at least they make our worst times look like a honeymoon in comparison.

For the first time in my life, I was on the receiving end of other people's *huh*s, *what*s, and *okay*s. I wasn't observing a crazy world anymore—I *was* the crazy one. I never thought I'd find myself in that position.

51

THE DAY I BECAME A COMEDIAN

"**S**o you're telling me that I should talk about what's going on with Torrei?"

"Damn right." Keith and I were on our way to New York again. "Every time we're in the car, you're telling me about all this shit you're going through with her and getting mad cause I'm laughing at your dumb ass. But it *is* funny. Problems are funny. You think you're the only one in the world that's going through relationship problems, dummy? How many guys will breathe a sigh of relief if they can look at their woman during your set and say, 'See, we ain't the only ones who get like that. There's other couples that's crazy too.'"

The problems in my relationship felt like something I should be hiding, not talking about. But the truth was, Torrei was one of the only things I was qualified to talk about, besides sneakers. People call this *the elusive obvious*: It's right there in front of your face, so close that everyone can see it but you.

"Talk about shit that people can relate to," Keith went on. "You don't have to make it up. Your life is funny, stupid. You're making up a story about being robbed by a midget when you don't have to make up a story about calling the cops on your girlfriend cause you're scared of her. How many times do I gotta tell you to talk about your *real* life before you get it? Use real names, real conversations, real feelings. Tell 'em what Torrei looks like. What she said, what you said, what you felt. It's so easy that it's hard."

I listened in silence. I didn't have a rebuttal. I could see his genius. Finally, after so long, I truly understood what Keith had been saying since the day we met—and what I'd been moving toward in small, reluctant steps. After that conversation, I started thinking differently and performing differently.

The next day, while Torrei was at work, I sat at home talking out loud about our fights and the police coming to our house. I was terrified to share this part of my life in public, afraid that I'd be judged harshly by the women in the audience. This was stuff I didn't even want my mom to know. Most of all, I was nervous about the scariest piece of advice that Keith had given me: *use real names.*

I ran through the stories of our arguments over and over—they weren't jokes. They were the shittiest parts of my life. But they passed the Keith test:

Is this person real? *She's my girlfriend.*

Did this story really happen? *It happened yesterday.*

Did the police come? *They sure did. I'll never forget it.*

There was no question Keith could ask that would receive the answer, "I made it up." For the first time, I was truly going to be *me* on stage, talking about *my* life, not a life I'd made up.

That night, my heart was pounding through my shirt as I told a roomful of strangers about fighting with Torrei and the evening I called the cops. To my relief, the audience cracked up through the whole painful mess. It wasn't the loudest laughter I'd ever received, but it was deep, rich belly laughter. Just on its own, the situation was as preposterous as the joke about the midget robber, but it was real and it was true, so it had an integrity and believability that the other story didn't.

I understood then what Keith had meant about the audience needing to know who I was. All along, I'd been trying to write jokes. This was another level: I was finding my pain points and transforming them into something that could touch and maybe even help other people. An entertainer makes you laugh, I realized, but an artist makes you understand.

The butterflies in my stomach settled as I painted a picture of me standing in the house, blubbering to the police, "I just want y'all to take her as far away as possible!"

On the surface, it wasn't a funny line at all. It was just a comic exaggeration of something I'd said. But the look on my face and the image of me begging the police to save me from my girlfriend were all the audience needed to laugh. I didn't need to be clever.

That night led to perhaps the biggest epiphany of my career: The audience wasn't laughing at the jokes. There weren't really any punch lines. The situation itself might have been funny, since it was a role reversal, but it wasn't *that* funny. What they were laughing at was *my reactions.* The humor was in my uniqueness, my personality—not the way I *saw* life, but the way I *did* life. That was the payoff; that's where I struck gold. For the first time, I could see it wasn't my jokes or my delivery or my ideas that were funny. *I* was actually funny.

52

SNAP-YOUR-FINGERS FAMOUS

After that breakthrough night, I started to observe my life and what was going on around me in a way that I hadn't before. I started looking not externally but internally. Over time, my set became more about the situations I found myself in and my responses to them. The smallest thing could turn into a hilarious story if I noticed that my response to it was way out of proportion.

That's when I started to get consistent headlining slots in New York. Being myself was actually paying off. The money started rolling in: four hundred, sometimes five hundred dollars a week. I began not just paying my rent on time but saving money so that I could pay off the overdue bills that had gone to collection agencies. Things were finally turning around.

After a headlining set at Carolines one night, I was downing a Ketel One and tonic at the bar. A couple of guys approached me and said, "Hey, man, Dame Dash wants to say what's up to you."

I scanned the back tables and, to my surprise, saw Damon Dash, who founded Roc-A-Fella Records with Jay Z.

"Hey, man, I think you funny as hell," he told me. "You made me laugh. I think I got a movie for you."

A movie? You want me to act? Is this, like, a bit part as a stand-up comic, or a real role? Do I need to check with my manager? Why me?

These were some of the hundred questions that went through my mind in that moment. But I only spoke one word: "Okay."

"You got a number or something so we can meet?"

"Yup." I gave him my number, and the next afternoon, my phone rang.

"Can you meet Dame in New York?" boomed the caller.

"Sure, when?"

"Tomorrow, two p.m. At our offices."

I caught an early bus to New York the next day and went to the Roc-A-Fella office. There were framed multiplatinum album awards all over the walls. Everybody was dressed in Rocawear. They were all talking excitedly about new albums, artists, and deals. Jay Z walked through the front door and right past me.

This was a level of success I hadn't seen before, even on the *Def Comedy Jam* tour. I made mental notes of what it looked like, so I could strive to reach that level too. One day, when I succeeded in comedy, maybe I could have an office buzzing with employees and awards and people making deals.

A receptionist brought me into Damon Dash's office, where he sat in a brown leather armchair, wearing a white T-shirt with sleeves down to his elbows. He got right to the point: "We got a funny idea for a movie. I wanna do it, and I think you'll be funny as the star."

"Huh?" He wanted me to be *the star*?

"There's just one thing: Y'all gotta write the movie first."

"What?" He wanted me to be the star *and* the writer—after seeing me perform just once.

"Capone. Smokey. Charlie Murphy. They'll all be writing with you."

"Okay." Charlie was not only a great comedian, but Eddie Murphy's older brother.

It was a crazy conversation. He was talking to me like I was already on board and best friends with everyone involved. I didn't ask about a contract or how much I was getting paid. Even if he was going to exploit me, it would be worth it for the experience.

He put me in touch with the other comedians he'd mentioned—Capone Lee, Smokey Edington, and Charlie Murphy—as well as a staffer from

Roc-A-Fella who would oversee the process. We started going to Charlie's house two days a week to work on the script, which was about a good kid on parole trying to make ends meet by robbing houses.

I came to love Charlie, except for four things:

1. He lived in New Jersey.
2. His house was two miles away from the bus stop.
3. He had a car.
4. He refused to pick us up.

So twice a week, Smokey and I would take the bus to Jersey, walk two miles to Charlie's house, work for four or five hours, and then walk two miles back to catch the bus to Manhattan.

It took us less than two months to complete the script. When we turned the script in, Dame didn't ask us to change a single thing. He just found a director and started planning production. Dame was the first real doer I'd met: He didn't overthink things or try to make them perfect or worry about everything that could go wrong. He just made things happen.

The movie, *Paper Soldiers*, was the first film set I'd been on. With the exception of me, the cast was mostly accomplished people: Beanie Sigel, Memphis Bleek, Michael Rapaport, Stacey Dash, and Jay Z.

When I showed up to work on the first day, Dame was there with the director, who never really got a chance to direct because Dame kept talking over him. I don't think many people on that crew had much experience making movies.

"What do you want me to do?" I asked as we prepared to shoot the first scene.

"Yo, B, just be funny. Just be you."

"All right, I can do that."

That was the only kind of direction I got all day: "Yeah, man, y'all got some funny shit, just do it. Do the funny shit."

Dame had no idea how to direct, but he was a genius within that lack of knowledge. If I ever did something he didn't like, he'd say, "Naw man, that shit-ass. Don't do it like that. Do some funny shit, yo."

"Was there anything specifically that you didn't like about it or would like to see?"

"Yo, just do the same shit but be funny."

The dialogue I had walked so many miles to write was barely used. Instead, we improvised all day. Though the process was loose and unstructured, it was amazing to be trusted with the freedom to do whatever I wanted and be my best. It would come as a shock later when directors wanted me to follow a script word-for-word. I never felt like the scenes turned out as well.

I was new to being around so many high-profile people, so I was careful never to overstay my welcome—even when I was actually being welcomed.

Memphis Bleek: Kev, you wanna come out tonight? We going to this club.

Me: I got spots.

Memphis Bleek: Get the fuck outta here with your spots. What the fuck's a spot?

Me: It's a show at a comedy club.

Memphis Bleek: Have fun. I'll be getting laid.

Even though I was spending less time in Philadelphia than I ever had, Torrei was understanding. Filming a movie made sense to her: That was work. She even drove to New Jersey one day to watch me act, and her support meant a lot to me.

Two and a half weeks after we started filming, we were done, and I was back on the New York grind. I nearly forgot about the film until, one day, Dame called out of the blue and said, "Yo, the DVD is about to drop, man. Y'all be on the lookout for it."

He invited me to a screening with the cast and crew. And I was shocked: It was funny. It was moving. It had heart. It was actually good. To this day, I still don't know how it turned out like that. Dame had no film-producing experience. I had no acting experience. It was never released in theaters. There was no marketing for it. There was no publicity. But it worked.

A few weeks later, I was performing and a group of guys came up to me afterward, yelling, "Yo, yo! Oh, shit, from the B & E gang. You funny as shit, man!"

"Huh?"

"Oh, you funny," they said and moved on.

At another club that same night, someone stopped me: "Oh, shit, the dude from *Paper Soldiers*! Damn, what up, man? You crazy."

That was how I learned that the DVD had hit the streets and become an instant hood classic. As it continued to spread, I became snap-your-fingers famous. People would see me in the street and start snapping their fingers: "Oh, shit, that's my man from . . . uh . . . oh, shit (*snap, snap*)."

I think Dame Dash paid me $175 for the whole thing. And it was worth it.

53

SQUEAK CRUNCH SMACK

During my year of craft honing, Dave occasionally sent me to small auditions—not because he wanted me to get a certain part but because he wanted me to know what an audition room, casting agents, and the overall process were like. It was a way to get comfortable with something that's an uncomfortable experience for anyone: being judged.

I didn't get any of the parts, but I didn't expect to. However, after my third audition, Dave called with an opportunity he felt like I had a good shot at landing:

"Look, it's very hard to get an audition for *Saturday Night Live*, but I got you one. I told Lorne Michaels that you were a new, hot young comic on the scene, and he said that's exactly what he wants and asked to see you."

"What? *Saturday Night Live*? This could be game changing. *Life* changing."

Holy shit, I'm about to get SNL, I thought—until Dave added: "They want you to come in and do three characters."

"Characters?"

"Yeah, find three impersonations you're great at. You got this!"

I didn't have shit. Maybe Tommy Too Smoov would have gotten it, but I'd never done a goddamn impersonation in my life.

I spent the next two weeks thinking about characters I could handle. I eventually settled on one basketball player, Avery Johnson, and two actors, Robert De Niro and Denzel Washington.

That was the moment my fate was sealed.

First of all, no one in that room, or probably any audition room, knew who Avery Johnson was. When I did my impression—"Dave, I'mma pass you da ball"—no one gasped and said, "Ah, that's Avery Johnson!" I might as well have been impersonating Tommy Too Smoov.

Next I did my De Niro. I figured I had to do a white guy, and he seemed like the easiest one. So I squinted and screwed up my face, then looked at Lorne Michaels—the gray-haired legend who created *Saturday Night Live*—and promptly forgot everything that De Niro had ever said in any movie. As for my Denzel Washington, I extended the pointer fingers on each of my hands as if they were guns, waved them in the air, and yelled until I was embarrassed enough to stop.

There was total silence in the room, except for the sound of Lorne Michaels eating popcorn and licking the salt off his lips. He seemed more interested in his snack than in me. I went into some of my best stand-up material, but no one even smiled. I just heard the *squeak crunch smack* of Lorne and his popcorn.

Sweat started trickling down my back. I wasn't used to performing comedy in total silence. Even when people hated what I was doing, they at least booed or threw chicken wings.

When I was finished, Lorne said, "Thank you," and I walked out of the room.

Even though the audition didn't feel good, I didn't know what anyone else's had been like. Maybe Lorne was like that with everyone. Maybe my personality was more important than my impersonations. Maybe he saw my potential. Maybe I'd nailed it. Maybe they saw a young Eddie Murphy or Tim Meadows in me.

Every day after that, all I could think about was *SNL*. What would happen if I got it? On the comedy circuit, I'd see Tracy Morgan and Chris Rock, who had both jump-started their careers on *SNL*, and I'd think, *Aw, man, if I get this, I'll be a star.*

54

THE GREATEST PILOT THAT NO ONE'S SEEN

Thanks to Damon Dash's willingness to take a chance on me, one day I found myself sitting in first class on a plane to Los Angeles to meet with a young director who'd just gotten a television deal with ABC. His name was Judd Apatow.

Judd had told Dave that he was looking for a young black comedian. I might not have even been considered for the meeting if I hadn't acquired an edge over other comics at my level of inexperience: *Paper Soldiers*. Every comedian had footage of them performing at a club, but none had footage showing that they could not just act but hold down a film as the lead.

Before I knew it, I was in Los Angeles for the first time. I drove around Hollywood for hours, staring at the palm trees and the mansions, the Hollywood sign and the luxury cars. Then I walked back and forth along Hollywood Boulevard, taking in the stars on the Walk of Fame, the handprints outside Grauman's Chinese Theatre, the street performers dressed as Marilyn Monroe and Michael Jackson—and thanking God and comedy for getting me this far. When I went to bed that night at the Hyatt on Sunset Boulevard, I couldn't sleep. I just kept thinking: *Holy shit, I'm in Hollywood.*

I met Judd in his office the following day and liked him instantly. The audition was the exact opposite of the *Saturday Night Live* experience. I wasn't a jester being asked to amuse the royalty. Judd was curious, excited, and enthusiastic. He explained the idea of the show, which was about three struggling roommates living hand-to-mouth in North Hollywood and hoping to make it big. But the story was less important to him than the characters in it. He asked me what my character would do in different situations, and I would answer—or, more often, act it out—and he'd laugh at everything, even when it wasn't funny. He seemed to enjoy the process of watching a character come to life. In fact, he enjoyed it so much that I got the part.

It paid twenty-five thousand dollars, which blew my mind. That was the equivalent of roughly three years of shows at Sweet Cheeks.

I called my mother. "Mom, I did it! I made it. I got a pilot deal. I'm going to do a TV show!"

"I'm so proud of you, son," she replied. "I'm happy that you're doing your best." There were probably times when she'd lost faith in me, but now all the work and struggle she'd put into making me a responsible, respectable person appeared to be paying off.

At the time, the most famous actor doing the pilot was Judge Reinhold, who had starred in *Beverly Hills Cop* with Eddie Murphy. The rest of the cast I'd never heard of before—a funny little improv comic named Amy Poehler and a big, goofy twenty-one-year-old named Jason Segel. Though they're household names now, and they had more experience than I did back then, they were relatively unknown at the time.

In the show, Amy paid her portion of our rent by working as a personal assistant to Judge, who played himself. She'd walk his dog, pick up his dry cleaning, and get moldy food out of his fridge. Jason made his money by dressing up as Frankenstein to greet tourists at Universal Studios. And I was the roommate who got lucky: I'd landed a popular Bud Light commercial and lived off the residuals from that. My character's famous tagline from the ad was, "I love the way it tizzaste."

In order for me to develop a stronger camaraderie with my costars, Judd asked me to live with Jason Segel in real life while we were putting together the pilot. I returned to L.A. with my bags and moved into his house. I wanted to be a good roommate, so on my first mornings there, I cooked him pancakes, but he never woke up in time to eat them.

Almost every day, a friend of his named Seth Rogen came over, and they smoked a shitload of weed in the living room. It was the first time I'd hung out with productive stoners. They talked about the show, got excited about other projects they were auditioning for, and came up with hilarious movie ideas, most of which were still funny when the high wore off. We were often joined by more of their actor friends, January Jones and Charlie Hunnam. Jason Segel's living room turned out to be a better introduction to L.A. than the Walk of Fame.

As I studied my lines before the first day of shooting, it struck me as ironic that the guy who hated tests more than anyone in school had ended up with a career that required him to study and memorize things on a regular basis.

It was my first time on a Hollywood set with a director who actually gave direction, and the taping came surprisingly easily to me. There were only four things I really needed to do:

1. Know my lines
2. Show up on time
3. Pay attention
4. Be positive

We shot the pilot in seven days, which flew by quickly. I tried to bring good energy to the set and be easy to work with, because I hoped this would be my job for a long time. When the pilot wrapped and I left L.A., I gave Jason a check for groceries and rent.

He never cashed it. My best guess is that he either lost it while he was high or smoked it.

Back home, I phoned Dave every day: "Hey, did ABC call yet? No? What do you think, though? You think it's gonna get picked up? What about my chances of getting *Saturday Night Live*? I mean, like, no, I know you don't *know*, but if you had to put a definition to your feeling, what would it be?"

Finally, Dave called me.

Dave: I just heard from ABC. You're a star!
Me: *North Hollywood* got picked up?
Dave: No, they passed on it.
Me: Then how am I a star?
Dave: Because it's *in* you. You have that special something, and whether
    something goes or it doesn't go, you'll still be a star.

His words felt like something a father might say to encourage a depressed kid. I'd already told my mom, Torrei, and my friends to get ready to watch me on TV every week. Though maybe there was still a chance they could watch me on *Saturday Night Live*.

When the twenty-five thousand dollars came in for the *North Hollywood* pilot, which was more like twelve thousand after taxes and commissions, the first thing I did was math. I figured out how much I still owed my mom for the rent she'd paid for me when I was first starting out and gave her a check for the exact amount. But she didn't want to accept it.

Since that time, I've seen people work hard to become successful, only to have entitled parents exploit them for as much money as they can get. My mom actually *was* entitled to that money, and I still had to persuade her to take it. My goal in life is to have a heart as big as hers.

Unfortunately, I don't. Here's how I know that: Later, I'd find myself in a situation where the thought would occur to me, *I damn sure need that money back.*

55

HOW I BECAME AN INTERNATIONAL SUPERSTAR (IN CANADA, FOR ONE WEEK, AND NOT ACTUALLY ALL OF CANADA, AND NOT REALLY A SUPERSTAR, BUT THEY DID MENTION ME IN THE PAPERS SO THAT'S GOTTA COUNT FOR SOMETHING)

Just as Dave had promised, the year passed quickly and I was given another opportunity to perform in the New Faces showcase at the Just for Laughs comedy festival in Montreal. This time, thanks to Keith Robinson, Damon Dash, and Judd Apatow, I was ready—except for one thing. I had no experience performing outside the United States. For all I knew, people were completely different in Canada than here.

I told Dave that I wanted to go to Montreal early so I could get some stage time in and make sure audiences there could identify with my material. Then Dave asked a question that showed me just how unprepared I was.

Dave: Do you have a passport?
Me: Huh?
Dave: A passport.
Me: What's that?
Dave: A passport is a document you need to travel to another country. If you don't have a passport, you can't go to Canada and you can't get back into the United States.
Me: How do I get one of those?

Dave gave me the address of a government office where I could get a passport. Standing in line there, I was amazed by what my life had become:

A day ago, I didn't even know this thing called a passport existed. Now I'm get-
ting one so I can go to a foreign country and do comedy internationally!

In the days leading up to the trip, I barely slept. Sometimes I was excited.
Other times I was nervous, especially when I heard that some people in Montreal spoke French. How were they going to understand my jokes?

Traveling out of the country for the first time, going through customs, arriving in a strange city where I knew nobody, getting welcomed with a sign
that had my name on it, being taken to a luxury hotel, and getting introduced
to all these Just for Laughs people who respected me as a performer—it was
all so incredible that I couldn't stop smiling.

I got my feet wet with my first international show and was relieved that
everyone seemed to understand the material. However, the laughs didn't
seem as big as they did at home. A comic named Dean Edwards, who had also
auditioned for *Saturday Night Live*, was in Montreal as well. After one of my
warm-up shows, Dean pulled me aside. "Kevin, you're doing great," he said.
"There's just one thing: slow down. Make sure everyone can understand you
and you're not breezing through your material. In New York, maybe you can
talk that fast, but if you want everyone to relate to you here, you need to at
least pause sometimes."

That simple pivot was just what I needed. There were twenty-four other
comics in the New Faces showcases besides Dean and me, and each of us was
scheduled for two performances. They weren't the biggest shows at the festival in terms of audience size, but they were the biggest in terms of industry
turnout. This was where the heavyweights came to answer the question:
Who's the next big thing?

I obliterated the audience at both showcases so decisively that, afterward,
the festival's bookers added me to every event where they had space. Newspapers were writing about me. Strangers I walked past at parties were buzzing *Kevin Hart, Kevin Hart, Kevin Hart.* I felt like the Godzilla of comedy—I'd
destroyed Montreal.

And then, like in every Godzilla movie, I got destroyed.

I was walking through the hotel lobby carrying two newspapers, both
with great reviews of my sets. I wanted to save them and show them to my

mom. Then I ran into Dean Edwards, who was also on a high from his amazing reviews. We went to the bar for a drink, and suddenly his phone rang.

"Hello? . . . Hold on a second—Kev, give me a sec, real quick."

He stepped away and I overheard: "Yo, you lying, Jason—you lying! . . . Jason, don't tell me that, man. Oh my God, man, you gotta—*ohhhhh!*"

It sounded like he was having an orgasm.

He hung up, then stood there, like he was catching his breath. As he walked back to me, he said, "I got it, man."

"Got what?"

"*SNL!*"

It took me a second to process what he was saying. Then it clicked. "Give me a hug, man. Amazing!"

If he'd passed the audition, that meant I'd been rejected. One way to know you're in a society that's not equal is when there's only one slot for a new black person in an ensemble cast, or in any group. It's a sign that people are more concerned about *looking* equal than actually *being* equal.

Granted, Dean could do impressions. He'd done Scottie Pippen and Spike Lee on television before. And his De Niro had to be far better than mine. Anyone's De Niro probably was.

"The best man got it," I told him honestly, though deep inside I could hear the sound of my dreams being smashed to pieces.

"You the first one who knows, man," Dean grinned. "Like, I ain't even called my lady yet. This is crazy."

I ordered celebratory shots and held mine up to toast him. "Dean, there's enough spots out there for everybody, but goddammit, you got first place today. Go out there and show them, man. I'm proud to know you. Here's to your success."

An hour later, Dave called me. "Hey, buddy, I just wanna let you know that Dean Edwards got *SNL*."

"Did they tell you why I didn't get it?"

"No, but it's all right. These things happen. You know, there's a lot more out there besides *SNL*."

"I'm fine. I just wanted the feedback. It's all good."

Dave seemed surprised that I was shoulder-shrugging it. "Boy," he said, "I don't know how you take this shit the way you do, but I wish everybody had whatever you call this emotion. Just keep doing you, and I'm telling you, Kev, you're gonna be all right."

SNL was and remains a massive launching pad for comedians. And that door was now closed. It was the second time my dream of becoming a star was dashed—though it wouldn't be the last. But Dave was right: The shoulder-shrugging kept it from leaving a bitter taste in my mouth.

Besides, I understood their decision. I would have rejected me too. Even Avery Johnson wouldn't have recognized himself. To this day, I still can't impersonate celebrities.

56

OH MY GOD, I'M FUCKING RICH

When I returned from Montreal, Dave Becky used my success there as a way to set up meetings with directors, casting agents, production companies, and television networks. Most of the entertainment industry is in Los Angeles, a city full of dreamers hoping for just one of those meetings, so booking appointments with some people was still a challenge.

However, *Paper Soldiers* saved me again. Between my set at Just for Laughs and a reel from the film, Dave was able to get me in the doors of the biggest executives at the biggest networks.

"They're talking to you because they're already interested," Dave advised as we flew to Los Angeles together. "You already blew them away on stage and on your tapes, so just be yourself."

But I want to be more than myself, I thought as I sat there. These gatekeepers had probably met with thousands of hopeful kids with stars in their eyes and then forgotten about them as soon as they left the room. So I prepared by essentially putting a set together that they'd remember. I planned answers to the questions they were going to ask—about my background, my goals, my ideas—and thought of good questions to ask in return. I thought about being funny, likeable, vibrant, charming, interesting, positive, exciting—you name it, and I wanted to be it in those rooms. Most importantly, I knew that *what* I said mattered a lot less than *how* I said it. It was a job for *the fun guy*.

In office after office, I poured on the personality. Every executive in every room was Ms. Davis, and I was in a battle to charm them into letting me do what I wanted. These weren't meetings. They were seductions.

By the time I landed back in New York, Dave had already gotten calls from the people I'd met with: Many of them were interested in working with me. My childhood had trained me well for this moment.

"So what do we do now?" I asked Dave.

"We wait for them to make an offer."

"Can we take more than one offer?" It was like Christmas for my career.

"What we want to do is start a bidding war. Let them know there's competition, and they'll have to show how serious they are."

"How do they show they're serious?"

"With money."

So this was how people afforded those big homes and nice cars in Los Angeles. It wasn't from multiple sets at comedy clubs. It was from Hollywood bidding wars.

I was ready to make another twenty-five thousand dollars, maybe even fifty thousand. I started thinking about all the things I could buy with that money.

A few weeks later, Dave called with the news.

Dave: Hey, man, it's confirmed: NBC is gonna give you two hundred and seventy-five thousand for a holding deal.

Me: Oh my God, I'm fucking rich! Wait, what's a holding deal?

Dave: That means they have the exclusive right to use you in their
   programming for a year. You can't work with any other network.
Me: So there's no pilot? I don't have to do nothing for the money?
Dave: No.
Me: Oh my God, I'm fucking rich!

I probably could have used a good warning next. I was twenty-two, and I had no idea about money or how it worked. I just knew that in a year, I'd gone from making $175 a deal to more than a quarter of a million dollars. It was more money than I could imagine.

Life's amazing, I thought. The way to break into film is to have an acting reel, but you can't put together a good acting reel if you're not in any films. It's a catch-22, and somehow I had gotten around it, thanks to Damon Dash. It was almost as if God was looking out for me, saying, "All right, man, I'm gonna have you do this random, low-budget street movie. You may not know why now, but trust me, later it's gonna get your foot in the door."

A lot of my philosophy is that life is about making the right choices in the dark. Many people ask me what to do if they have doubts about their career or how talented they are or what their passion is. My answer: When it comes to the future, it's *impossible* to have any certainty. I may appear to be certain, because I've learned to have confidence in my abilities and faith in my will to succeed. But what I don't know—and what no human being knows—is how we will fulfill our destiny as individuals and what that destiny will be.

If you wait for certainty, you will spend your whole life standing still. And if you grow discouraged and give up when things get rough, you'll miss out on your best possible destiny. So the secret is to be excited about what *is* in your power to control, be accepting of what's *not* in your power to control, and then move with certainty into an uncertain future.

This of course leaves open the question of what direction you should move in. The answer: Pay attention, dummy. Life is pulling you there automatically. You don't have to know. You don't have to understand. You just have to trust. There is a flow to life, and all you have to do is make the decision to follow that current—even if it seems to be carrying you away from everyone around you.

That's why I made my next decision quickly and without a second thought, even though it was the biggest decision I'd ever made. I decided to move to the place where the current was pushing me: Hollywood.

I told Torrei that if she wanted to move with me, I'd get everything set up so we could live together. Though we'd had such rough times in Philadelphia, I couldn't imagine *not* being with her. She was my rock—although at times, a very loud rock. And every now and then, that rock hit you in the head. But we still loved each other in our crazy way. A relationship is strengthened not by experiencing good times together but by surviving the bad times.

And there were plenty of those coming.

Life Lessons FROM OPPORTUNITIES

The only way to prepare for what you want is to believe that what you want is coming tomorrow . . . or maybe the day after that. If not, then it will come pretty soon. If it hasn't come by that point, then you should change your want before you waste any more time. Shit, I'm talking to YOU, Tanya.

With the cast of The Big House

© *American Broadcasting Companies, Inc.*

57

REMEMBER HOW I SAID I WAS RICH IN THE LAST CHAPTER— WELL, NOW I WASN'T

A quarter of a million dollars is a lot of money—until you spend it all.

We live in a culture where it's so hard to make money, yet so easy to spend it. Whoever designed the system is a genius: I never even saw the money itself. It was just a big number on a small piece of paper.

But that number made it possible for me to sign a rental contract for an apartment on Poinsettia Place in Hollywood and a lease agreement for a two-door Ford Explorer Sport. Then I got a magic plastic card that fit in my pocket with my keys—except it was better than a key, because it could unlock every item in every store in the world. It wasn't even really my card: My credit was so bad from all the bills that had gone to collections in Philadelphia, I had to get a card through Torrei's mom's account.

With that magic plastic, I picked up a watch that was priced expensively (which I now know is different than an *expensive watch*) and enough throwback jerseys for every day of the month. I furnished my new apartment with the biggest bed, the nicest couch, and the most expensive coffee table I could find, so that I felt like the Godfather every time I walked in the door. Everything was so easy to get, it seemed more like stealing than shopping.

Of course, the person who was really being robbed was me. Because it didn't *feel* like I was spending money, I didn't think I was. If I'd had a stack of hundred-dollar bills in a drawer and no credit card, I'd have been able to see that stack rapidly shrinking and know to slow down. Instead, what happened was that the stack got smaller, but the magic card kept working.

Meanwhile, Torrei gave notice at work and I booked a flight for her to make the move. This meant I'd now be supporting two people in Los Angeles. And that was fine with me: I was going to be the next prime-time star.

Whenever I drove down Sunset Boulevard, I thought: *Man, I can't wait until I'm on one of those billboards . . . Man, I can't wait until my face is on the side of that bus . . . Man, I can't wait until that celebrity tour is stopping outside my apartment, saying, "That's where Kevin Hart used to live when he was doing all those hit shows for NBC."*

———

As I was setting up my new life in Hollywood, my mom came out to see where I was living and how I was doing. Though my money was already starting to get tight, I made sure to take her to nice lunches and dinners so that she felt like her baby had made it.

She gave me some wise advice before she left: "If you ever hear the words *no* and *can't*, ignore them. They don't exist. Don't let them get in the way of the goals you need to accomplish."

It was advice she followed herself: While working at the university, she was also studying for a master's degree. "Mom, why do you even need a master's degree? Like, what are you studying for?" I asked.

Her answer: "Everything."

She loved learning, which is something else she passed on to me. I must have attended four different graduation ceremonies to celebrate degrees she'd earned.

Eventually, NBC cast me in a pilot. It was called *Class of '06*, and was described to me as "a younger *Friends*, with freshmen roommates on a college campus." It also happened to be written by one of the writers of *Friends*, so of course it was going to be huge.

It ended up being as huge as *North Hollywood*—we poured our hearts and souls into it, and it didn't get picked up.

With stand-up comedy, the better I was on stage, the more successful I became. With television, it seemed that talent had nothing to do with success. Because a corporation was making the decisions, the criteria were different: The decisions were based on numbers. We didn't talk about ratings measurements and quarterly earnings at The Table.

After the pilot failed, NBC didn't bring me any more work. A holding deal, it turned out, is exactly what it sounds like: NBC held me. And I couldn't do anything on television for the rest of the year.

While waiting for my freedom, I decided to hit the comedy clubs and work my way toward becoming Multi-Set Hollywood Kev. After my first performance at the Comedy Store, I spoke to one of the other comedians and tried to figure out where the L.A. equivalent of the Comedy Cellar comedians' table was.

Me: So, what are you doing afterward?

Him: Going to where the women are at.

Me: Is there a table where all the other comedians hang out after their sets?

Him: What you talking about?

Me: Y'all don't hang out? Discuss material?

Him: You can come to Xeni.

Me: What's that?

Him: A dance club with bangin' women.

Me: But where's *The Table*?

Him: Naw, you don't wanna pay for no bottle service!

The comedy scene in L.A. was different than in New York. Comedians didn't shuttle through the city doing spots at multiple clubs in a night. There were good places to perform: the Ha Ha Cafe, the Improv, the Laugh Factory, the Comedy Store, a few others. But I was lucky to get a booking a month. A lot of performers there were bitter. They'd been in Hollywood for ten, twenty, even thirty years and hadn't made it, so they had no patience for a young, enthusiastic kid with a holding deal. Rather than trying to elevate the art of comedy, they were trying to elevate their mood with clubbing, drinks, and women.

So I adapted and became Multi-Party Kev. Every night, there was a different club, lounge, or mansion that was going off. There was always something to do—anything but work on the craft.

During the day, I killed time on the basketball court, at the gym, and playing video games with other young comedians I met, like Nick Cannon, Rodney Perry, and a guy named Harry Ratchford, who soon became one of my closest friends.

Since the bowl-cut years, one of the most important things to me has always been a good haircut. But every place I tried in Hollywood was an overpriced beauty salon where some hairdresser to the stars fucked up my shit.

Finally, one night at Xeni, I was bitching about it to some guy, and he said, "You can't get your hair cut in Hollywood. Might as well get it cut in a mall. You gotta go down to Inglewood, man. I got a goddamn place for you there!"

He sent me to a hood barbershop called Platinum Cuts on Manchester and La Brea. He didn't give me anyone's name, so I parked my Explorer and walked inside to check it out.

The first rule of the barbershop is, never go with the motherfucker in the first chair. That guy's always the hustler, hitting up people first when they come in: "Yo, yo, what you need? I got you." The guy in the second chair is better. He's competent and has some regular clients. But whoever's in the last chair, *that's* the man who's confident in his skills and the demand for them.

I went straight to the last chair. The dude standing there looked like Ice-T—if Ice-T worked a nine-to-five job, never exercised, and smoked so much weed that he could barely keep his eyes open. He was with a client and talking about how Busta Rhymes was one of the greatest lyricists of all time.

"Hey, man, how many you got?" I asked him.

He said three people were in front of me, so I waited. I knew it would be worth my time.

When my turn came, I hopped into the chair and introduced myself. He said his name was John. When he finished, I looked in the mirror, and just like when Greg cut my hair in middle school, I felt like a new and better person. "Hey, man, can you be my barber? I just got out here. I'm a comedian. I don't know where else to go."

"Yeah, yeah, I know you. I saw you at the Improv a few weeks ago. Somebody was heckling, and you said, 'Man, shut your ass up with your teeth over there looking like baby shoes.' You was right: They looked just like baby shoes. I thought, *Yo, this little motherfucker is funny as shit.*"

That was the last time I received a compliment at Platinum Cuts. As people grew to know me there, I'd walk in and they'd go, "Oh, you think you a comedian? What's funny about you, nigga? You just look funny."

"Man, get the fuck out of here with your damn lopsided head," I'd snap back. "You look like a stop sign that someone hit with a baseball bat!"

Finally, I'd found a place in Los Angeles that was like the Comedy Cellar table, where I could keep my skin thick and my wit sharp. Platinum Cuts became my church. I spent every Sunday there, talking trash and learning about the world.

———

To keep my New York edge, I began letting my friends from the Comedy Cellar crash at my place when they were in town performing or auditioning. One day, when Patrice O'Neal was staying with me, I came home from the barbershop and called out, "Patrice?"

Silence.

I went to my bedroom, put on my slippers, and sat on the edge of the bed. It was the middle of the afternoon, and I wanted to hang with Patrice. Maybe he was here somewhere.

I went to the back room, opened the door, and saw that big motherfucker slumped in a chair, intently focused on something.

"Hey, man, what're you doing?"

He jumped out of the chair. "Shut the door! Shut the door!"

"What the fuck's going on?!"

"Shut the damn door so I can clean myself up!"

That's when I noticed that his pants were open and there was a bottle of baby oil on the desk. "Oh, oh no, man, my bad. Aw, shit . . ."

I backed out and closed the door.

Fifteen minutes went by before he emerged from the room.

Patrice: Hey, man, there's nothing to say.

Me: I think I'm permanently scarred.

Patrice: I'm sorry. I didn't know nobody was back.

Me: Okay.

Patrice: Just don't say shit, man.

Me: You're my friend, so of course I have to honor that friendship . . . and never let you forget the moment we just shared.

Patrice: Come on, man.

Me: I'm gonna put this in my set. I'm going to put it in my movie. I'm gonna put it in my book. Just you wait and see.

Patrice decided not to wait and see. I love him with all my heart—and that's why I never let him forget it or all the other great moments we shared. He's somewhere in heaven right now, jerking off with the angels.

58

IF I THINK I'M TOO GOOD FOR YOU, BUT YOU REJECT ME, THEN WHO'S TOO GOOD FOR WHO NOW?

As the expiration date of my holding deal approached, I felt like a racehorse ready to charge through a starting gate.

What I discovered, however, was that on the other side of the holding deal was something called *waiting for another deal*.

The auditions I went on when my holding deal ended were different than the meetings I'd had after Just for Laughs. In a meeting, they were interested in who I was. In an audition, they usually weren't. It was a cattle call for actors. One of my first big auditions was so bad that the casting director took the script out of my hand and said, "Okay, that's enough, sir."

"Would you like me to try it another way?"

"We don't want you to do it any other ways. That's enough for us."

The word "no"—or sometimes the more polite two-word rejection, "thank you"—became as much a part of my life in L.A. as traffic jams and parking tickets.

"Kev, what happened to that audition you went on?"

"Didn't get it."

"What about that pilot?"

"Didn't get picked up."

"How about the—"

"Nope."

A new routine settled over my life. It consisted of going to casting calls and not getting the part. More auditions, still no part. Finally getting a part, shooting a pilot, and waiting for the pilot to get picked up. The pilot doesn't get picked up. More calls, more auditions, more testing, more pilots—nothing happens. Hey, there's a call for extras. *I'm desperate. Why not?* Show up and hope it turns into a speaking role. It doesn't. *Maybe I'm not a good enough actor?* Get acting coach. Start cycle from top.

One of the reasons I was able to survive all the rejection was because it was so familiar from my childhood. *Can I play with my friends? No. Can I go to a movie? No. Can I check out that party for just a few minutes? Hell no.*

Every experience is a potential life lesson. Even if you don't appreciate it at the time, each struggle in the present is preparing you for something else in the future.

Hollywood is a horrible place for a relationship, especially since Torrei and I had packed all our emotional baggage and brought it with us. Any problem between us was exacerbated by living in a city where we had no family or close friends.

The nightlife swallowed us up. It wasn't like going out in Philadelphia: *Everything* in Hollywood had shine on it. It was full of the most beautiful women, the most expensive cars, the hottest clubs, the classiest restaurants, and an endless parade of celebrities and wannabe celebrities.

Most of the people could barely afford to even be in these places. Just about anywhere else in the world, what they were doing would have been called partying. But in Hollywood, it was called work. People justified spending all their time and money on going out, drinking, drugging, and fucking because it was *networking*. One day they might wake up with that special someone who would make their career—though more likely, they'd be passed around, used up, and spit out.

And I was right there with them, throwing my life away. I didn't want to be home. I didn't want to be in a relationship. I didn't want to be arguing all the time. I didn't want to be stressed out about my career. I wanted to be at the clubs drinking.

When Torrei and I went out together, I drank even more. And every time we drank, bad shit happened. We'd wake up, try to put the pieces back together, and promise not to drink again, then go out a few days later and do the exact same thing.

One day, we came up with a way to put a permanent stop to this pattern of partying, drinking, arguing, retaliating by flirting with other people, occasionally hooking up with those people, denying it, and then screaming at each other for hours. At the time, it seemed like the most logical idea ever. The thought process went something like this:

1. We keep fighting over jealousy issues.

2. That must mean we really care about each other.

3. If we had an honest relationship without jealousy, then we'd be happy together.

4. Jealousy is a fear that one of us will abandon the other.

5. So to get rid of the jealousy, we need to make a real commitment to each other that's undeniable.

6. Let's get married.

The first person I told about the decision wasn't my family but an old friend. This was his response: "Hey, dummy, you don't need to be getting married. You're too young and stupid. Get your career figured out first. *Then* decide if that's what you want. You have no idea what you're in for with marriage, so don't be stupid, stupid. Call it off before it's too late!"

Then I told my brother: "Are you sure? My shit didn't work out, and you guys already have worse problems."

But I shoulder-shrugged the advice. "Yeah, I got it. It's gonna be cool."

The only person who didn't disapprove was my mother, who just asked if I was sure I wanted to do this. When I said that I was, she told me to be honest and loyal, and to treat Torrei well.

I wish I could say I followed her advice. I saw the marriage as another attempt in a long line of efforts to make the relationship work by making bigger and stronger commitments. I also thought it would be the coolest thing ever to elope to Vegas, then come back to L.A. as a married man.

But there was a big gap between my intentions and my actions. I started our new life out with a lie that, to this day, Torrei still isn't aware of.

Most of my lies came from my desire to keep Torrei happy, but they always backfired and made her unhappy. So I don't know why I kept telling them—probably because they at least made her happy in the moment.

In this particular case, she kept asking for a proper diamond wedding ring with a gold band, so I told my first lie—that I'd gotten her a special one. She was happy and stopped asking me about it.

The day before the wedding, I told her I was going to the casino to gamble. Then I ran to the jewelry stores, where I discovered that I couldn't afford a single ring with any type of diamond on it.

I didn't want her to know that I'd lied about the ring, so I lied about the ring again. It made total sense to me at the time. I returned to the room and told her I was on a streak in blackjack, but bet too much on a bad hand and had to pawn the diamond wedding ring to pay the debt.

Now she was unhappy, but my previous lie had at least delayed this by a couple of weeks. I promised to get her an even better ring as soon as I could afford it. That didn't console her much.

The next day, I bought a cheap ten-dollar ring as a placeholder. The ceremony, if you can call it that, was at the casino's wedding chapel. Torrei's parents and sister could afford to fly in for the ceremony, so they were our only guests.

I had on a pair of Diesel jeans, white Air Force 1s, and a black T-shirt under a leather blazer. Torrei wore a beautiful sundress. I was twenty-goddamn-three years old and flat broke. It was fucking nuts.

59

LIARS GET LIED TO TOO

I was too young, too old, too good-looking, too ugly, too urban, not urban enough, or "just not what we're looking for in this role." I couldn't seem to get any work.

Dave had connected me with a talent agency, UTA, and one afternoon, the agents there called me in for a meeting. The room was full. It seemed like everyone in the company was there, talking about all the new movies they were going to get me auditions for: *King Arthur, The A-Team, The Hulk.*

I finally said something:

Me: Wait a minute, *The Hulk*? They want a five-foot-four-inch black Hulk?

Them: Well, who knows, look at Tom Cruise—

Me: You guys got me going out for B.A. Baracus in *The A-Team*? I'll never get that. There's nothing Mr. T–like about me.

Them: Well, you know, I can really see you reinventing Mr. T for today.

Me: Look, man, ain't nobody putting me in none of them damn movies.

Y'all don't have to Hollywood me.

The agents seemed taken aback by what I was saying, as if no one had ever called them out on it before. But I was starting to understand that auditions were less about nailing the part and more about nailing the casting agent. Some of those parts weren't for me; in other cases, they already had someone they liked in the part. The goal was to shine and to win over the casting agent, so that when the roles that *were* right for me came along, and I was further along in my career, they'd remember me.

"Just get me in rooms with the right people," I told them, "and I'll take care of the rest."

That talk, and that realization, changed my career. I started going to auditions with the intention of not getting *this* role, but the *next* role. To make an impression, I'd pop right away: "Hey, guys, what's happening? How's it been going so far? Am I the first black guy you've seen?"

Later I might say something like, "When I'm done, I'm gonna leave my phone here accidentally, with the recorder on, so I can come back for it and find out if y'all said I was good or bad." Or I might point to the guy who was lowest in the pecking order in the room: "If I don't get the part, I'm blaming it on Ray right there."

The goal was to break the tension and get them laughing, but without trying too hard. I'd still work to embody the part. Even if the role wasn't for me, I wanted them to see how prepared I was and what I was capable of. I'd mix it up and play the character in ways that weren't right for the film, just to show them that I had different levels.

I almost always got a callback, and to this day, I'm still close with a lot of those people. The leading actors in Hollywood may change, but the players behind the scenes often remain the same. Even though they didn't give me parts at the time, some of them ended up giving me great roles later.

Though people say to live in the moment, each moment leads to other moments. So treat each moment like a seed, and care for it so that something beautiful can grow from it. That Ray kid you joked around with when he was just starting out may become a studio head ten years later, and will remember that you noticed him and treated him special.

One day, my agents called and said that a casting assistant I'd met had alerted them to a situation where I could potentially get a role. But it wasn't an audition. It was what's called a table read, which is when actors sit in a room and read a script in character so that everyone can get a sense of how the dialogue will sound when it's performed. This one was for the horror movie parody *Scary Movie 3*, and my agents said that if I knocked it out of the park, I might be considered for a part.

I walked into the table read like I owned the world, and the director, David Zucker, gave me three small parts to recite. There wasn't enough dialogue in any of them for me to show much of my personality, so I improvised extra lines when I saw opportunities for humor. The movie was a comedy, so I figured at least I was helping everyone get in a good mood.

Afterward, Zucker called Dave Becky and told him, "I think Kevin's our guy. He's very funny. He did an amazing job with the part of CJ. It's just a small part, but we'd like to meet with him and see if we can build this character out a little more for him."

Zucker is a comedy legend. He directed *Airplane!* and other classic Leslie Nielsen comedies. I met with him and the screenwriters, and they said that there were two friends in the film, played by Anthony Anderson and Simon Rex. "What if we add your character to the friendship? You guys can be a trio."

"I love it," I replied. Of course, I would have said the same thing if they were suggesting that I play a tree. I was just glad that I was going to be in a legitimate Hollywood film. Progress.

When they asked if I wanted to write my own scenes into the script, I just about passed out. I'd personality'd my way into the movie.

There was a parody of the *Ring* series in the script, and Anthony Anderson's character, Mahalik, had a line about someone who "woke up dead." I'm a logical person, and that phrase didn't make sense to me, so I played with the dialogue afterward:

CJ: How in the hell do you wake up dead?
Mahalik: Because you're alive when you go to sleep.
CJ: So you're telling me that you can go to bed dead and wake up alive?
Mahalik: You can't go to bed dead, man. That shit would be redundant.

Working on the script was a good distraction from my marriage, which, to no one's surprise but ours, hadn't improved our relationship. Every week, we made promises to each other about what we were and weren't going to do. Yet, a few days later, we were yelling our *fuck you*s, storming out of the house, exchanging phone numbers with anyone who seemed interested, and then coming home and accusing each other of cheating. We'd fight, fuck, wake up, and then start all over again with the promises.

One weekend, my childhood friend Spank visited. He went out with Torrei and me one night, and the usual happened. We were having a good time, we did a few shots, and then Torrei started laying into me: "I went into the bathroom and there was some bitch talking about you. That bitch in the white dress."

She wanted to know who she was and why she was up in my business. I looked over and I had never seen the woman before in my life.

"Yo, we out, man," I told Spank.

With Spank in the back seat, Torrei and I fought the whole ride home and then on into the house. Spank finally pulled Torrei into another room and pleaded with her: "Come on—not in front of me. Just go somewhere else if y'all have to do that."

According to Spank, Torrei responded, "Spank, I ain't even hear nothing in the bathroom. I just like to push his buttons."

Fortunately, I was able to get out of town and start filming *Scary Movie 3* in Vancouver. It was the first time I saw the professionalism of a film with a decent budget. Every comfort and luxury was taken care of. All

I had to do was show up. My scenes turned out to be some of the best on-camera work I'd done. Because I'd written my own lines, it was easy to be authentic with them.

In the process of filming, I came to understand why none of my pilots had been picked up: They weren't my material. If I wanted my next pilot to get picked up, maybe I should write it myself. It could be honest, like my comedy, and the audience would know something about me by the end of the show.

I thought back to an idea I'd once discussed with Na'im, my comedian friend from Philadelphia: We thought it would be cool to do a show about my family, but to make them rich instead of poor. We quickly dismissed it because it sounded too much like *The Fresh Prince of Bel-Air*. But on set, where I was so attached to being treated like a star and sad to think it would end, I figured out a solution. The show should be *The Fresh Prince* in reverse: Instead of being about a poor kid moving in with rich relatives, it should be about a rich kid who loses everything and has to move in with his poor relatives.

Sometimes you have to get outside of your environment in order to see it more clearly. Though I was disappointed when filming in Vancouver ended, I was excited to get home and make this show idea work.

60

MY NUCLEAR FAMILY

"I know we've been having bad luck with these pilots," I said to Dave when I saw him next. "But what if I have an idea for a pilot? Will they take an original idea that I have?"

"Sure. Do you have one?"

"Yeah, it's loosely based on my family." I explained as much of the idea as I'd worked out: a wealthy, spoiled version of me is living in Malibu, but his mother passes away and his dad gets thrown in prison for a financial crime. The only other family he has lives in a poor neighborhood in Philadelphia, so he has to move in with them.

"So I go there expecting my own apartment with a cook and a maid," I concluded, "but instead I have to sleep on, like, a couch in the basement with my cousin."

"I think there's a show there. I wanna pair you up with a showrunner to develop the idea."

I had no idea what a showrunner was, and I felt like the idea was already developed, but getting paired up with one sounded like a good thing. So I agreed.

A showrunner, I soon learned, is a writer who's in charge of making the creative and production decisions on a TV show. I was introduced to Stephen Engel, who'd worked on *Mad About You* and other sitcoms. Through talking with him, I began to see that all I had was a premise—not a show. He filled in the world until it felt like a sitcom that could generate new episodes for decades. He gave the characters more depth and created meaningful relationships between them.

Most importantly, he gave the show a theme. Kevin Hart, as we creatively decided to name the main character, defined himself through his valuable toys—cars, watches, clothes. But his relatives in Philadelphia defined themselves by *internal* values. The show would be about Kevin discovering who he was and what he stood for. The big idea was that losing everything materially would ultimately make him rich spiritually.

We named the show *The Big House* because it worked on many levels: It was the mansion Kevin left, the prison his father was in, and the packed home overflowing with relatives that he moved into.

I loved it. Dave loved it. And soon, ABC loved it.

But a network like ABC doesn't just buy your idea and put it on the air—there are hoops to jump through first. Usually, they pay you to write a script. If they like the script, then they give you the resources to record one episode of the show for them to evaluate, which is the pilot. If all the right executives like the pilot, then they green-light your idea as a series and order a certain number of episodes for broadcast in the next television season.

Fortunately, ABC believed in the script and gave us the go-ahead to tape a pilot. We put together an amazing cast to play my Philly family: Yvette Nicole Brown, Keith David, Aaron Grady, Arnetia Walker, and Faizon Love from *Friday*.

I flew my actual family to Los Angeles for the live studio taping. It ate up a good chunk of my advance from ABC, because I didn't just bring in my mom, dad, and brother. I also flew in my aunts Patsy and Mae and my cousins Darryl, Kimberly, Michelle, Thelma, and Shirrel. If they were a Hart, I invited them to L.A.

Besides wanting them to see the Hart family brought to life on stage, I wanted to give them a taste of the Hollywood lifestyle. I picked them up at the airport in a limousine, took them to the best restaurants, and saved the front rows of seats for them at the taping.

They arrived on set like a herd of elephants. My dad spotted the craft services table, where there were chips, candy, and other snacks piled up for the cast, crew, and guests to eat. He snuck over to the table and filled his hands and pockets with goldfish crackers and cupcakes, then brought them back to the family to share, as if he'd just robbed a convenience store.

While the rest of my relatives were telling stories and laughing hysterically like they were at a family dinner, Dad kept going back and forth from the food to the seats, making conversation to distract anyone who was near the table. "Yeah, that's my son Kevin right there. He turned out to be a fine boy, even though Nance always be spoiling him." While his lips were moving, his hands were grabbing as much food as he could carry.

Eventually, a production assistant told him: "You know, Mr. Hart, you don't have to take that stuff—"

My dad grabbed him by the collar before he could finish. "What are you, a rat? You trying to drop down on me, man?"

I had to come over, break it up, and tell my dad that everything was complimentary. He looked at me like I'd just said that it was free-money day at Citibank. He started gathering everything he could—staplers, pens, stickers—and running it back to family members to hold for him. I think he was worried that other people would find out this information and start taking everything for themselves.

As Dad was pocketing a fistful of Red Vines, Faizon Love walked by. My dad recognized him from *Friday* and shouted, "Oh, I know that fat motherfucker right there!"

"Whoa, Dad, you can't say that! Don't embarrass me."

"No, I need a picture with that fat motherfucker right there!"

That fat motherfucker clearly heard every word my dad was saying. "Who's that?" Faizon asked.

"Faizon, I give you so many apologies right now. That's my dad. He's never been on a set before."

"It's okay, Kevin. Don't forget, I've read the script—and now I know you weren't exaggerating. I'll take a picture with him."

I'd never seen my dad so excited. At a live taping, audience members are supposed to just applaud and laugh on cue. They're not supposed to yell, "Naw, you gotta be kidding me. That's Nance right there!" or "What? Ain't no way in hell that's me!"

Even my mom's side of the family started hooting and hollering like I was doing impressions just for them. Eventually, a nervous producer pulled me aside. "Hey, we're glad that your family's enjoying themselves, but we just wanna let you know that we're gonna have to ask them to just kind of keep it down a little bit."

When we edited the show, the biggest problem we faced was finding ways to cut and fade out my family's comments. On the raw tape, you could actually hear the specific verbiage. After one joke, I distinctly heard my cousin Darryl cackling, "They got you good on that one, Shirrel!"

It made me wonder if the characters on the show were too normal. But if I'd written them just like my family, no one would have believed it.

After the taping ended, the waiting period began. Once again, someone was going to make a decision that would either make me a star or put me back at square one.

While I was hanging out with my family, I got the call. I could just barely hear Dave Becky over the sound of my dad offering to copy his latest bootleg DVDs for my cousins:

Dave: They wanna pick up your TV show.
Me: What?
Dave: They wanna pick up your show.
Me: Who?
Dave: ABC just green-lit the show. They want twelve episodes for their fall
    season. They're revamping the network; you're gonna be one of the
    shows in their new "Thank God It's Friday" lineup.
Me: Hey, everybody, shut up! Mom, I'm about to get you a house. Kenneth,
    I'm gonna get you a house, a car—I don't know what you want. Dad, I'm
    gonna set you up. This is it. I finally hit it! Y'all told me to go to commu-
    nity college and focus. Look at me; I'm focused now, bitches! . . . Sorry
    about the language, everyone.

According to my contract, I'd get paid twenty-five grand per episode as an actor, then something like ten grand for other duties like executive produc-ing. So that was some thirty-five grand an episode. At twelve episodes, that was $420,000!

There was nothing that could bring me down after that. I was about to be on buses, billboards—everything I had dreamed about when I first landed in L.A.

Oh, Mr. Hart, can I please have your autograph?

Sorry, young lady, if I give one to you, then I'm gonna have to give one to all those other fine ladies screaming over there.

But please, Mr. Hart, I'm your biggest fan. I've memorized every episode of Big House.

That's The Big House. *Don't forget the* The . . . *Oh, no, don't start crying. I'm sorry. Here, look, I'll sign your Kevin Hart-throb poster.*

Thank you, Mr. Hart. You're the best!

Call me Kevin . . . No, actually, keep calling me Mr. Hart. I like the way that sounds.

———————

A few days after my family left, I got my third callback for a movie audition I'd gone on. The director, Jessy Terrero, told me at the end of the session: "Look, this is a big movie for me, and I think it can be big for you. I want to put you in the lead role. I'll make sure you look good, and we'll knock this out of the park."

It was a "black version of *Airplane!*"—as he put it—about a guy who sues an air-travel company and wins enough money to start an airline modeled to his own taste, N.W.A. The film was called *Soul Plane*, and the producers agreed to pay me one hundred and fifty thousand dollars to play the lead, Nashawn Wade. Ol' Kevin Hart's time had finally come. I had my own prime-time sitcom and a leading role in a feature film. This was the year that was going to break me.

And break me it did, though not in the way I was expecting.

Life Lessons
FROM OBSTACLES

*Sometimes you got to take three steps back
to know that there's a lot more steps you
can still take backward.*

At the Soul Plane *premiere party*

61

MAKING TELEVISION HISTORY

You can always tell who's just landed their first big deal in Hollywood by the change in their transportation. The Civic or Jetta disappears, and they roll up to the valet stand of that month's hot restaurant or club in a new BMW convertible or Range Rover with the dealer plates still on.

I was that cliché.

When the *Soul Plane* and *Big House* deals closed, I still had my two-door Ford Explorer Sport. I went out to celebrate and pulled up to the valet in front of a restaurant on Hollywood Boulevard. "Bring it around to the back," the valet said.

"Nah, man, I'm trying to valet."

"Go around to the lot and self-park."

"Come on, man. I got the money!"

"Uh-uh, go around."

Even valets didn't want to be seen in my car. Hollywood was so shallow.

Conveniently, I was shallow too. The next day, I took out a lease on a black Tahoe Z71. One of the sponsors of *Soul Plane* was Lexani Wheels—if you watch the movie closely, you'll see a Lexani symbol on the plane wheels. A guy named Leonard who did product placement for the company told me that since I was the film's star, he'd hook me up with a set of wheels for my new truck.

As soon as I picked up my Z71 and Lexani wheels, the first place I went wasn't the hot restaurant or club. I went to a place where approval was even harder to get: the barbershop.

Cars were what made the men there. When my barber, John, pulled up in his classic Mustang or Chris Mills of the Golden State Warriors parked outside in his '59 Impala, everyone would run over to check out their ride. "Oh, shit, Mills got the mothership!"

Now it was my turn. As I approached the barbershop, I called John: "Hey, report to the bridge, because it's about to blow up. Make sure you're wearing something to protect your eyes."

"What're you talking about?"

"Just come outside, motherfucker."

I pulled up to the shop, ready for the boys to start freaking out. However, John was the only guy outside. And he was unimpressed. "Okay," he said when I leapt out of the car.

"What do you mean, *okay*?"

"Okay, I like it, but yo, you gotta get rid of the rubber sides, and you gotta black out these panels, and you gotta . . ."

He gave me a long list of what I had to do to get the car to meet his standards. It wasn't a critique; it was an education. I told him that when my movie hit it big, I'd hire him away from the shop so he could be my personal barber.

"Last week, you were driving a two-door Sport. This week you come in with a Z71 and think you the second coming of Jesus!" He laughed. "I'll tell you this from experience: Cars are like breast implants for men. Don't let it go to your head."

After I left the shop, I went straight to 310 Motoring and asked them to do every single thing John had recommended and more. You couldn't tell me shit after that. I'd bought confidence. I rolled back to that restaurant on Hollywood and up to the valet stand with an attitude: "Yeah, remember how I used to drive a Ford Explorer Sport? You remember that? Well, look what the fuck I got here now!"

They were unimpressed.

Torrei wanted her own car too, so I leased a BMW Z4 for her. My credit was so bad that the leases were ridiculously high, but, hey, I was rich. This meant that it was time to fulfill two promises I'd made: I put a down payment on a house for my mom and I bought Torrei a proper wedding band. One night, in the middle of a fight, I pulled the ring out of my back pocket and slipped it on her finger. She froze as she tried to process what was happening. Then she broke down in tears of gratitude.

I made a note to myself to buy about fifty more rings.

As I was working on episode ideas for *The Big House*, an ABC executive called. "Kevin, we want to fly you to the upfronts so you can announce the show."

I bombarded him with questions.

What are the upfronts? *The biggest television industry event of the season.* Where does it happen? *New York.* What happens there? *The big networks unveil their new shows to press and advertisers.* Should I get a suit? *Look your best.* Is the rest of the cast coming? *No, they only want you.* Wait a minute, that's not right. *The network doesn't have the budget to bring everyone. I'm sorry.*

I wasn't going to leave my *Big House* family behind. I wanted them to experience the excitement with me, so I told the network that I'd fly them to the upfronts on my own dime.

I got plane tickets and hotel rooms for everyone. Then I went to the Hugo Boss store on Rodeo Drive and bought every item of clothing that was on the window mannequin, from the brown pin-striped suit to the camel-colored shoes. It cost eight hundred dollars, the first designer outfit I ever owned.

When I stepped out of the airport in New York with the cast of the show, there were cameras flashing everywhere. At the hotel, another mob of photographers was waiting. On the night of the upfronts, there was a red carpet laid out from the hotel to the car services waiting outside. My heart was pounding with excitement. I couldn't stop talking. I never wanted to walk on any other color of carpet again.

I got out of the car at the event, and—*pah, pah, pah, pah*—more cameras, more reporters asking questions. Publicists and handlers led me this way and that way, celebrities said hello, flashes kept going off. E! asked to do a red-carpet interview with me. *That's something famous people do.* I did it. I felt famous.

This is my life now, I thought as I waited to go on stage and introduce the show to the nation. I was twenty-three and ready to own the world. This was my time.

There was a tap on my back, and I turned around to see a guy in a headset. "Excuse me," he said, then held up a finger. "Wait a sec." Someone on the headset was speaking to him, probably giving the cue for me to go on stage. "Mr. Hart? Uh-huh, I'm with him now."

I'm about to go up. Into the spotlight. There's no going back after this. I made a note to always remember Headset Guy—my escort into television history.

"Where do you want me?" I asked him.

"Mr. Hart, can you step back?"

"Okay, sure—like here?"

"No, you need to clear the walkway. They're not gonna use you."

"Huh?"

"They're telling me your show isn't part of the lineup anymore."

All my excitement knitted into a tight ball and landed with a thud in the bottom of my stomach. "I-I-I don't understand."

"Your show. They're telling me it's canceled. It's not happening."

"That can't be right, cause I'm here. I'm about to go on stage and talk about it."

"They're gonna go with the Kellys instead." He pointed to a group of suburban-looking white people who were being rushed past me. They walked on stage, and the room filled with applause. *My* applause.

"Hey, I'm sorry, I'm just the messenger. I'm sure someone will talk to you about it later, okay? So sorry. I gotta go."

He left, and I stood alone backstage in my eight-hundred-dollar Hugo Boss outfit, trying to process what was happening.

Wait! What the fuck? Hold on, everybody stop. Is this a joke?

I saw Dave running toward me, like a football coach ready to help an injured player off the field. "Buddy, are you okay? I just heard. In all my years in the business, I have never seen anything like this happen. I'll get to the bottom of it. Let's get you out of here and back to your room."

In the car, Dave called and emailed everyone he knew from the network until, finally, he got off the phone and confirmed: "Okay, look, they're not picking up the show. They apologize for that. They're saying they moved your flight and you can go back home tomorrow."

"That's it? It's over?" If anything was a sure thing, it was this show.

"They're saying it doesn't make sense for the network right now. This is so fucked up. It's the most unprofessional thing I've ever seen!"

"I flew the whole cast here. Who's gonna tell them?"

"I don't know, Kev. These are answers I don't have. I've never seen—"

Suddenly, something in me shrugged. It was a shoulder. That shrug sent a signal to my brain: *The decision has been made. What's getting to the bottom of it going to accomplish? Nothing. What's moping about it going to accomplish? Nothing. You're still you. Nothing's changed. Look how beautiful New York is outside that window right now.*

I interrupted Dave. "I'll let everyone else know. I'm fine, whatever. Tell them not to change my ticket. I'm down here for the weekend for the upfronts, and I'm gonna experience the upfronts."

Over the course of the night, I got in touch with each cast member and broke the news. I told them that either I could change their flight to the next morning or they could stay to make the best of the weekend.

I was the only one who chose to stay. I was determined to show the industry that I wasn't defeated, slumped over, depressed, complaining. That wasn't gonna fix anything.

I went to every event and every party possible. I danced, drank, socialized, and had a blast. From managers to agents to studio heads, it seemed like everybody came over to see how I was doing—"Are you all right? I heard what happened, buddy. I just wanna say it's so unfortunate." Everybody, that is, except the executives at ABC.

"I'm fine," I always answered, truthfully. "These things happen. It's the business we're in."

In the process, an interesting thing happened: Once people saw that my confidence in myself wasn't rattled, they understood that I had more going for me than that show—and instead of feeling sorry for me, they became more interested in me.

I wondered as I flew home on Monday: *Where did I get this from? Who was it that jumped into my body at that moment to hold back the hurt and the tears?*

It must have been my dad. If it ain't no big deal to get chopped up with an axe or walk out on your family, then it definitely ain't no big deal when something as minor as a sitcom gets canceled.

Besides, if *The Big House* didn't work, there was still *Soul Plane*. I could bypass television and go straight to film.

62

THE NOSE SMOKER

You could not tell me that *Soul Plane* wasn't going to launch me to fame. I had my own trailer on set. I was number one on the call sheet, above people who were more established than me: Sofía Vergara, Snoop Dogg, Mo'Nique, and Method Man. They even built little ramps for me to walk up and stand on so I wasn't dwarfed by those tall-ass actors.

Everyone knew I was inexperienced, so they were all encouraging, especially Mo'Nique, who became my set mom. We had Popeyes chicken for lunch, In-N-Out burgers for dinner, and laughter all the time. Every day on set was a great day.

Except the day I got high with Snoop Dogg.

I was sitting in Snoop's greenroom with him, Method Man, legendary pimp Bishop Don "Magic" Juan, and a bunch of humidifiers. All they did in there every day was smoke.

Bishop lit a blunt, put it in his nose, and inhaled. I thought my eyes were playing tricks on me at first. I'd never seen anyone smoke through their nose before—and I haven't since. He passed the blunt to me. "That's yours," I told him. "I'm not putting that in my mouth, brother. That is yours for life."

"Smoke with your unc," Snoop said, handing me his blunt. "Come on, nephew."

"Sure, I'll smoke a little with you." I didn't think at the time that it was like telling Evander Holyfield that you'll go a few rounds in the ring with him.

All I remember is that Snoop kept smoking and passing me the blunt, smoking and passing, smoking and passing, until I could only see smoke and couldn't see the pass. I felt him nudging me, and through the haze, I forced my mouth to form words. "How high are we trying to get? Because I think I'm there."

Pretty soon, I couldn't see the smoke. My eyes were closed, and I couldn't remember how to open them. I got scared. How was I gonna explain this on set? *Snoop got me so high that I forgot how to open my eyes.* No one was gonna believe that. My career was over. I'd let everyone down. *Why did I do this? I'm an East Coast guy, I shouldn't be fucking with the West Coast. Maybe they can just write a part into the script where I get blinded by exhaust from the plane. Do planes even have exhaust pipes? Fuck, I'm so high. I want my mom. Oh, there she is.*

"Hi, Mom."

"Here, take this. You'll feel better."

She handed me a blunt. I put it in my mouth and inhaled deeply. I could taste the end of it. It was slimy. Then I heard Bishop laughing.

That fucking nose-smoker! I'd just introduced his snot to my digestive system. I got even more paranoid. My dick started itching. I began to worry that I'd caught something from him. It started spreading. I couldn't see, and my whole body was itching. I scratched my chest. It felt like there were sores everywhere. I mean, why was he smoking through his nose? Probably because he had some disease in his mouth. I was done.

All I remember about the filming that day was that when I climbed the ramp to get to eye level with Sofía Vergara, I fell off.

That was my first and last time smoking with Snoop.

While we were editing the movie, I got a phone call from Dave: ABC had changed its mind again. They'd decided to cancel *Married to the Kellys* and wanted *The Big House* to take its place.

"Get it in writing!" I insisted. I'd completely let go of the show by that point, consigning it to the garbage can of oh-well-I-tried along with *North Hollywood*. For weeks after Dave called, I felt certain ABC was going to cancel the show again at the last minute.

Though I was wary, when the cast got back together, the excitement returned. We started taping episode after episode, having a great time. It felt like we were creating something undeniable, and it was all rooted in the truth of my life. In one episode, the mother of the family kept her son at home and wouldn't let him go to a concert. To guilt him into obeying her, she even pretended she had saved his life by donating a kidney. Pulling from a more recent incident, I had the father stuff his pockets with free food from the hospital.

Each week before the show aired, I called everyone I knew and told them to watch it. Afterward, a check rolled in. I was back in business.

63

KEEPING UP WITH THE JONESES

This new routine lasted six weeks, until another phone call came. Since I'd moved to Hollywood, it seemed like every call had the potential to make or break me. This one went exactly like this:

Dave: ABC is canceling the show.
Me: Okay. Thanks for letting me know.

I didn't feel shock, anger, or disappointment. But this reaction was different from a shoulder shrug. With a shoulder shrug, you let the information in and process it. Maybe it even feels bad for a moment. Then you shrug your shoulders and realize that life goes on and you'll be just fine. With this *okay*, I didn't let the information in and process it. Something was changing in me, but I didn't know what it was yet.

It would have been better if ABC had just never picked up *The Big House*, because when a TV show doesn't get picked up, it's not a failure—you just got unlucky. When a TV show gets canceled, everyone knows that you had a chance and you failed, and the ratings were probably terrible.

Meanwhile, I'd spent nearly all the money I'd earned—most recently on watches, jewelry, bottle service at clubs, and meals at expensive restaurants—in an attempt to keep up with the Joneses. I wished I could find this Jones family and ask how they managed to stay ahead of everyone without ever having to worry about money. That would be a good TV show.

No, fuck TV. It was all about the movies now. *Soul Plane* was coming out in a few months, so maybe its success would overshadow the failure of *The Big House*.

Meanwhile, *Scary Movie 3* was released, and though it didn't even come close to making me a star, it did give me enough buzz to get a few more bookings from colleges and comedy clubs. One day I was at the airport, waiting for my flight to a college show, when someone I didn't know clapped me on the back: "Nashawn Wade!"

"Excuse me?"

"*Soul Plane*! Wassup, man? I saw that shit."

The movie wasn't due in theaters for months, but somehow this guy knew my character's name. "Do you work in the industry or something?"

"Naw, man, I got the bootleg!"

"The bootleg?" We hadn't even finished postproduction yet. It wasn't possible for a bootleg to come out that early—was it?

A few days later, I was back in L.A., hanging out with Rodney Perry, Harry, and a comedian we'd befriended named Joey Wells. While we were playing *Madden*, Joey got a call from his teenage son. He put the phone on speaker.

"Say that again, son."

"They watching Kevin's movie right now."

"How's that possible?" Joey asked.

"Somebody got a bootleg. Everybody in class is watching it."

Soul Plane, it turned out, was about to make movie history—as a landmark case of a bootleg coming out so early and spreading so quickly that by the time the actual film was released, it already seemed old. One of the people with those bootlegs was my father, who'd made copies for half the family.

While I was sitting in the theater at the premiere, someone actually came up to me and asked me to sign the bootleg DVD. It was no surprise when the movie came and went without even making its budget back. It was a flop. I was a flop.

Here's what happens when a movie you play the lead in bombs at the box office *and* a sitcom you star in gets canceled midseason: You become poison.

No one in Hollywood wants you in any of their productions, because they feel that anything with you in it is going to be toxic.

Up to this point, my whole career had been a climb—sometimes fast and sometimes slow, but always uphill. Now that it was plummeting, I didn't know what the next step was supposed to be. I hadn't considered that failure was a possibility.

Instead of shrugging, my shoulders began to sag.

"What happens now?" I kept asking Dave. "What do we do?"

"Pilot season is right around the corner. We'll go out and book you something."

"So I'm just supposed to wait?"

"Don't worry about it. Everything will be okay."

I couldn't tell anymore if Dave was my manager or my therapist. Every day, I called him, trying to get something going. But no one in the industry wanted to meet with me. All those casting agents and producers who I thought I'd been charming left and right suddenly had no interest. Everyone in the business had moved on to the next New Face from that year's Just for Laughs. I was an Old Face now. In Hollywood, just like in relationships, it's easier to get a first chance than a second chance.

64

YES, I REFER TO MYSELF IN THE THIRD PERSON AGAIN. BUT THAT'S ONLY BECAUSE IT FEELS LIKE I'VE LIVED THREE LIVES.

They say that bad news comes in threes.

I don't know who said that, but they got their math wrong. I think it's that you're in either an upward or a downward phase of your life. And if you're going down, bad news comes more than three times. It's just that after three, you stop keeping count because it's so familiar. It's like counting how many socks you own.

My third sock came from the worst possible person: the one handling my money.

Business Manager: I just got off the phone with the IRS. They need you to pay your back taxes.

Me: Taxes? Don't they take those out of my checks?

Business Manager: Sometimes they do and sometimes they don't. It depends on whether you're being paid as an employee or an independent contractor.

Me: Huh?

Business Manager: I'll just cut right to it: You only have $30,000 in your account.

Me: So pay my taxes with some of that.

Business Manager: Kevin, you owe almost $400,000.

Me: Wait, what?

The last time I'd done a *Wait, what?*—which is much bigger than a regular *What?*—was probably when my dad told me he was leaving my mom.

Business Manager: I'm going to be frank with you, Kevin. You overspend. You haven't *ever* saved enough to pay your taxes. I've been able to work out an installment agreement with the IRS for you in the past, but you made so much last year, the IRS won't do an agreement for you again.

Me: What happens now?

Business Manager: I'm gonna have to wipe out your accounts to make your payments so they don't seize your assets.

Me: Wait, wipe out what? That's gonna leave me with nothing. How am I gonna make my rent?

Business Manager: You'll get more work, I'm sure. We've seen people go through this before. You'll be—

Me: Hell no, I won't. I can't pay that right now. I'm gonna keep that thirty grand I got left and just owe it all. Whatever happens happens.

Nobody ever told me how taxes worked. I figured that when I made the money, they removed taxes and the rest was mine to keep.

When I was younger, my mom did my taxes. In Hollywood, my business manager took care of them, along with the rest of my bills. But no one ever called and told me about these installment plans.

That's when the enemy of success started looking for me, trying to see if there were any weaknesses in my armor. His name was bitterness.

Suddenly I knew the TV lineup for every day of the week. I could recite the Monday morning shows, the Tuesday afternoon shows, the Wednesday evening shows. Every halfway-decent and hardworking comedian's name seemed to be on that goddamn schedule but mine. Not only was my name now a liability, but so was my attitude. I'd lost my confidence.

Struggling when you're going somewhere is exciting. Struggling when you're not getting anywhere is challenging. But struggling when you're going backward is hell.

Pilot season came and went, and I didn't book anything. My only opportunity came from Judd Apatow. He was working on a new film, *The 40-Year-Old Virgin*, and asked me to audition for one of the leading roles. I loved the character and felt Judd had written it for me.

I killed the audition, then found out two weeks later that another comedian, Romany Malco, had gotten the part. As what felt like a consolation prize, I was given a small, two-minute role in the film.

I thought my career was over after that. *This was my last chance. How could I not get that part? If the director who's been my biggest supporter isn't giving me a starring role, then I'm definitely not getting a part from someone I don't know.*

One of the most stressful things in the world is to live outside your means. As my savings dwindled to nothing and I went into debt, I started getting stomachaches that were so intense, I'd double over in pain. I worried that I was developing ulcers or irritable bowel syndrome or worse.

Occasionally, I'd get a college or out-of-town club gig that would help me pay the bills, but half the time I only made enough money to cover the expense of traveling there.

Outside of Na'im, who I brought as an opener for my out-of-town shows, I didn't tell anyone how much I was struggling. Even if I was failing, I could at least *look* successful. I still had my car, watches, and jerseys—at least for now. I didn't even let my mom know how broke I was. Lord knows the level of worry she would have had if she'd found out her son was going through hard times twenty-seven hundred miles away on the West Coast. I knew she would have sent me a check, but I didn't want to be in debt to her again. I was determined to figure a way out of this by myself.

Then one night, my Z71 was stolen.

This was my bottom. It felt like God had parted the clouds, sat down, taken a giant yearlong shit on me, and then used my car for toilet paper.

I was talented. I was funny. I was likeable. I was experienced. Yet none of those things was doing me any good. I was wasting my life away in clubs where I couldn't afford the drinks anymore. I was, I had to admit—for perhaps the first time in my life—doing everything wrong.

That's when I learned the biggest lesson of all: humility. In the depths of my disappointment and failure, I understood that nothing in this life is guaranteed. One day you're hot, the next you're not. One day you're rich, the next you're poor. One day you're free, the next you're in jail. One day you're alive, the next you're dead.

You can work hard. You can be talented. You can know all the right people. You can follow all the right lessons. You can be smart, rich, beautiful, everything—and still, life can deal you a bad hand.

So what are you to do in the face of a reality that can be indifferent, cold, even cruel? All you can do is play the odds. If you choose to give up, you can be fairly certain that life will pass you by. But if you choose to try your best, you can at least tip the balance significantly in your favor.

Life is not about the result—we all have the same outcome in the end. Life is about the effort you put into it. And I wasn't putting effort into my craft anymore. After months of spiraling debt, domestic disputes, and career rejection, it was time to take a hard right turn and start doing the work myself.

Fuck being someone else's plus-one at the same clubs every night. Fuck calling Dave Becky every day, hoping that some executive saw something special in me. Fuck paying sixty-five dollars an hour that I can't afford for an acting teacher when I'm not getting booked for anything. Fuck living a lie with Torrei and having the same argument over and over. Fuck all this idle time. It was time to get out of this city, take my career back into my own hands, and get on my grind again.

If I was going to call myself a comedian, I needed to actually be doing comedy. I called Dave. "Dude, I just wanna do stand-up for a while. I need to get out of L.A. and work the road for as many nights as I can. I wanna go everywhere."

After asking five times if I was sure that this was what I wanted to do, Dave finally said, "I can find a booking agent to help you, but the shows aren't gonna be glamorous."

"Just book me anywhere. I don't give a shit where it is. I'd rather be performing for five dollars again than sitting around waiting for the phone to ring."

Within a month, I was on the road—and that's when the quiet storm of Kevin Hart began.

Life Lessons
FROM LOSS

If you experience loss, it doesn't mean you lost.
It means you've been blessed with an opportunity
to take a moment, realize how special someone
or something has been to you, and go through
new doors that were closed to you before.
No jokes here. Just wisdom.

Me and Kenneth with Mom

65

THERE ARE TWO KINDS OF HUSTLERS, AND BOTH ARE WORKING FOR ME

Thus began the Road Warrior era: seven straight years of touring, practically nonstop.

While I booked myself into clubs, Dave found me a personal appearance agent named Glenn Ruskow, who put me on comedy package shows at small theaters. On paper, these looked like a great opportunity. I was performing with comedians like Bill Bellamy and Katt Williams, and each show paid around five thousand dollars.

But I was always at the bottom of the bill, as "Kevin Hart from *Soul Plane.*" I'd show up and do a fifteen-minute set for a few hundred people, then slink off stage. Usually, by the time the headliner came on, the theater would still be only half-full, and the promoters would bleed money while Glenn got his guaranteed payment. At the worst of these shows, only fifty people showed up.

After a period of doing one or two package shows a month, I became frustrated. Promoters and audiences were associating my name with bad experiences. I mentioned this to Glenn, and he responded, "Don't sweat it. You're making *your* money, brother."

There are two kinds of hustlers. There are the hustlers who work inside the business, like Glenn Ruskow: You look them in the eye and you know you can trust them. They follow the rules but they know the loopholes. They're in it for the money, and they'll do everything in their power to get as much of yours as possible, short of actually doing anything dishonest. What keeps them in check is that they want money so that they can be safe, comfortable, and accepted by the Joneses (yeah, them again), so they're not willing to take any risks by ripping someone off.

Then there are the hustlers who work outside the business, like Terrence Lock. Na'im introduced me to him. He was booking gigs for a few other comedians on the scene, and he started pursuing me as a client. You look these kinds of hustlers in the eye and you know you *shouldn't* trust them. But you start listening to their words, and they say exactly what you want to hear, and you see that they can make anything happen by flapping their mouth, so you forget about your first instinct and decide to trust them anyway.

These hustlers don't know the loopholes because they don't follow the rules. They're not actually in it for the money but for everything else—the fame, the sex, the love of the hustle. They don't want safety or stability, because they need the high of living on the edge of being broke, arrested, or shot at any moment. They're your best friend, as long as you serve a purpose—and when you don't, they've never heard of you before.

"Hey, Kev," Terrence told me, "I don't know what kind of work Glenn got going for you, but I can get you some spots on the side."

I didn't like the work Glenn was getting me, and there wasn't enough of it, so I decided to try an outside-the-system hustler. With the amount of debt I was in, I didn't have much of a choice.

"Okay, Terrence, let's see what you can do."

The first thing Terrence did was set about spending my money. "You need a road manager," he insisted. "I got someone for you."

"No, I don't. I've been doing this by myself just fine. I'm not one of those pampered artists who needs someone else to dress him in the morning and drive him everywhere."

"Let me ask you: How much money are you leaving on the table because you aren't negotiating the best deals with the clubs? How many times do you finish a gig and the owner says he'll pay you later, and you never hear from him again? A road manager is an investment. The money you give him, you get back times ten because his job is to make sure you get paid. And he frees up time for you to do what you do and be an artist."

Terrence went on: "A road manager's job is also to take care of everything for you so that you have no problems when you get to the venue. There are the problems of flights, hotel rooms, and transportation from airport to hotel, from hotel to venue, from venue to party, from party back to hotel. All this stuff can be coordinated by a road manager and tailored to your likes and dislikes."

He had a strong case. Then again, every time he opened his mouth, he had a strong case.

A few days later, I found myself at lunch with Terrence and someone who looked like the guys I'd seen sniffing seats on the public bus in Philadelphia. He introduced himself as Nate Smith. He was thin but had a potbelly and graying, uneven muttonchop sideburns. When he spoke, he said ten words for every one he actually wanted to say. "You know, Kev, it's like this, you see what I mean, I do the work, right, I ain't, like, one of them kind of, you know, them damn guys who you see all the time out there like that who's not doing what you call the work, if you know what I'm talking about."

The only way this guy is gonna get me my money is if promoters pay him to stop talking, I thought.

After the meeting, I told Terrence: "Nate's too old."

Nate was working for another comedian at the time. This comedian was obsessive-compulsive, and treated him like a piece of shit, calling him names and threatening to fire him every day. If Nate handed him a stack of money and every bill wasn't facing the same way, he'd throw them all on the floor and make Nate pick them up.

When Terrence told him that I wasn't interested, Nate responded: "You tell Kev he doesn't have to pay me. Just let me get out with him and show him what I can do."

As soon as Terrence said this, I knew that Nate, despite my first impression, was a rare find: dedicated, persistent, and willing to work hard and be judged by the results. "If he wants to do this on a trial basis and see where it goes, then fine," I told Terrence. "But I'm gonna pay him."

The three of us were going to beat those clubs up together. We had the future all planned out. Then Torrei got pregnant.

66

CHAPTER 8 + CHAPTER 58 = CHAPTER 66

In the Hart family tradition, it was an accident. Torrei was feeling nauseous in the mornings, so she went to a convenience store and bought a pregnancy test. We broke the Hart family tradition, however, by being excited about the news.

I wasn't ready. She wasn't ready. But no one is ever ready. You become ready by experiencing it, and I couldn't wait to experience fatherhood.

We weren't in the best place in our relationship, and once the mood swings kicked in, we were in a worse place. A cloud of permanent rage settled over the house. Some nights, I had to wait until Torrei was asleep before going to bed, because I was worried that she'd try to harm me in my sleep. One day, after neighbors called the cops on us because we were arguing so loudly, I made a questionable decision. The math was as follows:

Torrei + Kevin = Fighting
Baby + Fighting = Miscarriage

Torrei − Kevin = No Fighting
Baby − Fighting = No Miscarriage

I rented an apartment a few blocks away and moved out. I didn't know what else to do.

Torrei was hot about it, and I didn't blame her. But my intention was solely to keep everybody—her, me, the baby—from getting hurt.

When I first moved out, it was like paradise on earth. It was so quiet in

that apartment. No one was mad at me for anything I said and did—or didn't say and didn't do. No one asked me twenty questions every time I left the house and required proof of where I was going. I couldn't remember feeling so free since I'd moved out of my mom's place.

There must be a part of me, I reasoned, *that stays with Torrei because it's so familiar.* I'd spent years under my mom's strict control, getting beaten if I stepped out of line or even thought about stepping out of line. So as much as I hated the drama with Torrei, I was also addicted to it.

The sweet taste of living free and alone, however, was soon soured by guilt. I was disappointed in myself for abandoning Torrei when she was pregnant. And I didn't want my daughter to be born into a broken home. Surely I could be understanding of what Torrei was going through right now—emotionally, physically, and hormonally—and stay strong. Going back was the right thing to do.

After a month on my own, I moved back in with Torrei. I kept my lease on the other apartment, just in case, and sublet it to J.T. Jackson, one of the funniest actors in Los Angeles.

In the meantime, I started doing my first shows with Nate as road manager. Traveling with him was an uncomfortable experience at first. Nate had been so overworked and exploited by his last employer that he did everything: He was my driver, navigator, publicist, security guard, caterer, accountant, and valet. He did so much for me that it was embarrassing.

I've never shat on a person once, even when I felt they deserved to be shat on, but Nate chewed out club owners and promoters on my behalf like I was Mariah Carey or something.

Eventually, I had to speak up. "Nate, people keep coming over and saying my tour manager's an asshole."

"Kev, listen to me, man—I get shit done. Don't ask me how I do it, but I always do it, know what I'm saying? If I ain't do what I had to do to get the shit done, the shit wouldn't be done. But you don't wanna know how I get it done. As long as they mad at me and not mad at you."

"I don't want them to be mad at *anybody*. You're a reflection of me."

We would get into it all the time, but I appreciated where his heart was at. So I stuck with him, and kept reminding him not to be a dick to people.

Then, on March 22, 2005, it happened. I stood in the delivery room and watched the doctors guide my daughter into the world. As soon as I saw her, tears ran down my face. I couldn't remember the last time I'd cried. The little boy who'd spent half his childhood in a fort made of bedding in Ms. Davis's basement was now a father. This beautiful baby was mine to love, nurture, and raise. To succeed, all I had to do was not do anything my father had done.

I wanted our daughter to have a name similar to Kevin, so I told Torrei we should call her Kevina, which, by the way, is a totally valid woman's name. It's the female form of Kevin, in the same way that Roberta is the female form of Robert. But Torrei wisely slammed the door shut on that dream. Instead, she came up with the best name I could ever imagine for a daughter: Heaven Leigh Hart.

It was a happy day for us. While Torrei and Heaven were recuperating in the hospital, the nurse asked if I had a car seat for the ride home. I had no experience with babies, so I didn't know this was a legal requirement.

I immediately drove to Target and spent probably two hours reading each box, asking employees questions, selecting what I thought was the safest seat, and then struggling to install it.

You want to know what heaven is like? It's like putting Heaven in that car seat for the first time, making sure the padding and straps are set just right to protect her tiny body, and knowing that we're taking her home to be part of our lives forever. It was my first daddy task, and I took it as seriously as her life.

Torrei was in a wheelchair, so I helped her get into the car as well. Before I slid into the driver's seat, I looked at Torrei sitting in the front and Heaven in the back, and suddenly I didn't feel trapped in a crazy relationship anymore. I felt privileged to be part of a family.

When we got home, there was no fighting. It was all about taking care of my two girls. The fact that such an angry time in our lives had produced such a sweet, gentle, beautiful soul seemed like a miracle.

Every time I saw Heaven in those first weeks, I told myself: *I need to make this work. For her.*

67

USING MY GODDAMN BRAIN

For a month, my relationship with Torrei felt miraculously normal. We woke up together, usually to the sound of Heaven. We ate our meals together, watched television together, went out together, and took turns each night putting Heaven back to sleep when she woke up crying. We were a team.

But there was one thing missing from this team: Someone had to go to work and earn money. I still had a mission, but it was one I now needed to balance with this new responsibility of being a father. As soon as I told Torrei that I was going away to perform, we fell right back into our old pattern.

Torrei: Who you going to go fuck?
Me: Terrence booked me some spots. Really.
Torrei: Whatever, whatever. You probably got a bitch waiting for you right now. What am I supposed to do?
Me: Someone's gotta stay with the baby.
Torrei: So you get to do whatever you want while I'm stuck here?
Me: We don't have a choice. If I don't work, we can't feed the baby.
Torrei: Okay, you go "work." Just don't get that bitch pregnant.

I had a lot of shows lining up. Terrence was such a talker that he'd sold me to bookers who'd never heard my name before. His argument was the same every time: "You may not know this here guy, but he's the next big thing."

I was "the next big thing" for years as Nate and I went back and forth, side to side, around and around the country, hitting up the small clubs that Glenn wouldn't touch. Outside of carving a couple of days from each week to spend with Heaven, I didn't say no to stage time. I ended up doing every college you've never heard of and every shit comedy club you wouldn't take a date to.

At first, the goal was to get back to the craft and be productive. But eventually I noticed that there were people at the shows who knew me: mostly from *Soul Plane*, sometimes from *Scary Movie 3*, even occasionally from *Paper Soldiers*.

Those movies had come and gone, but each one had captured a few fans. That, I recognized, was more valuable than a holding deal, because a true fan pays dividends for life. So if at every show I could pick up a few more fans, then leaving Hollywood to tour might turn out to be the best possible thing I could do for my film career: I could overcome the stigma of being a proven failure by becoming too popular for the entertainment business to deny. I needed to build myself a following so big that, instead of worrying that saying *yes* to me or one of my projects was a mistake, the gatekeepers would worry that saying *no* was a mistake.

At the time, Dane Cook was one of the most popular comedians in the country. I met him at the Improv one night and asked him how he'd grown his audience. His answer: by getting email addresses; using the social media of that era, like MySpace; and having the patience to stay engaged in the lives of his fans.

When you have somebody who's created a blueprint that's working, all you gotta do is copy it. So Nate and I went to a copy shop and had three-by-five cards printed. As I ended each set, he'd pass them out and ask people to fill out their contact information—email, street address, phone, social media, everything. Then he'd add each person's name to a database for that city.

The next time I came through town, we'd hit up everyone on email, on MySpace, by phone—everything short of knocking on their door. Before the show, Nate, Na'im (when I could get him an opening spot), and I would go to malls, barbershops, and shopping streets to hand out flyers.

After each show, I'd treat the audience just like customers at City Sports. I'd spend some time talking with them about their life, and make sure to remember their names and stories if they came to another show. Sometimes I'd even exchange phone numbers with them so I could reach out in a more personal way next time I was in town. Afterward, I'd start seeing them in the audience all the time—some of them still, to this day.

My new business manager had worked out a payment plan with the IRS, and I needed to make more money at the shows. So Nate and I set up a merchandise table at each club. We couldn't afford actual merchandise like T-shirts, so instead we bought a Polaroid camera. After each show, Nate would stand there with the camera and talk audience members into paying twenty dollars to take a photo with me, which I'd then personalize and sign.

Desperation is the best motivator there is. If I hadn't sunk so low, I wouldn't have been willing to work so hard. But I was happy busting my ass on the road. We were creating a business that was completely *ours*.

68

THE MANY FACES OF KEVIN HART (ALL OF WHICH ARE LOOKING AT EACH OTHER, CONFUSED)

Here's a life lesson: If you're having problems in your relationship, getting married or having children is not going to solve them. It's just going to create new problems.

This may be common sense to most intelligent human beings. It wasn't to me. So I continued to learn it the hard way.

Torrei's and my endless argument about my work took on a new dimension. Now she resented me for leaving her with Heaven and making the baby her sole responsibility, and I resented her because she didn't seem to understand that parenting isn't just about being physically present with a child. It's also about providing for a child—food, clothing, shelter, education, opportunities. I thought about how hard my mom had worked to provide for me. She wasn't present all the time, but she was the most caring mother I could imagine.

Almost every time I left for a show and every time I returned, there was an argument. And one night, as my parenting, my career, and my mother were all being attacked, I ran out of patience. *Do I have so little self-respect that I'm allowing someone to talk to me like this?* Instead of leaving, like a man who actually had self-respect would do, I began yelling back at her. Between the two of us that night, hairbrushes were thrown, mirrors were broken, and our only television set was smashed.

Heaven somehow slept through this, thanks either to the white-noise machine in her room or the fact that she was so used to it by now that it sounded like white noise. Our neighbors, however, called the cops on us again, and soon there was a loud knocking on the front door.

I opened it as calmly as I could and saw two cops standing there. "Officers, we're fine. It's no big deal."

They looked around the house and saw the mess. "No, no," one of the officers said. "We need to separate you two."

He seemed to know our situation. All of a sudden I realized that it was the same officer who had shown up when Torrei and I were fighting during her pregnancy.

He looked at me like I was a piece of shit, which is exactly what I was—the kind of guy who's always got cops in his living room breaking up domestic disputes. "We're taking you in," the officer said.

When I was released the next day, I moved back into my old apartment, where J.T. was still living. After a few days, I visited Heaven, and ended up staying with Torrei again for a week. I went back and forth between the two apartments, wrestling with myself.

Single Kevin: We're always fighting. We're always going at each other. One of us is going to end up in prison for real one of these days. Our shit's still not right, and it's never gonna be right. Fuck this. I'm outta here.

Relationship Kevin: How can I be so selfish? I'm not only walking out on my wife, I'm walking out on my daughter. There's a name for people who do this: deadbeat dads. I can't be a deadbeat dad. I don't want my daughter to come from a broken home. I'm going back.

Single Kevin: This is worse than before. We're not united as parents. We're not happy together. It's fine for us to destroy our lives, but we can't destroy the life of this innocent child. I'm out!

Relationship Kevin: Why did I leave? I can deal with any heckler in any crowd, but I can't handle my own wife? Put yourself in her shoes: She left her job and came to L.A. because *I* invited her. Now she's here. She has no family and no job, and she's trapped with my child. How could I be so selfish? I need to go back to that poor woman and apologize.

Single Kevin: I just wanna be happy. I'm—

Relationship Kevin: No, I'm not. I'm not gonna be happy if I'm a fucked-up father who abandoned his family. I'm . . .

Single Kevin: . . . going.

Relationship Kevin: . . . staying.

Both Kevins: Fuuuuuuuuuuuck!

It was relationship Ping-Pong. I was in, I was out. I was there, I was gone. I felt good, I felt bad. I loved Torrei, I hated Torrei. I loved God, God hated me.

In the end, the same tenacity that enabled me to take so many whuppings from Hollywood and keep coming back for more also kept me coming back to Torrei, hoping that if I worked harder, things would go differently.

69

MY EIGHTEENTH LUCKY BREAK

One day, I got lucky.

Katt Williams had gotten a role in an action movie called *Fool's Gold*, which was shooting in Australia. But he'd gotten in trouble with the law and wasn't allowed to leave the country. The casting agents called Dave and said they needed a comedian as soon as possible to play a villain in the film named Bigg Bunny.

Dave mentioned my name, and they asked him to send an audition tape. Instead, Dave insisted that they meet me in person. It was the first big role I'd been up for in a while, but I had no experience playing James Bond–style supervillains. I was desperate to get the part, so I went to a pet store, bought a big bunny, and took it to the audition. I did the entire Bigg Bunny scene sitting in a chair, stroking the rabbit.

It was a gamble, but the casting agents loved the courage it took and ended up giving me the part. The writers even incorporated a bunny into the script. It was more proof that only your mother thinks you're special; to all other people, you look the same as everyone else unless you make the effort to stand out—and that effort is always worth it.

I kept the bunny and took it home as a reminder of this lesson.

Fool's Gold was a seventy-million-dollar tropical action movie starring Matthew McConaughey and Kate Hudson. When I arrived in Australia, the producers gave me a rental car, keys to an apartment, and a sheet with call times. They then informed me that people drive on the opposite side of the road in Australia. But because I wasn't the star, the rest was up to me: to be professional, show up on time, kill the material, and make the director, Andy Tennant, feel that I had a future in the business. I'd been given another chance.

Being so far away from home for three months, I missed my family—even Torrei. So she came out with Heaven, and in the paradise of coastal Queensland, Australia, she told me she had bad news.

My bunny rabbit, my lucky reminder to always be different, was dead. She'd killed Little Bigg Bunny, though she said she didn't know how it had happened. I figured that they'd probably gotten into an argument because he was tired of eating carrots at home and wanted to go outside to hunt for wild carrots.

Outside of that, though, we got along the whole time. I felt like things were turning around: my movie career was starting up again. Torrei and I weren't fighting. Heaven was growing into a beautiful girl. And Na'im, who was house-sitting for us, decided to move to Los Angeles permanently.

Then my brother called in a panic.

70

THERE ARE NO WORDS TO SUMMARIZE THIS ONE

"Look, man, Mom told me not to tell you this," my brother began. I braced myself for something painful. "She's sick."

I could feel myself getting ill as I heard the words. "How sick?"

"Real sick. She didn't want you to find out, because she knows this movie is big for you and you wouldn't have done it if you knew how bad it was."

"How bad is that?"

"As bad as a death sentence. If you don't come home soon, the next time you'll probably see Mom is in the grave. I'm sorry for telling you this so late, but if you're mad you gotta deal with it, because those were her wishes."

It felt like the world stopped spinning. I drifted in and out as he continued: "Ovarian cancer . . . a year ago . . . I only found out by accident . . . family . . . when . . . Kev? Kev?"

"I'll be on the next plane home."

As soon as I hung up, I explained the situation to the producers. Fortunately, Bigg Bunny wasn't in a lot of scenes that week, so they were able to adjust the schedule and let me go home for a few days.

My brother picked me up at the airport and told me that Mom was refusing to get treatment. She believed in God's will, he reported, and if God wanted her to get healthy, she'd get better. And if God wanted to take her in the same way her own mother had died of ovarian cancer, she'd get sicker. "I'll let God handle it," she kept telling him.

I felt all my childhood frustration rise to the surface as he went on about Mom's stubbornness. If God really wanted to handle those things Himself, without human participation, then he wouldn't have created doctors.

Kenneth pulled into the driveway of my mom's house and I ran inside. My heart broke when I saw her. She was sitting in an armchair, and her stomach was so swollen that she looked pregnant. She was in a lot of pain and wasn't even able to go to the bathroom.

"I didn't want you to know," she said softly. "It's wonderful that you're out there doing your thing. My little Kevin! You've made me so happy."

Tears filled my eyes. I asked her if she could please go to a hospital—not for herself, but for me and Kenneth, so we would know we'd done all we could—and thankfully, she agreed.

We took her to Temple University Hospital, the same place my brother and I were born, and she began chemotherapy. But she was unhappy there. She'd built her life around working hard, being around loved ones, and participating in her church community. Here, everything seemed cold and clinical and far from God. You weren't seen as a soul on your way to paradise, just as a chart on a clipboard.

"These people don't want me here," she insisted. "Take me home!"

With the money from *Fool's Gold*, I was able to set her up at home with a hospital bed and around-the-clock nursing. When possible, we had a doctor come in and do treatments at her bedside.

The day I was flying back to Australia, my brother called: "You gotta come back over to the house."

"Why?"

"There's a bird in the basement."

"Huh?"

"You heard me: *There's a bird in the basement!*"

"Oh my God, I'll be right there!"

When we were young, Mom had filled our heads with dozens of superstitions. One was about splitting a pole being bad luck, and another was that if a bird flies into the house, it was a sign of death.

When I arrived at the house, I asked for clarification. "If a bird gets into the house but you catch it and take it outside, does that mean that you got death out of the house too?"

"Well, *if* you can get the bird," my cousin Shirrel answered. Evidently, they'd all tried.

"If that's all it takes, we'll go get that bird right now. Get his ass out the house, and Mom will be okay."

Kenneth and I went downstairs. The bird was huge: It really looked like death.

My brother was armed with a mop; I had a broom. The plan was to swat and chase the beast out of the basement. Kenneth swung the mop at it, and it swooped in my direction. I dropped the broom and went running up the steps so fast I fell at the top.

However, a true hero never gives up. I bravely picked up the phone and called the Society for the Prevention of Cruelty to Animals to come get the bird. "That still counts, right?" I asked Shirrel afterward.

Not long after I returned to Australia, I was speaking with my dad on the phone, and he told me he'd gotten "what they call a pap-something" and found out he had lung cancer. Where my mom didn't like getting treatment and kept saying "I'll leave it up to God," my dad wanted every treatment available and kept saying "God, why me?"

I was able to take a few more days off, so I flew back to Philadelphia to visit my folks. I was worried I was going to lose them both, until I spoke to my father's doctor, who explained to my relief that even though Dad was talking like he was gonna die any day, he was going to pull through just fine.

Mom, however, was back in the hospital because the cancer had progressed. No one mentioned it, but we all knew what was going to happen. I sat with her each day, happy to be near her. Every time I left her bedside, I made sure to tell her that I loved her.

They were hitting her hard with the chemo, and she was having relatively good days and really bad days. On a good day, my brother and I got the most loving version of Mom there was. On a bad day, we were verbal punching bags for whatever she was angry about at that moment.

One afternoon, after Kenneth gave her some water, she said he was the greatest son in the world. She showered him with all the praise she'd never given him growing up. It filled his soul with exactly what it had needed all these years. The next day, he was giving her water again, and she choked on it.

Instantly, he became purse-snatching Kenneth again: "You're trying to kill me! I know what you're up to, boy—you wanna murder me so you can get that insurance money!"

Mom began insisting that we stop the treatments, take her back home, and let God get on with his work. There was no convincing her otherwise. Dad even visited her, tried to tell her that his God wanted her to do chemo, and ended up in an argument with her that seemed just like the old days.

On my last day in Philadelphia, Kenneth and I sat with Mom for hours. He was on one side of her chair, and I was on the other side. While she was speaking, Kenneth dozed off from exhaustion. Suddenly, Mom summoned strength from God knows where, reached out, and smacked him across the face. "You better wake up," she rasped. "These could be the last words I ever speak, and you're falling asleep!"

After I returned to Australia, I got the call from Kenneth. Mom was no longer in pain. She was in a better place. I instantly said a prayer, from me to her, thanking her for her love; letting her know that I was in this great position in life because of the lessons she taught me; and promising to continue honoring her by keeping her wisdom, compassion, and leadership alive in me.

The producers allowed me to go back to Philadelphia one more time to make arrangements for the funeral and bury my mom, my rock, my teacher.

I'd never lost a loved one before, but I noticed that I processed it differently than everyone else in my family. I knew that my mom had wanted to stop suffering, and her wish had been granted. It was only us, those left behind, who were still suffering. And we had just two choices: to stop living or to go on living.

It was strange to travel back to Australia after the funeral and see that nothing had changed: Airport security still yelled about traveling with liquids. The plane still smelled like old carpet. Couples still kissed and bickered and ignored each other. The sky was still blue. The movie crew was still scurrying around, coordinating the same tiny details through their radios. Everything was different for me, but in the world, everything was the same.

When you mourn, when you hurt, when someone you love—or everyone you love—passes, it may feel like a void has opened up in your universe. But in *the* universe, energy can never be destroyed. So if the pain and the absence existed only in my mind, then it wasn't real. It was imaginary, and me being hurt or angry about it wasn't going to change anything. There was nothing I could do except let go of a tragic story and embrace one that served me—and her—better. So I did.

I chose not to lose my mom, and instead to gain an angel. In my mind, my heart, and my life, she is still completely present to this day—and as wise, compassionate, and stubborn as ever.

Life Lessons
FROM
INDEPENDENCE

Waiting for other people to make your dreams come true is like waiting for a bus on a corner where there's no bus stop. Sometimes the bus driver may feel bad for you and stop anyway, but usually he'll speed right past and leave you standing there like an idiot.

With Nate

71

WHEN LIFE HANDS YOU SHIT SANDWICHES, KEEP YOUR MOUTH SHUT

When someone dies in your family, traditionally there's a period of mourning. This is generally followed by a period of amazement. This period begins when you start going through the possessions of the deceased.

Sometimes the amazement is positive: "Oh my God, Dad's Coke bottle collection is worth a million dollars!"

Sometimes the amazement is negative: "Oh my God, Dad's wanted by the FBI!"

And sometimes it's just confusing: "Oh my God, why does Dad have three boxes full of pubic hair?"

In our case, we experienced all three kinds of amazement.

The positive: Kenneth found a box of memorabilia from both of our careers. There were videotapes of *The Big House* that Mom had recorded every week, newspaper clippings from my appearance at Just for Laughs, advertisements for my performances at the Laff House. Any accolade I'd received, if Mom had access to it, she'd clipped and saved it. From Kenneth, she'd saved fliers announcing pool tournaments that he'd started competing in and even articles about the military drill accident that restarted their relationship. She'd never mentioned being aware of some of these things, yet it turned out that she'd been following our lives more closely than we'd thought.

The negative: Kenneth found a lot of pictures of Mom and Dad in intimate situations that no child ever wants to see.

The confusing: We found a family tree that Mom had made. On it, she'd written names of my dad's relatives who I'd never met, as well as how they'd died. Peaches got stabbed at a block party. Booby got stabbed in jail. And I forget where James got stabbed. But anyway, most of them were gone.

The confusing part kicked in when we saw the list of seven names underneath my father's branch of the tree. Two of those names were Kevin and Robert, which is my brother's birth name: Robert Kenneth Hart. The rest were the names of Dad's other kids. Some I knew about, others I didn't. But next to those seven names, Mom had written the number eleven and circled it. It was a mystery. Neither of us could figure out what the number eleven meant, but it felt significant.

The next time we spoke to Dad, Kenneth asked him about it.

Kenneth: What does this number eleven mean? I don't understand.

Dad: Just leave it alone.

Kenneth: No. Mom is gone—somebody has to keep this information alive. We need to know where the fuck we come from.

Dad: Well . . . you're the oldest of the Roberts.

Kenneth: What do you mean "the Roberts"?

Dad: There are more Roberts than you. There's four of 'em that Nance knew about, but there may be five.

Kenneth: Why would you do that?

Dad: I wanted to name everybody Omar, but only one of them women would let me. When they didn't go for Omar, I tried Robert, cause that's my dad's middle name.

Kenneth: You've got five sons named Robert? You're nuts.

Suddenly we understood why Mom had started calling my brother by his middle name: The name Robert had become a reminder of all my dad's affairs. My brother was the first of his children, but almost every other one was born while he and my mom were together.

Meanwhile, Torrei was pregnant again. Coming right after the loss of my mom, it felt like a sign to keep building the next generation of Harts. "We gotta get a house," I told Torrei. "That's what we need to be a family: a real home. That'll fix everything."

With the money I had left from *Fool's Gold*, I rented a house on Lemona Avenue in Sherman Oaks for forty-five hundred dollars a month. And instantly the relationship changed: Instead of arguing in an apartment, we were arguing in a house.

Torrei named our son Hendrix, to do a run on the Hs for our kids' names, and I got in Kevin as his middle name: Hendrix Kevin Hart. By trying to give the same name to all my kids, I guess I was more like my dad than I thought.

Then the inevitable happened. I had to get back on the road, and the shit hit the fan: "You're never here!" "I'm gonna find me a job, and *you* stay home with the baby!" "All you do is party with your friends!"

I left for the airport, with the usual thoughts running through my head. *Oh well, I'm gonna get served a big shit sandwich for taking off to do more shows, and I'll eat it. But I'm not gonna stop focusing on what I believe is gonna change my life and get us financially secure and give a good education to our kids.*

In New York, I'd had very little real-world experience to talk about on stage. But now I had the one thing that comes to all people with age: more baggage. I was trapped in an unhappy marriage with an angry wife, two beautiful children, and bills that I couldn't afford to pay. I had problems and a struggle that were relatable to many people, and I was living them out at a level so intense that I didn't need to exaggerate a thing.

I didn't have a voice in my relationship, but I had a voice on stage. I could speak my mind, acknowledge the insanity of my situation, and be understood on such a raw, uncomfortable level that it elicited knowing laughter. I was careful, though, never to humiliate or belittle Torrei, but instead to make me—my reactions, my cowardice, my inability to be the man in the relationship—the butt of the jokes.

All this set up a vicious cycle: The better I got at comedy, the more bookings I got. The more bookings I got, the worse things got at home. The worse things got at home, the better I got at comedy.

Before long, my set was forty minutes of solid material. I invited Dave to a show, and he was blown away. "I think you're ready to do an hour-long special," he said afterward.

An hour-long special is the holy grail of stand-up. Do a tight sixty and you get to join the annals of giants: Richard Pryor's *Live in Concert*, George Carlin's *Jammin' in New York*, Eddie Murphy's *Delirious*, Bill Hicks's *Relentless*, Chris Rock's *Bring the Pain*, Dave Chappelle's *Killin' Them Softly*.

I told Dave that I didn't want to pour my heart and soul into something, only to have some executive's assistant calling two days before it's supposed to air and saying, "We decided this isn't right for us and we own all the rights, so no one's ever gonna see it."

I wanted to own it. I wanted to control it. I wanted to do it myself.

The only problem was that I couldn't actually afford to do it myself. So while Dave worked on finding someone to help finance it, I kept touring and wrecking my marriage.

72

REMEMBER WHEN I SAID I HAD TWO HUSTLERS WORKING FOR ME? THAT WAS A BAD IDEA. I GOT HUSTLED. WHAT DID I EXPECT, REALLY?

While I was building my special, Terrence Lock cooked up a plan to make me—and him—better money.

"I know you hate those package shows Glenn has been putting you on," he told me as we sat backstage at another empty theater, "so let's put together one that features you and has enough big names that it will sell out those theaters. You can do twenty dates in a month and walk away with two hundred thousand dollars, easy."

Terrence and Nate lined up six other comedians they represented and knew. Each of us stood to make six figures from the whole road show. Terrence said he had collected the guaranteed money up front so that nothing would go wrong.

He was doing such a good job that I let Glenn go and I went all in with Terrence and Nate.

Just before the tour was supposed to start, I reached out to Terrence for my first check so I could make my nut—and learned that only a nut would trust Terrence Lock with his money. He didn't answer the phone that day, the next day, or the next year. No one could find him anywhere. This motherfucker had disappeared—along with the money he'd supposedly collected.

The tour fell apart and everyone went their separate ways, pissed off. I didn't see Terrence's face again for eight years. When I did, I found out he'd been diagnosed with multiple sclerosis. He didn't say anything about the missing money, but I figure he hadn't been insured. If he had just told us, I'm sure everyone would have helped him.

After Terrence disappeared, I found myself in a familiar situation: home, car, and tax payments due; nothing in my pockets; and another box-office failure. *Fool's Gold* launched and quickly sank even deeper than the buried treasure in the film. Critics destroyed the movie, most giving it one star. They called it "stupid," "tedious," and "excruciatingly lame."

I was out with Nate one night, talking about ways to make more money, and he said: "Hey, look, I can do all *that* for you, you know. I'm a hard worker. I'll put cash in your pocket, man."

"What exactly do you mean by *that*?"

"I can make calls on your behalf—book gigs for you, man. I can bring you dates. Allow me to hustle for you, know what I'm saying? Damn."

This was one of those right-or-left moments: I could either make a decision based on what everyone else said about Nate or I could trust a guy who had been tirelessly busting his ass for me.

I decided to trust him. "Okay, do your thing."

"Damn, Kev, you won't regret it. Give me six months, and I'll get you double what you're making. Shit, I'm not shitting you, shit."

Immediately, Nate started hustling. He had me doing bars, banquets, marching-band rehearsals, even a pimp-and-ho convention. I don't know how he was finding half that shit, but I was paying my bills on time and putting food on the table, so I didn't ask.

But then I noticed that I'd walk into gigs and everyone would be pissed at me: the booker, the owner, the host, the waitstaff. They'd all be looking at me like I was a volcano that might erupt at any moment.

It didn't take much time to get to the root of it. And the root of it, of course, was Nate. I heard him on the phone one afternoon, getting aggressive with a club: "Either I get the money tomorrow or there ain't gonna be no show, okay? . . . Look, I don't give a shit. Fuck y'all. Fuck this whole damn thing. If Kevin Hart don't see that money, Kevin Hart's not gonna show up, and you can tell all them people in that club of yours the show is canceled and Kevin Hart ain't coming."

I'm sure that threats are an effective way of doing business for the mafia, but I don't want to be feared. I want to be *enjoyed*. That's why I got into the business in the first place.

However, I wasn't very enjoyable when I found out that Nate was using my name like that. The biggest fights I've ever had with him, or anyone who's worked with me since, have been when I've caught them using their involvement with me to disrespect somebody else. Even if things don't happen the way they're supposed to, there's a professional way to talk about it.

It took Nate a long time to understand that. Yet he did keep his word: He got me twenty-five hundred dollars for a weekend—double what I'd been making—two months earlier than the deadline he'd set. I have no idea what his dealings were or how it happened so quickly. All I know is that he's the angriest asshole with the best heart that I've ever met in my life.

73

ONE OF THOSE MOMENTS WHEN EVERYTHING COMES FULL CIRCLE, EVEN THOUGH I'M CONTINUING TO MOVE FORWARD, WHICH I THINK IS GEOMETRICALLY IMPOSSIBLE UNLESS I JUST WENT AROUND THE WORLD. NEVER MIND, I THINK IT'S ACTUALLY POSSIBLE.

Whenever I was back in L.A., I continued auditioning for small parts so that I could stay on screens and in the faces of casting directors. Eventually, I landed a bit part in a movie called *Meet Dave*, which wouldn't even be worth mentioning if not for the fact that the star of the movie was Eddie Murphy.

I hung around the set every day hoping to meet the legend who started me down this path. But everyone guarded him like he was the president. "Hey, don't go over there . . . He don't like to talk . . . When he comes here, just be ready to work."

Months after the movie came out and bombed, I decided to ask Dave for Murphy's number and tried calling him, just to see if he would speak with me. My heart was thudding through my shirt when he answered. I explained that he was a big reason why I was doing stand-up and that I was about to do my first hour-long special, *I'm a Grown Little Man*.

"My advice is don't ask for advice," he responded patiently. "Trust yourself and your own way of doing things. Just because something worked for someone else doesn't mean it's gonna work for you."

It was good non-advice advice, which he has continued to give me over the years. With the blessing of the man responsible for the first comedy special I ever saw, I felt ready for my big show.

I had a solid hour of material. I had a producer, Michelle Caputo, to take care of the filming. I'd rented the Skirball Center for the Performing Arts in New York. And I'd given away all eight hundred tickets for free to make sure the house was full.

However, a week before the taping, Torrei's mom called. "I want to remind you that the credit card bill is due," she chirped. "I see you all had a good time this month."

The bill, which was usually in the hundreds of dollars, was in the thousands—the maximum allowed on the card—and I didn't have enough money left in my account to pay it. It just so happens that the previous month, I'd discovered a loophole that allowed me to get an additional card for the account in Torrei's name.

I stormed into the bedroom. "What you been doing with that damn credit card?" It took every ounce of restraint I had not to grab it and snap it in half. The only thing stopping me was that I knew it would bend instead of breaking, and I'd end up struggling like an idiot to snap it.

"What do you care? You get to buy whatever you want for yourself. I never get anything."

"You maxed out the card. How are we gonna get to New York now?"

I still hadn't booked plane tickets and hotel rooms for me, Torrei, the kids, Nate, and Na'im, who was opening the show. But my bank account was nearly empty. The credit cards were done. And I had thirty-five dollars in cash for food until then. We were fucked.

I swallowed my pride and called my opening act:

Me: Na'im, man, I need some money.
Na'im: Wow—what for?
Me: Does it matter? I'm asking. It's that bad.
Na'im: All I got is three hundred dollars.
Me: Sorry, man, but can I borrow that?
Na'im: All right, but just so you know, I need it back.

I went to the bank and withdrew the rest of what I had, leaving seventeen cents in the account to keep them from closing it. I then went to a travel agency to buy tickets.

I didn't have enough money to fly to New York. But the agent found a cheaper flight to Philadelphia that I'd be able to afford if I brought one fewer person.

I asked Torrei if she was cool with staying home, and she flipped out. So I broke the news to Nate that I couldn't afford to bring him. I needed him there, but I needed the peace and quiet at this time more.

Next I had to figure out the rest: hotel, transportation, food, and an outfit for the show. I could ask Torrei's parents to drive us from the Philly airport to Manhattan, and then to the show itself. But short of everyone sleeping in the car, I couldn't think of a legal way to take care of the rest of these things.

I'd have to do it illegally.

I called hotels in New York until I found one that accepted checks, then returned to the bank and asked for a set of checks for my account. Fortunately, they gave them to me without asking about my balance of seventeen cents.

I had a college show the weekend after the taping, and maybe I could get that payment into my account quickly enough to keep some of the checks from bouncing.

Torrei's parents met us at the airport. Her mom was so pissed that I couldn't afford to cover the American Express bill that she didn't speak to me the whole ride, except to say: "I trusted you when I got you that card. I told you not to ruin my good credit. What's the matter with you?"

I agreed. I apologized. I promised her I'd call American Express and work something out. She was right to be upset.

We pulled up to the hotel, poured out of the car, and walked to the reception desk, where I needed to deliver one of the best acting performances of my life:

Me (*whipping out checkbook confidently*)**:** So, who do I make this out to?
Receptionist: Just make it out to the hotel.
Me: And, um, when does it clear? Just so I know, for me to get a little more clarity on how it works here.

Receptionist: I'm not sure. Probably the next business day.

Me: Okay, great. And does the hotel have a happy hour at all, with free
snacks and drinks?

Receptionist: No, I'm sorry.

Me: Not that it matters. It's just a nice thing sometimes. For my wife. She
loves those. (*To family.*) Come on, y'all, let's get up to the room. Hurry
it up.

It was my worst performance since the *Saturday Night Live* audition. I'm
sure she knew exactly what was going on. I didn't even have enough money to
tip the valet.

I wrote so many bad checks that weekend that if they could actually
bounce, some would have cleared a football field. I just needed to make it to
the Skirball Center the next night without getting arrested. I could find a way
to dig myself out of all these holes afterward.

Twenty hours later. Skirball Center. This was it. Lights, producers, cameras. My first big special was about to go down. *I'm a Grown Little Man.*

I checked to make sure the seats were filling up. Still too many empty
ones. There was my family, though. Torrei's family. Na'im's family. Many fans
I knew by their first names. And many I didn't.

Okay, showtime.

I walked out. The audience jumped to its feet applauding, screaming.
Normally a good thing. But we told them to do that for the special. Will look
like they actually paid to be there.

I grabbed the microphone. The stand was too high. No one had adjusted
it after Na'im's performance. If Nate were here, this wouldn't have happened.

First joke. Me trying to pick up women with baby seats in the back of the
car. Big laughs. More jokes about my kids. Bigger laughs.

I spotted Riq, Na'im's brother, in the audience. Couldn't look at him. He's
too critical. Always tells me whether my delivery is good or bad—and where
I've performed the joke better. He's usually right.

Damn, he caught my eye. He nodded and smiled approvingly. As if to say,
You're doing it, Kev, you got this!

That was just what I needed to get in the zone and stay there. When the show ended, I brought Heaven and Hendrix on stage. "Anyway, this is just so y'all can see that what I tell is the truth," I began, and then got choked up. A flood of joy and relief roared through me and lifted me up. I'd done it.

I went to the theater lobby afterward to thank everyone who came. "I saw you at Boston Comedy Club back in the day," one woman said excitedly. Then a guy nearby: "Boy, I remember you performing to a hundred people at Carolines!" To know that there were individuals watching my career, invested in me, rooting for me, on the journey with me—that was the icing on the cake.

The cake, of course, was the show itself. And the blown-out candles on the cake were my bank account and credit.

Back in Los Angeles, we stayed home for the rest of the week and ate everything on the shelves until it was time for my college show.

I got paid for it with a check. Since I now had a negative balance at the bank, I cashed the check elsewhere and began to rebuild my life. I bought food for the family and worked out a payment plan with American Express.

It took a long time for Torrei's mom to forgive me for dinging her credit. But American Express held its grudge even longer. Years later, when I was one of the highest-paid comedians in the world and had a great credit rating, I applied for a card and was still denied.

Comedy Central ended up buying *I'm a Grown Little Man* for fifty thousand dollars, which, after commissions, allowed me to pay off some of my expenses and debt. Though I was proud of the work, the special didn't explode into the world like I'd hoped. It came and went like everything else I'd done. I was just another comic with an hour-long special—and a DVD and CD to sell at my merchandise table.

But I was fine with this outcome, because by now, I'd come to accept that endurance is key. If I stayed persistent and on my grind, I would make it out of this hole and my dreams would come true.

I just didn't know when.

Life Lessons

FROM TEAM BUILDING

I know I just said that you gotta do things alone, but make sure you do things alone with a team. That may not seem like it makes sense, but it makes total sense once you've read this section. And if it still doesn't make sense, I suggest you get a team to help you understand it.

With Joey, Harry, Wayne, and Spank

74

I'M THINKING THAT I SHOULD GET AN HONORARY DEGREE FOR ALL THE COLLEGE SHOWS I'VE DONE. CALL ME IF YOU CAN MAKE THIS HAPPEN. (NOTE: WOULD PREFER A DOCTORATE.)

The thing that saved my ass, more than the fifty thousand dollars from Comedy Central for *I'm a Grown Little Man*, was NACAC.

NACAC is the National Association for College Admission Counseling. That may not sound like much, and it didn't to me either, but they organize an annual convention for six thousand professionals from different high schools and colleges around the country.

Nate and I set up a booth at the convention. After I performed a showcase there, people from different colleges stopped by our table to ask about hiring me. I took every show they offered. As a result of that convention, I ended up booking some fifty-five colleges that year, with each show paying between seven hundred and twenty-five hundred dollars.

Those shows gave me many opportunities: to pay off more debts, to work on a new hour of material, and to go to practically every state in the union and make people laugh.

Nate and I worked hard to get the contact information of everyone at each college show. Then we'd ask if anyone had connections at local comedy spots, so we could come back and pick up an adult audience in the town as well.

As we worked this system, however, club promoters began pulling me aside and telling me they were going to stop booking me if they had to continue to deal with Nate. They complained about being threatened, distrusted, and micromanaged. They wanted to do business with someone else.

I sat down with Nate in my hotel room one night. "Listen, people are saying they won't book me again if you're the one doing the business. So this is what I'm gonna do: Because I like you and I'm loyal, I'm gonna get us a personal appearance agent."

Nate flipped out. "Naw, hell no. *Hell no*. That's what I do. I'm the one that do that. Damn, man!"

"Nate, listen to what I'm saying: We don't have a choice."

"No. Ain't no way in hell you gonna let them white boys take this over."

"Nate, you're not listening to me. The clubs will not work with you. We have to slowly get you back into a position where they're comfortable dealing with you. Let me do what I gotta do."

"I don't know, Kev." He shook his head. "I don't like it. I don't like it one bit. You don't need nobody else."

The reason Nate had done so well for me up to this point was because he'd been as tenacious with the promoters and bookers as he was in this conversation. But I needed to make this change if I wanted to still have a touring career. It took me four more years to get that motherfucker to work civilly with people. The only other person in my life I've argued with more than him is Torrei.

Dave Becky soon found me a new personal appearance agent named Mike Berkowitz. I told Berkowitz that I didn't want to do any more package shows—even if it meant turning down big-money offers. "I can have you working as much as you want by yourself," he said.

"Good, cause I want to work a lot—but not alone. I want to build my *own* team."

ry Ratchford was a friend I met on the Los Angeles comedy scene. He
ped performing soon after that, but we kept hanging out. He was loud,
oing, and a naturally fun guy. He made people around him smile and feel
l. His marriage, like mine, was crumbling into open warfare, so whenever
gs got rough with Torrei, I'd call Harry and we'd drive to Crazy Horse Too
as Vegas, where it was impossible to stay mad. Meanwhile, his wife and
ei became close friends. I have no idea what they did while we were
e—probably went to *Thunder from Down Under*.

When Harry was promoted at his graphic-design job one day and then
the next for reasons that neither of us understood, I told him: "Right
, I'm making twenty-five hundred a weekend. I wouldn't mind giving you
ece of the pie if you wanted to write with me and help me build on the
erial I have, until you can figure things out."

I'd never hired a writer or felt like I needed one, but I was willing to do
hing to help a friend. It turned out, however, that I *did* need a writer, and
ry was more of a help to me than I'd expected. After each show, we'd run
ugh the set together:

'That part where the girl you're on a date with tells you milk makes her
was funny, but what if you said 'me too' afterward?" he'd suggest.

'Oh, damn, that might be funny. Or not. I'll try it, though. Let's see what
pens."

Over time, Harry came to understand my voice as well as I did. As my set
he next hour-long special came together, I'd find he had just one or two
gestions after a show, but each would make the material stronger.

Harry never found another job, either because he believed in me or be-
e he was unemployable. To this day, he's still my writer. He also keeps my
in check, for free.

"Spank" Horton has always thought he was better than me—ever since
net as kids. He used to heckle me in clubs when I was starting out, but
that I was making it, he wanted to get in on the act. Since he was sure
he was funnier than me, he decided to become a comedian.

"Yo, I been doing this shit for a while, man," Spank called to tell me after

75

WHAT NAPOLEON AND I HA
IN COMMON (AND IT'S NOT HI
BECAUSE HE HAD TWO INCHES

I've had a lot of families in my life. I had the family I was bor
my dad, my brother.

I had the family I married and fathered: Torrei, Heaven, I

Then I had the family I worked with: my fellow road w
whom are still warrioring with me today.

War is definitely the right metaphor for what we did:
country. Any town in the United States with a comedy clut
the afternoons, we hit the streets, the barbershops, and the i
recruits. In the evenings, we murdered and killed (and occas
And at night, we conquered the bars, the clubs, and the nigh
other kinds of recruits.

Combat turns men into brothers, and that's what the con
to us. Like most brothers, we came to love each other, but w
learned to respect each other, but we also formed resentme
Above everything, we were dedicated to the mission: to m
right-hand road to success. Shortcuts may get you there qu
experience you gain on the long road allows you to stay ther

In everything that has happened in my life since then,
been there for me. Besides Nate—who's more like our cre
are four more of them. It's time for you to get to know them

Na'im Lynn has already been mentioned many times. You
him in the Philly scene, he was my first road warrior, and h
ing with me ever since, so nothing more needs to be sa
enough space in my life. He doesn't need to be taking up a
my book.

Soul Plane came out. "I'm starting to pop, baby. You gonna start fucking with me—just watch."

The next time I performed in Philadelphia, he did a guest spot, and I was impressed by his charisma and presence. Because he's so outgoing and vibrant, he can "personality" his way through a set and get big laughs even though he neglects the craft.

Afterward, Spank called and asked if I had any room for him in my next show. I said, "It's in Atlanta, but if you can get yourself there, no problem."

He got himself there. Turns out he had a college friend named Wayne who worked at Philadelphia International Airport, so he had a hookup for cheap flights.

Before the show, Spank went to the greenroom, made himself a drink, and met Nate, who greeted him with his usual charm: "Don't be touching that, man. That's Kevin Hart's liquor!"

Back at the hotel that night, I asked Spank what he wanted from comedy. He told me that he wanted a career. So I thought carefully about what I was getting myself into, on account of the fact that he doesn't shower until someone complains about the smell, and made him an offer: "Right now, it's just Na'im and me on stage. We wouldn't mind bringing you out with us. We could take over a whole night and make it our shit. But you'll have to find a way to get to these spots yourself. I don't have the money right now."

"Dude, I'll figure it out," he replied. "Just tell me what I gotta do."

Joey Wells was hosting a night at a place called the Comedy Union when I first arrived in L.A. I performed there, and he soon became a part of the *Madden* games that Harry and I played at Rodney Perry's house. We put in so many hours on the game that sometimes Rodney's wife would have to cut the power in the house to get us to stop.

Then Joey had a streak of bad luck: a bunch of his gigs got canceled, his relationship fell apart, his car got towed, and he didn't have enough money to pay his rent or even to get his car back. It was a story I could relate to.

For months, Joey was walking and taking buses everywhere, but pretending like he still had a car. He didn't want to ask for help. Not because he was too proud, but because he was too nice. Joey is one of the most gentle, thoughtful guys you'll ever meet. Eventually, Harry and Rodney had a secret meeting with me about Joey. They explained the situation, then suggested that I throw him some work.

That night, we went to see Joey at the Improv, and—*boom boom boom*—he slayed. Afterward, I pulled him aside. Actually, I don't pull people aside. I got a loud mouth, so it was more like a public announcement. "I'm trying to get an hour together. You wanna do some fucking writing with us? I talked to Harry. If something's going on, you can always tell me, man."

Joey said he was all right, but I kept insisting, until finally he looked me in the eye and said: "When do I start?"

"How's tomorrow?"

I could see the relief in his face. I didn't have extra money to pay him with, but I knew I'd find it somewhere. I later found out that he'd already had his bags packed and was about to return to his hometown to become a teacher.

One of the problems with touring clubs is that sometimes the local hosts are terrible, and we have to perform to a dry crowd. We solved that problem by bringing Joey along to MC the shows—and he's hosted with us ever since.

Eventually, he even got his car back.

A year after Joey joined, we came up with a name for this ragtag group of otherwise unemployable misfits.

We were in Vegas complaining about our relationships and drinking tequila out of red plastic cups—the ones that are always stacked next to the free alcohol at parties. I suggested that we all run away and move to Jamaica together. As we toasted to that, Harry burst out: "We the Plastic Cup Boyz!"

"What the hell is that?" Spank asked.

"Nigga, we always got plastic cups. When you see these red cups, it's always a party or a good time. So we the Plastic Cup Boyz."

I was tired of saying I was bringing my "crew" or my "team" or my "package" to each club. We needed a name. So from that day forward, we were the

Plastic Cup Boyz and Nate had a new responsibility: making sure we had red plastic cups everywhere we went.

76

I THINK THAT LAST CHAPTER TITLE WAS THE ONLY HEIGHT JOKE IN THIS BOOK SO FAR

It was an amazing setup.

Joey hosted, Spank opened, Na'im featured, and I closed. I wasn't touring as a comedian anymore, but as an entire traveling show. It worked for the clubs, because they didn't have to do any more work to book the night, and it worked for the audiences, who got a solid, consistent show.

The downside was that traveling with a group this big was expensive. At first, we weren't making enough money to fly, feed, and lodge five people. But once we sold out a few clubs, Nate asked, "Kev, I got a question for you: Are you bold enough to go percentages at the comedy clubs? That's my question that I want to ask. Damn."

"What do you mean?"

He explained that he wanted to work out a deal with the clubs where instead of getting a flat rate for performing, we'd be paid a percentage of the money the club made at the door each night. It was a risk, because we'd make less on a bad show but much more on a good show.

Being a gambling man, I took the bet.

The biggest challenge was making sure the clubs didn't lie about attendance, so every night Nate would walk through the crowd with a mechanical counter. On more than one occasion, I caught him checking the bathrooms just to make sure he hadn't missed anyone. At least, that's what he told me he was doing in there.

After every show, he'd be in the manager's office with his counter, calculator, #2 pencil, and bill-counting machine. He'd go over all the numbers, asking questions about every line item. Then he'd count the money three times just to make sure it was right. He'd be there so long settling, a manager or promoter would pull me aside afterward and say: "You know, there are computer programs that can do all that stuff."

Almost half the time, though, Nate would discover that the numbers were off in the house's favor, so he'd ask for what was right. If that didn't work, he'd yell for what was right. If that didn't work, he'd threaten for what was right. And once, when that didn't work, and a promoter started pushing him, Nate stabbed him with his pencil. We never played that club again.

As we toured more, we put together a system that enabled me to walk away with thirty-five hundred dollars a weekend. Add in another fifteen hundred a week in merchandise, and we were making twenty thousand dollars a month.

Then came Wayne.

Wayne was Spank's hookup from the airport. Since he could fly for free, he started coming out to join us on weekends. The thing we liked most about him was that he never kept his money in the bank; he kept it in his pocket. This made him the ATM for everyone on the road: "Hey, Wayne, give me a hundred."

At the end of the weekend, Wayne would get his cash back from Nate. Eventually, he wanted to get more involved.

"Hey, Kev, you know how you're always going to clubs after these shows. I don't mind making sure y'all are safe and keeping people off you. If things get crazy, I can handle it."

On the particular night when Wayne said this, we were at the Improv in Fort Lauderdale, and there were probably a hundred open seats in the house. There was nothing I needed to be protected from other than my own spending habits.

On the other hand, Wayne was a big guy, and maybe this would keep Nate from trying to pretend like he was my security. At every club I went to, I had an out-of-shape middle-aged man walking behind me with his stomach poking into my back and one hand thrust into his pocket like he was packing. "Nate, what you 'bout to do?" I'd laugh. "You gonna shoot that man with the fingers you have balled up in your pocket? Back the fuck off, so people can stop thinking I'm a human centipede."

Everyone in the group liked to keep me in check, but Wayne more than anyone had no problem telling me, "Hey, man, sit your stupid ass down!" So I figured he'd be better at the job, just because he was clear when he spoke. Though I didn't need any security, having a bodyguard made it look like I was succeeding. And in entertainment, perception is reality.

So I told him: "Okay, yeah, I probably need that. I can break off a couple dollars and pay you for security."

Wayne eventually became our travel agent too. One day, we were checking into a hotel and I overheard Spank saying, "Yo, Wayne, stop being a bitch and tell him."

Wayne didn't say anything, so Spank did: "Wayne got fired from the airport."

"Yeah," Wayne cracked, "you bitches was calling me like an hour into my shift—nonstop, every motherfucking day. So yeah, I got fired. I'm spending all my time helping y'all."

"Tell 'em how long you been fired for."

Wayne wouldn't say anything else, but Spank ratted him out again: It had been months. Wayne's car had even been repossessed. I'd been paying Wayne just two hundred dollars a week, so I have no idea how he was surviving.

"Come on, man, I got you," I said. "We'll figure it out."

And now there were seven of us Plastic Cup Boyz.

77

YOU'VE HEARD IT BEFORE, NOW HEAR IT WITHOUT JOKES

The one time we needed Wayne as security, he hurt us a lot more than he helped.

We were in Austin, and I had flown Torrei out to spend the weekend. The guys weren't happy about this. There were times when Torrei and I would be in the middle of a full-blown screaming match as I was waiting to go on stage. I'd tell her to wait a minute, I'd do my set, then I'd walk off stage and pick up with her right where we'd left off.

A local promoter and his girlfriend took us to Sixth Street after the show to do the club crawl. While we were drinking, his girlfriend began flirting with Wayne, and the promoter got mad and took off without her.

She started asking us for cocaine. I explained that drugs weren't our thing, unless she was looking for Tylenol, in which case we went Extra Strength. As we headed out to another club, Torrei said she had to use the bathroom.

"We were just in that place for two hours, but the minute we leave, you gotta go?" It's always a bad sign when you get upset at your wife for something you wouldn't get upset at anyone else about.

Torrei and the cokehead girlfriend ran to a bar across the street to use the bathroom, and Nate went to get the car while we waited for them.

When Nate pulled up, Torrei and her new friend still hadn't come back. We checked the bar they'd gone into. They weren't there. I called Torrei—no answer. We fanned out to search for them.

I walked into a bar a little ways down the street and spotted the girls. A tall, bearded fifty-year-old dude who looked like the bar manager was trying to kick them out. I found out later that it was because Cokey had been asking everyone for drugs.

I ran over: "Hey, my fault. That's my wife. I got her."

The bearded guy shouted, the veins in the folds of his neck bulging, "They need to get the fuck out of my place now!"

"Hey, chill, I got 'em."

Drunk, the girls were annoying, even to someone who wasn't married to one of them: "We're just having fun! What's his problem?"

The manager grabbed Torrei's arm as she tried to walk deeper into the bar.

I shoved him away from her. "I said, 'I got her'! Get your hands off my lady!"

Two security guys appeared out of nowhere and instantly put me in a full Nelson, or a half Nelson or some sort of Nelson—whoever the fuck Nelson is, he had it in for me that night. He's probably part of the Jones family.

The guys carried me out of the bar by my neck, ripping my shirt in the process, and then held me up in the air. Moments later, the manager burst through the door with Torrei, pushing my face out of his way with the palm of his hand.

My friends saw what was going down and ran over. "Get your fucking hands off him!"

"Yo, I'm good. I'm good. Just let me go." The security guys released me. But I wasn't good.

I walked away as calmly as I could pretend, then quickly pivoted and ran back toward the bar, where the manager was still holding on to Torrei.

His eyes widened as he saw me coming for him like young pygmy dynamite. (If I ever get into wrestling, Young Pygmy Dynamite is gonna be my ring name.) He put his head down as if to tackle me, so I stopped running and, *boom*, I hit him. Then I got a few more shots in. It was a rare opportunity, because I've never hit anyone whose head was at a lower level than mine. Usually I have to swing up, like I'm saluting.

In summary, I whupped the ass of a fifty-year-old man. It's pathetic, I know. So far in this book, I've only been in fights with women, children, and old white men. If Young Pygmy Dynamite actually *was* in a wrestling league, he'd definitely be the villain.

The security guys went to get the cops, and my crew turned and ran. I dashed to the SUV and yelled: "Nate, let's go, let's go, let's go!" We did a head count, made sure we weren't missing anyone, and then noticed the car wasn't going anywhere: Fucking Nate was adjusting the mirrors. "Fuck it, Nate, just go!" He flipped on the turn signal, then sat there waiting to pull out. He eventually crept into the traffic lane, driving like an old man, which I guess he technically was. I hadn't seen a car go that slow since I last took Heaven on the kids' rides at the amusement park.

Suddenly, I spotted a faint flash of red lights in the rearview mirror.

"Everybody chill!"

I turned around to see two cops on bicycles pedaling in the distance and gaining on us. With Nate at the wheel and Sixth Street traffic, we were no match for them.

I pulled out my wallet, removed my money, and handed the bills to Spank in the front seat. "If I go to jail, come get me. Here's everything I've got. No matter what happens, none of you know shit, okay?"

The police pedaled up alongside us and asked us to pull over. A cop came to the window.

Cop: They're telling me there was a fight going on back there. Do you know anything about that?

Spank: I don't know nothing about that.

Cop: How about you? You know anything about this fight?

Nate: I don't know what you're talking about.

Cop: And you, in the backseat, do you know who was fighting?

Wayne: We was all fighting.

Everyone: *What the fuck, Wayne?!*

Cop: Get out of the car!

After that, Wayne was dead to me as a security guard.

The officer told us all to sit on the curb. His partner sauntered over, looked at me, and exclaimed, "Hey, it's Kevin Hart! I loved you in *Soul Plane*."

I could tell right then that he was a crooked cop, because the only way he would have recognized me from that movie was if he'd seen the bootleg.

"Look, man, none of them did nothing," I told him. "The situation is that my lady here was drunk. She was asked to leave that bar, and as she was coming out, someone put his hands on her. There was a little tussle. It's not—"

"Then why's your shirt ripped?"

"That was my lady did that."

"The guy back there says you assaulted him."

"What?" It was time to show this fan some acting. "Why would I assault that man? Like, why would I put myself in that situation? You know who I am. I wouldn't risk my career like that."

"All right—stay here." He walked away and spoke with his partner. Then they talked with the manager and came back.

"Listen, it sounds like the situation got out of hand. If you go over there and apologize to that man, we're good. I'm not going to cause you any trouble."

I walked over, apologized sincerely, shook his hand, apologized again, realized he was probably more like sixty, apologized one more time, and then returned to the car.

"All right." The cop waved us off. "Y'all stay out of trouble."

That was the moment I knew that I was making progress in the world. I was officially famous enough to get out of going to jail, but not so famous that I was taken to jail as an example.

I also had new material. I figured the story would be good for at least five minutes of the hour I was putting together for my next special. Though when I added it to the set, I conveniently left out the fact that the bar manager I punched out was pushing sixty.

78

IT TOOK ME HALF A DAMN HOUR TO COME UP WITH A WAY TO EXPLAIN WHY IT'S IMPORTANT TO COMMUNICATE WELL, SO I HOPE I COMMUNICATED IT WELL, OTHERWISE IT WOULD BE KIND OF IRONIC

After the Austin incident, I sat down with Wayne. "You're no goddamn security guard, Wayne. You're a good guy, but you're not the protector. You can't be security no more."

"Thank you, brother. I'm tired of standing in the corner while y'all are having fun. I'm gonna figure out some better shit I can do for you."

He thought about it for a moment and then said: "I'm more of a guy who can help with business. After some of these shows, what if we did afterparties? I'll find a club, broker the deal, and set everything up."

From that day forward, Wayne and Nate started arranging events at nightclubs after the shows, and we'd work to bring over as much of the audience as possible. The clubs kicked us a commission off the cover charge, and I divided the money among the guys.

With the picture business, the CD and DVD business, and now the afterparties and T-shirts (which we could finally afford to get made), the money I made from incidentals was starting to match the money I got for performing.

Wayne soon took over on the promotions front. MySpace was dying, but Twitter and Facebook were coming up, so we started doing guerrilla marketing on those networks. Wayne and I would sit there with our laptops open—copying and pasting messages to random comedy fans in each city on our itinerary, introducing myself and letting them know I'd be in town. Out of a hundred people, ten would reply and say: "Sure, I'll come down and check you out." And that was ten more people than we'd had before.

Wayne helped improve the flyering process as well. By the time we arrived in each city, he had identified every mall within a twenty-mile radius of the club. We'd drop our bags at the hotel, he'd hand us each a hundred flyers, and we'd fan out. The rule was, don't come back until all your flyers are gone.

We'd make sure to tell anyone we gave them to our name and say, "Let the person at the box office know that I sent you." At first, it was just to see which one of us had the most charm. But soon it became a way to find out someone's area of strength. Then we could say, "Hey, you gotta go talk to those girls, cause you been doing well with them. You're great with the guys, so go to the barbershop. And you . . . I don't know . . . you should go to the dog park or something."

At one point, I came up with the idea of giving people five dollars off their ticket if they came to the club with the flyer. I figured the club could take that amount out of my share. However, I forgot to pass this information on to the venue. So dozens of people showed up that night with flyers and started arguing when the person at the box office wouldn't give them a discount. The manager ended up honoring the agreement, but he was pissed at Nate and me.

This incident taught me one of the most important business lessons there is: Communication is the key that unlocks a plan. Everyone should know your intentions at all times, as well as any changes to them. A good idea with bad communication is as useful as a phone with a dead battery.

In each city, we were able to see the results of our work. The first time we'd perform there, we'd sell out Fridays and Saturdays, but Thursdays and Sundays were light. The next time, Thursday would be sold out too, but Sunday was still light. By the third visit, every night would be sold out.

Online, our work was also paying off. I'll never forget being in Cincinnati when I first hit ten thousand followers on Twitter. It felt like such a huge achievement. I was walking on air all day.

As our reputation grew with the clubs, Wayne got the comedy promoters to find a street team for us. We'd send them five hundred flyers in advance, and they'd plaster the city with them. It cost us a few hundred dollars, but it saved us a lot of time that we then used to promote the shows online.

It was on these tours that the entrepreneur in me was born. When I was on my own, I knew that whatever ups and downs occurred, I'd survive. But now that I had people whose salary I was paying, I had to think differently. I couldn't fuck around with *their* rent and car payments. I had to learn the crafts of business, entrepreneurship, and brand building as well as comedy. Figuring all this out early in the age of social media, before people started brand building on the day their parents gave them their first phone, gave me a huge advantage over other comedians.

There was another lesson too: When I increased my overhead by hiring all these guys whose expenses I couldn't afford, everyone said I was being stupid and wasteful. But as an unexpected consequence, this expansion ended up increasing my personal profit. Because now it wasn't just me working to survive, it was a whole team working to survive. They believed that I could grow—and knew that as I did, they would grow too. A team is going to survive better than an individual, just as a team is always going to beat an individual in a sport—that is, in a team sport. I'm not sure how that would work in an individual sport. In fact, forget I mentioned it. My point is: It's all about community, people. We are stronger together.

The seven of us must have gone to every comedy club in the country. It didn't matter if it was good, bad, or sketchy. When we got to the last club, Nate or Berkowitz would call the first ones we'd gone to and book them all over again. We did that four times in a row, until we'd built up a fan base so large that the clubs couldn't hold them anymore.

The long road, it turned out, was tens of thousands of miles: four times around the country. What finally ended up launching my career, though, was something that I never would have predicted. In fact, it was something I didn't even want to do.

79

SOMETIMES YOU HAVE TO SAY YES TO THE THINGS YOU WANT TO SAY NO TO SO YOU CAN RAISE YOURSELF TO A PLACE WHERE YOU GET TO SAY NO TO MORE THINGS

In this period, I was invited to perform a fifteen-minute set for a comedy event Shaquille O'Neal was putting together in Phoenix during the NBA All-Star Game.

The night was being filmed for Showtime, which normally would have been a good thing, but I was still building my next special, *Seriously Funny*. If my new material was on Shaq's *All-Star Comedy Jam* special and DVD, then I wouldn't be able to use it for my special and DVD.

"I might just pass on it," I told Dave. He thought that was fine. I'd done a few other stand-up comedy showcases on TV, *Comic View* and *One Mic Stand*. They hadn't done much for me, so we figured this show probably wouldn't either.

But the producers kept coming back to us, eventually offering me the headlining slot. I folded and agreed to participate. "I don't wanna do it, so can you come with?" I asked Harry. "Maybe we can find a way to make something good out of it, get some new material or something."

I don't usually complain. I don't drag my feet. I don't resist things I have to do. This wasn't me. But I was worried that it would push back the timeline for my next special. It might take four months to get another good fifteen minutes together.

Just before the show began, Harry and I stood backstage with the other comedians who were performing: Tommy Davidson, DeRay Davis, and Cedric the Entertainer. It was stunning to me, and probably to them, that I was the headliner. Harry and I went back and forth, unsure whether to give away some of the *Seriously Funny* material or try to get away with using something from *Grown Little Man*.

The room was packed with celebrities, and each comic who went on destroyed. Fifteen minutes before my set, I still had no idea what I was going to say on that stage. I huddled up with Harry and said a small prayer I'd started reciting before each performance, thanking God for the moment and the blessings. As we leaned into each other, Harry asked, "What material are you most comfortable doing?"

"Well, all I've been doing lately is the *Seriously* jokes."

"So do those. We can write new material for the special."

"Yeah, you're right—we can just fucking write new jokes. I'm gonna go out there and give 'em the best shit I got."

It was another right-or-left moment, and thankfully, I went right.

By the time I danced onto the stage, the audience was so heated up that the room exploded after every phrase I spoke. I fed off that energy and grew larger and louder. When I hit the fifteen-minute mark, I wasn't ready to stop. So I pressed on: "I love the fact that my wife is crazy. I don't want a happy woman." Then I went off for another ten minutes on my relationship, and relationships in general. When I was done, I'd burned through twenty-three minutes of *Seriously Funny*, but just about all the people in that room were out of their seats, giving me a standing ovation that didn't seem to end.

When the *All-Star* special aired and the DVD came out with a relatively unknown comedian headlining after all these amazing performers, people started investigating.

"That motherfucker's funny. What'd they say his name was?"

"Kevin Hart."

"Never heard of him."

"He's the guy from *Soul Plane*."

"Oh, yeah. What else he done?"

"I think he got his own special."

"I'm gonna go back and watch that shit."

In the last year, I'd done *Comic View*, *One Mic Stand*, *Grown Little Man*, and more than a dozen films and television shows that I'd hoped would launch me. But everything either hurt me, did nothing, or helped just a little.

For some reason, this appearance—the only one out of all these that I didn't want to do—became the thing that propelled me to the next level.

When I did club shows afterward, I felt a heightened sense of anticipation in the audience. They weren't just seeing a comedian they were curious about or had heard about from a friend or recognized from a cult movie anymore. They were seeing *Kevin Hart*.

That was the moment that gave me the right to refer to myself in the third person, because that was when a public Kevin Hart was created, who is pretty much the same as the private Kevin Hart, which now that I think about it means I don't really have that right. But writing *me* above would look even more egotistical. You know what . . . Fuck it, that's my goddamn name, I can say it all I want. I don't gotta explain myself. Not that you asked me to—but some of you were thinking it. You know who you are.

In the end, I didn't regret giving away my material at all. In fact, it was one of the best worst decisions I'd made in my career.

I've learned so many valuable lessons in my life, and this was one of the most important: Do your best, *always*. Because you never know who's watching.

As Curtis Mayfield once said, "It may not come when you want it to, but when it does, it's right on time."

80

I DESERVE EVERYTHING THAT HAPPENS TO ME IN THIS CHAPTER AND MORE

When you're touring and you're in an unhappy marriage, your resistance to temptation is low.

You know that. Your buddies know that. Your woman knows that. So instead of her being your wife, she becomes your parole officer.

Her whole life becomes about trying to find out the truth. This can only go in one of two directions: Either she's right and she investigates you until she gets proof, or she's wrong and she investigates you until she drives you away. Either way, you both lose.

As for the cheater who hasn't been caught, a psychological miracle happens: The more he tells lies, the more he believes them. His secret life moves into a compartment in his mind that's locked and sealed when he's with his wife.

All this is my way of explaining that when I denied seeing other women to Torrei, I actually *believed* what I was saying. This may seem hard to buy, but because the *facts* Torrei was saying were wrong, I was able to be honest with her on a *technical* level. Here's how that worked:

Torrei says: "You're not doing a show. You're just sneaking out with one of your side bitches for the weekend!"

The facts are: 1. I am doing a show. 2. None of my side bitches are coming to that particular show. 3. This is because I invited three random women I met online.

I say: "You're crazy. I'm *doing* a fucking show. I'll take a picture of the damn club marquee and send it to you to prove it!"

Is that real honesty? Of course not. But everything I told her *was* true, so the fact that she distrusted me made me feel like I was the victim in the situation. Then I'd go to the show and feel justified in hooking up with one of those three women because I deserved it after being so mistreated. The lengths the human mind will go to deceive itself are incredible.

Some people know how to hit the brakes before things spiral out of control, but I was not one of those people. I'd never gone to college, so being on the road was my way of making up for it. I basically got a dual degree in business education and performing arts while living in a mobile fraternity.

Once, when I was in Louisville, Torrei and I were arguing on the phone about where I was the night before and what I was doing.

"I was with Na'im!"

"You wasn't with no goddamn Na'im!"

"I *was*. I'll call Na'im right now and prove it!"

I dialed Na'im on three-way. Na'im's not stupid—the moment I opened my mouth, he knew exactly why I was calling and who was listening in silently.

Me: Na'im, fucking *please*, real quick. Just tell me what we were doing last night.

Na'im: Hey, man, I don't like getting in the middle of this relationship stuff. Don't be lying to Torrei, saying you was with me, ever.

Me: . . .

Na'im: Why you be treating her like this?

Me: Wait!

Na'im: Nah, man, you gotta stop. Don't be making her look stupid when she's all alone out there in L.A.

Me: Whose fucking side are you on?!

I hung up the phone on both of them. *Fucking Na'im. Why does he have to be so damn nice, and honest. And shit, if he's nice and honest, what does that make me?*

I called Torrei back and . . . still didn't come clean. I spun an elaborate story about getting drunk, passing out in the street, getting sick all over myself, and being too embarrassed to tell her. She didn't believe a word of it. But she didn't have hard evidence that it wasn't true either. All she knew was that I'd lied and she was sick of it.

So was I. All this time, I'd been making Torrei into some sort of demon in my mind. But I was the one cheating, lying, leading a double life, and putting my friends in the uncomfortable position of covering for me. *I* was the demon. Fortunately, the proof Torrei needed to unmask me would come soon enough.

At a show in Columbus, Ohio, I spotted a woman who had one of the best bodies I'd ever seen. Throughout my set, she looked at me like a python waiting to strike a duck and swallow it whole. Later that night, I discovered that she actually had a snake tattoo on her back. I also discovered that she could swallow things whole.

The next afternoon, she emailed: "Oh my God, this is amazing. Did you feel what I felt?"

An hour later, she sent a long email about how this was destiny and we were meant to meet. For three days straight, she emailed love letters, sexual fantasies, even a photo of her with a dildo in her mouth.

I showed Na'im the emails.

Me: I think I got a stalker.

Na'im: Did you sleep with her?

Me: Maybe.

Na'im: That's what you get.

Me: What?

Na'im: You think these girls like you for you? Look at her body. Now look at yours. These girls are sleeping with you because they're obsessed with your fame.

Me: Hey, wait, does that mean I'm a star?

Na'im: No, it means you stupid!

I emailed her back and said something like, "Hey, you're being a little intense. Maybe you should chill out a little."

In retrospect, I should have said, "I'm falling so deeply in love with you that I don't know if I can see you again because I'm scared of getting hurt." Because instead of chilling out, she found Torrei's social media profile, sent her a message, and then emailed me a copy:

"You should know that your husband and I made love and are in love. He's not who you think he is. You don't mean anything to him."

She went on to provide details about that night: the date, the time, the name of the hotel, my room number, things I said, things I did—things you don't want your wife imagining.

I lost my shit. There were so many specific facts that there was no way for me to get out of this. My phone rang—it was Torrei. I let it ring through to voice mail.

When I finally got myself and my story together, Torrei wouldn't pick up my call. I took a moment to figure out which of my friends had any patience left for cleaning up my messes.

"Hey, Spank, do me a favor and call Torrei right now. Don't ask why. Just do it."

"She find out—"

"I'm not paying you to ask questions."

"Was it that girl with the snake tattoo?"

"You're killing me here!"

"Was it worth it?"

"Give me that fucking phone!"

Torrei started going off as soon as she picked up: "He shouldn't have crossed me. I'll make him sorry."

I spoke up, owned what I did, and apologized. Not because I'm a good person, in case anyone actually still thinks that at this point, but because I had no other option. Torrei laid into me for the next hour straight. I will never forget the last words she said: "You should never trust a woman with a snake on her back!"

From that point on, I had clarity on how to deal with women on the road. A few people have a snake on their back that you can see, but most people with a snake have one that you can't see. You don't know what someone is hiding—shit can go bad at any time and for any reason. So before getting into any situation, it's necessary to think: What are the worst possible consequences that could happen because of this? If you can live with them, then go have fun. But if you can't, then back the fuck away from that snake.

81

I CONSIDER MYSELF A SMART PERSON. I EVEN CALLED MYSELF A GENIUS IN THE SECOND CHAPTER TITLE. SO WHY HAVE I BEEN SO STUPID ABOUT THIS ONE THING? EVEN YOU, WHO ARE NOT AS SMART AS ME, KNEW I SHOULD HAVE DONE THIS LIKE A HUNDRED PAGES AGO.

Any small shred of hope I used to cling to, thinking that I could *force* my marriage to work, disappeared after the snake incident. Torrei now knew she wasn't crazy and felt justified in treating me like the lying sack of shit I was. I felt guilty for what I'd done and took it without protest.

Of course, I hadn't felt guilty when I was *doing* it—just when I got caught. So it's not like I *really* had a conscience in the situation. If I had, I wouldn't have cheated in the first place. At this point, I should have just left. I'd been over the marriage for years, and this would have been a good excuse to get out of it. But I couldn't bring myself to cut the cord because I didn't want to abandon the kids. I didn't want to lose the days I set aside each week to come home and spend time with them.

So I stayed and just tried to appease Torrei. I no longer argued with her. I no longer even disagreed with her. I became not a man but a pacifier.

The argument we'd had for so long—"You get to go out and live your life while I'm stuck here!" "I have to work to support this family!"—changed after I was caught cheating. It was now clear to her that I wasn't always working. So she wanted me on a tight leash; she wanted to be on the road with me more; and she wanted me to help her pursue her dream.

Me: Of course I'll support you. What's your dream?
Torrei: I want to be a stand-up comedian.
Me: Wait, what?

Torrei: I've watched you do it for so long. And I'm funny. I know I'd be great at it.

Me: It takes time to—

Torrei: Are you gonna help me like you said or not?

Me: Okay, I'll support you.

Torrei: Good. God knows you've given me more than enough material.

She got to work. She wrote jokes. She went to open mics to perform. And then she spoke the most terrifying five words I'd heard in our entire relationship—even more terrifying than "I am gonna kill you!"

"I wanna open for you."

That got another "Wait, what?" But I was the pacifier now, so I let her open a show for me. She got some laughs. She even did something on stage that I couldn't: impersonations.

Afterward, I gave her some notes to help her out. But she wasn't interested in that kind of support: "I don't need any advice. I'm not trying to be you. You do your thing, and I'll do my thing. I'll be successful my own way. Just you watch!"

After I'd gone out of my way to get her a spot, her words felt like a slap in the face. Though I understood that sometimes when advice comes from a person you're in a relationship with, it sounds more like criticism.

From then on, pretty much all Torrei talked about was how she was going to make it as a stand-up and get a television show and write a book and do it all much quicker than my dumb self. She soon started trying to insert herself into any opportunity I had.

The Torrei who'd moved to L.A. had no interest in being famous. I didn't know this Torrei. At one of my shows, a couple walked over and asked for my autograph. "Y'all want this motherfucker's autograph?" she asked them. "He ain't shit!"

A week later, I returned home from a run of shows to spend time with the kids and saw Torrei in the living room with a stack of scripts. "Hey," she called out. "I need you to read these. Let me know your favorite. If you agree to do it, they'll put me in the show too, right?"

In Hollywood, I'd met many sycophants who tried to befriend and use me to get opportunities—not knowing how hard I'd worked to get those opportunities for myself. I looked at my wife and it felt like she had turned into one of those people. She may have hated me as a person, but suddenly she loved me as a vehicle.

Then one day, my father called. We didn't talk about anything of substance. He just went on about how my mom had raised me too soft and that he wished he'd stuck with her so he could've made me a man.

I replied that I was happy with how things worked out. If he had stayed with my mother, and they had fought like they did throughout my entire childhood and adolescence—screaming, hitting, chasing each other with hammers—then I wouldn't be where I'm at today.

After I hung up, I thought about all the times I'd shoulder-shrugged the violence in my relationship: *It's all right, we just fist-fought a little bit and smashed some stuff. Let's put it behind us and move forward. I know we called each other bitches and motherfuckers all night, but that's okay. Let's sweep it under the rug and be nice to each other again. There you go! It's like nothing ever happened.*

Love isn't supposed to be violent. I'm not a violent person. Torrei's not a violent person. Even when we weren't loudly fighting, we were silently resenting each other. We had to end this cycle that my parents handed down to me and that we were now handing down to our kids.

Once I had these thoughts, my last rationalization for enduring the marriage was gone: I wasn't saving my kids from a broken home by staying with Torrei. The home was already broken—and only by leaving could I fix it.

A few days later, I walked out the door with just the clothes on my back. I was thirty years old and my head was finally clear. "Keep everything," I told her. "I got the rent. I got the bills. I got everything. But we are done."

I knew I wouldn't be coming back. Torrei knew it too. "After all you've put me through, you're just gonna walk out that door?" she asked.

"You may hate me today for this, but tomorrow you'll thank me for it."

"I'll hate you even more tomorrow."

She was right. It definitely took more time than that.

I checked into the W Hotel and wrestled with my conscience for weeks. I was still wracked with guilt and doubt at times, but what helped was spending time with my kids and seeing that I was a better dad to them without the distraction of trying to survive a bad relationship. You can be a great soldier on a battlefield, but you can't be a great father on one.

Slowly, over the course of years, we both became ourselves again. We learned to be much better parents. And we continued the process of growing up emotionally that getting into a relationship at such a young age had delayed.

The lesson learned from all this is that if you're not careful, your dick will get you into relationships that your head can't fix. But the deeper lesson is that what's important in a relationship is the bricks that every one of your words and actions lay down, because together they add up to the home that you're going to live in for quite some time.

Brick by brick, I'd built an unstable house with Torrei, one that was doomed to collapse. But the experience enabled us to build great homes afterward for our kids, our partners, and ourselves.

Life Lessons
FROM
BREAKTHROUGH

---

*Don't do drugs. Instead, prove everyone who
doubted you wrong. It's a bigger high. If this sounds
self-centered, that's because it is. I'm a selfish guy.
How else would it be possible to write a
book this big about myself?*

With Eddie Murphy at the Laugh at My Pain *premiere party*

82

I GOT NOTHING.
NAME THIS ONE YOURSELF.

Your dream is a huge boulder. It takes a lot of effort to get it moving. But if you can budge it just a few inches on the right terrain, then it starts picking up speed all by itself. And since Shaq's *All–Star Comedy Jam*, my career had started rolling.

My club dates began selling out on a regular basis, so we started stacking two shows a night in most cities. When I performed for four days at Carolines in New York, they had to add weekend matinees as well—and all ten shows there sold out.

Promoters noticed the number of tickets I was selling, and my booking agent Mike Berkowitz called one day: "I know you're not interested in doing package tours, but a lot of offers are coming in. There's a new *Kings of Comedy* tour they want you on, and they want you on a couple rap tours. The reason I'm calling is that these offers altogether are worth more than a million dollars."

When I first heard that, I had to sit down and catch my breath. Then I started thinking: I'd spent more than four years beating up the road to build a personal brand, one which I had total control over. I'd formed a brotherhood of loyal and talented friends. I'd told the guys that if they believed in me and stuck with me through the hard times, I'd reward them and take care of them when the good times arrived. I couldn't just throw away my name, work, and integrity for a big payday.

I told Berkowitz to pass on all of them. Sometimes a good opportunity can still be a backward step.

Instead, we decided to make a move that both excited and terrified me: If I was selling out ten shows at a 250-person-capacity club, then I could probably sell out one night at a 2,500-seat theater. So we started testing out theater shows—and although they didn't all sell out, they were successful enough to justify doing more.

Every time I waited by the side of a stage to perform on that tour, I had a flashback to standing in the same spot during the *Def Comedy Jam* tour at the Liacouras Center in Philadelphia, promising myself to get my shit together so that one day I too could be headlining big venues.

I booked the Allen Theatre in Cleveland to tape the *Seriously Funny* special. I knew I had made progress when I was able to sell tickets instead of giving them away, and I could afford the flight there. I was unfortunately traveling lighter than last time because Torrei, who I'd been separated from for almost a year, wouldn't let me bring Hendrix and Heaven to the taping.

"What if you come with them?" I tried.

"I ain't bringing them no-fucking-where."

It's the only special of mine that the kids missed.

Meanwhile, the Cavaliers were there. The Browns were there. Shaq was there. LeBron was there. And I lifted the lid off that theater, dropped a ten-ton thermonuclear device inside, lowered the roof, and then pressed the red button.

Okay, people, I'm running out of metaphors for good comedy shows. The point is that a lot of folks laughed a lot of times. But man, that doesn't sound as good as it felt up there on stage that night.

After the show, I rejoined the Plastic Cup Boyz and a local promoter backstage, poured myself some tequila, and informed them: "I'm about to write another set. We going out again. But this time, we gonna go bigger."

They looked at me like I was crazy—and like they needed a break.

"We don't rest after a success." I lifted my red plastic cup and put an arm around the woman I was with. Her name was Eniko. "We raise our goals."

We toasted to many more years of brotherhood. Then the promoter asked me: "Is that your wife?"

83

THINK I SHOULDA JUST DONE CHAPTER NUMBERS WITHOUT TITLES

Me: Hey, Eniko!

Eniko: What do you want?

Me: I'm about to tell the story of how we met. Remember, I was in DC at a nightclub after a show on the *Seriously Funny* tour and I saw you, but I didn't talk to you. You were wearing a purple dress.

Eniko: We kept running into each other that whole weekend. The next time you saw me, you cracked a joke because my friends and I were taller than you. It was the most random thing to say, and we just started laughing.

Me: First of all, I'm an attractive man, so I saw that I had caught your eye.

Eniko: Did you? No, I wasn't even really looking.

Me: I caught you looking!

Eniko: You had a certain charm about you. You did.

Me: That would have been the end of it, but on my last night in town, Na'im was meeting up with a girl and her cousin, so he took me along.

Eniko: And I was the cousin!

Me: It was crazy that she was the same woman I'd been running into for the past two days. I thought you were amazingly cute, so I serenaded you—I grabbed the mic in the DJ booth at this dance club we went to and I just started singing. Some of the worst singing you've probably ever heard in your life.

Eniko: It was silly. I liked it.

Me: You were laughing. After that, we had a conversation outside.

Eniko: I enjoyed it. It seemed natural, and I laughed a lot. I thought, "Okay, this guy's hilarious."

Me: See, I keep telling everyone that the fun guy always gets the girl.

Eniko: Whatever. We talked and exchanged numbers. But afterward, my girlfriends were like, "Girl, he married. You don't need to be around him!"

Me: I remember telling you, "On paper, I *am* married, but you have to understand that this is not what it looks like. I'm not living at home."

Eniko: Shady!

Me: Exactly. The fucked-up thing is, so many women have heard that from so many men that they don't believe it when it's actually true.

Eniko: We talked on the phone and Skyped for two months after that. I still wasn't sure.

Me: I'm a sex symbol. My body looks like somebody drew it. How could you not be sure about this?

Eniko: A *married* sex symbol. A month or so later, you were in Baltimore, and that was the next time I saw you.

Me: It was just a quick hi and bye. But we had an interesting chemistry.

Eniko: (*Laughs.*)

Me: Why're you laughing?

Eniko: It was just funny. You wanted me to hang out after the show, and I wouldn't do it. I'm not gonna be your hookup while you're in town.

Me: I'm what you call a ladies' man. The ladies know I'm a keeper, so they play that long game. I figured I'd wait it out.

Eniko: After that, a few months passed, and then I met you at that festival in Kansas City.

Me: To this day, that's still one of the most fun days of my life. You got on a plane to see me, so I knew for sure you were interested. We went to Gates Bar-B-Q and just ate and laughed. We went to the movies. It was like a high school date. Then I had a comedy show later. That was the weekend we hooked up, but when you look back, it took quite some time.

Eniko: It was just a few months. I don't know what you're used to.

Me: I was used to, "Hey, what's going on? You want a drink?"—then the next thing you know, *bam bam bam bam*. I had a plethora of those, so when you get someone who's different and your vibe with them is different, the other stuff stops mattering and you start thinking about just that one person.

Eniko: Well, it wasn't quite that easy.

Me: Okay, it took me a little while to get there. We were both stepping out of serious relationships. And I had the attitude of *She's definitely moving up to the top of my list, but the last thing I'm gonna do is be somebody's man again at this point. Y'all can kiss my ass. I'm a rolling stone.*

Eniko: But then . . .

Me: . . . you look up, man, and you just find yourself slowly falling into a goddamn relationship, and that's exactly what happened.

84

The moment I realized that my relationship with Eniko was getting serious was about seven months after we met. She came to Los Angeles a few times to visit me, and one day we got into our first disagreement. I don't even remember what we were arguing about. When the time came for Eniko to leave, her eyes started watering. And I thought, *You don't cry about what you don't care about.*

With any other woman, this would have been an alarm warning me to pull back. It was surprising when I felt moved by her level of emotion instead. I told myself: *This here is a good woman. It's time to invest more of myself and my attention in her and see if this can go somewhere.*

She was gorgeous—black, with pieces of Jamaican and Chinese. She had a great sense of humor; she could hold her own in a greenroom with the Plastic Cup Boyz; she accepted me as I was; she supported my career and touring; and even when we didn't agree on something, we always treated each other with respect.

She stepped into the picture at the worst possible time, which was actually the perfect time: My life was in debacle mode. I'd left my home. I was heading into divorce. And I was fucking around a lot on the road.

But the single life that I'd missed so much—it got old quickly. It was always the same thing:

I'd think, *Having a variety of women in my bed is going to make life better. This is what being single is all about, right? I got one for Mondays. One for Tuesdays. But, wait, it's Wednesday. I gotta go through my contacts and find someone.* "Hey, what're you doing today? . . . You got plans, huh? . . . Oh, okay." "Hey, girl, whatchu doing? Wanna come by and chill? Nope? Oh, okay." "What about you? Great, how soon can you get here?" An hour later: *She looks great. But damn, talking to her is like pulling teeth. Let's just take care of business. Bam bam bam. Okay. She still here? What time is it?* Finally, she'd speak the three magic words: "I gotta go." "Aww, so soon? All right, I'll see you around."

It was sad, and the saddest thing about it was that I had kids. I couldn't be the guy living this life while being a father. There was a reason why I never introduced any of those women to my kids. I wouldn't even introduce Eniko until I knew it was something very long-term.

Eniko was also cautious. She refused to put a name on our relationship until I was divorced. Twenty-year-old Kevin would have hated the idea of taking things so damn slowly. But thirty-year-old Kevin was grateful for it. That's how I knew I was actually growing up.

85

NO, I'M GOING BACK TO TITLES.
LET'S CALL THIS ONE:
SOME MORE GROWING UP

"It's some really heavy shit that happened to you growing up," Joey said.

He and Harry were at my house for a writing session, which, as always, was 5 percent writing and 95 percent *Madden*. They had great jobs: When we weren't on the road, they were basically paid to play video games with me.

"Yeah, man." I agreed with Joey. "But the last thing I want is for anyone to feel sorry for me, because I don't feel sorry for myself. I'm glad for everything that happened."

"Even losing your mom?" Harry asked. "Seems like you're still hurting over that."

"Of course, that was tough."

They asked about the funeral. It was a sad day, but since I'm not the type to wallow, I lightened up the story for them and started describing the characters in my family. They kept busting up, and every now and then, taking notes. It actually looked like they were working during work hours.

I riffed on my family and my dad's addiction for a good hour. As I did, I thought, *I'm supposed to be a comedian who isn't afraid to bare it all, so why have I been hiding this part of my life?*

By the time I was done, it was clear to all of us what the follow-up to *Seriously Funny* would be.

"Are you really ready to go to these places?" Joey asked.

"I guess. Some of the shit is so funny, I couldn't even make it up. The main thing that's important to me with this is that when I leave the stage, people know who I am and what made me."

I started popping up for unscheduled spots in the New York clubs where I'd cut my teeth so I could test different stories and approaches. Some nights, there were only ten people in the audience. Other nights, I'd do thirty minutes and I wouldn't hear a single laugh. A few times, I saw people on their phones when I was in the middle of talking about my mom's funeral. But I needed to bomb to succeed: I knew that if I could find a way to win over audiences in these tough, cold rooms, then I'd have no problem in a theater packed with people who were actually there to see me.

Through talking on stage about subjects I typically avoided thinking about, and receiving the immediate response of laughter—which to me says, *I can relate to what you went through*—I began to heal wounds I didn't know I had. It enabled me to accept even my father's worst behavior and finally go through the grieving process around my mom.

Choosing to talk about these deeply personal subjects on what became the *Laugh at My Pain* tour took me down a whole new road in life. People told their friends to see the show, and those individuals then told their friends. Groups of people came up to me in the street, yelling my dad's phrase from the show, "All right, all right, all right!"

Eventually, Mike Berkowitz called.

Mike: You know, I think we can add a second theater show in most of these cities.
Me: I don't know, man. I just want to be patient.
Mike: Let's try it.
Me: Uh, okay.
(*A few months later...*)
Mike: You can probably stop doing theaters and go to basketball arenas in a few of these cities.
Me: I don't know.
Mike: I'm telling you, you can. You sold out three nights in Boston. Let's try it.
Me: Uh, uh . . . fuck . . . okay.

The first arena show he booked for us was at the Mohegan Sun Arena in Connecticut, which holds ten thousand people. As we walked down the loading ramp and through the backstage door on the day of the show, I felt like every line of cocaine I'd ever turned down entered my bloodstream. I came on stage with so much energy that I had to slow myself down to keep from steamrolling over the jokes.

All the work we'd put in had created momentum, and for the first time it felt like we couldn't stop the audience from growing even if we wanted to. Our days of flyering were over. At this level, there was a machine working for us. Promoters had a budget for marketing campaigns with radio spots, billboards, print ads, and professional publicists. And I finally had enough money to make one essential addition to the Plastic Cup Boyz: John, the only barber who could do my hair right.

He left the back chair at Platinum Cuts, joined the Make-Up Artists and Hair Stylists Guild, and became a permanent part of the team.

Beyond the roadwork, the social media, the specials, and all the other promotion, another factor was probably responsible for this acceleration in my career. I was finally cleaning up the one area of my life where I was a jerk and a hypocrite and didn't live up to my own standards: my relationships. Without the guilt, fear, frustration, and resentment running through my mind all the time, I was free to be the best version of myself that I could be.

86

THAT ONE TIME I GOT CAUGHT CHEATING WITHOUT ACTUALLY CHEATING

The first time I saw how powerful the media's influence on my life could be was when I took Eniko to a Lakers game. The next day, there were photos online of us holding hands, with headlines like, "Caught Creepin'! Married Comedian Kevin Hart Brought His Jumpoff to Last Night's Lakers Game!"

My name had never been on TMZ. I'd never been someone who gossip sites were interested in. I was still so small time that some of those headlines spelled my name "Kevin Heat."

The instant the story broke, Torrei was on the phone:

"I can't believe you would do this to me!"

"Huh?

"How dare you humiliate me like that!"

"What? Torrei, we're separated. The only contact we've had for over a year is about our kids. Do you really think that I'm not doing anything? And if I am, that's not information I need to report to you or anyone else."

It was the first time I actually had solid moral ground to stand on with her. Torrei, however, felt otherwise. She became malicious in a public way that I'd never experienced before. She attacked me and Eniko on social media, on the radio, on *E! News*. She seemed angrier over this than she'd been about the girl with the snake tattoo—and in a way, it was understandable, because at this level, our private humiliations were becoming public ones.

This was the downside to the fame that I'd wanted. But I never wanted to be famous as a human *being*. I wanted to be famous as a human *doing*. I wanted my shows to sell out, my movies to top the box office, my television shows to get good ratings. I wanted to build on these opportunities to do more and leave my mark on the world through my accomplishments, not my personal life.

When I had that thought, I started to laugh. *Look at what people make important. Why does anyone give a shit about some comedian's relationship status? If they have nothing better to do, let 'em talk. I'm going to make the choices that serve my happiness, not their expectations, and that's all that matters.*

I soon got to the point where I could shoulder-shrug it. In fact, the whole situation ended up helping Eniko's and my relationship. When Eniko was dragged into the spotlight, and websites were calling her a home wrecker while strangers online called her a bitch, I got to see what her character was made of.

Though it was tough for Eniko to deal with, she didn't freak out, accuse me of ruining her life, or take it out on me in any way. She just told me how she felt about it—that it was hurtful, upsetting, overwhelming—and asked for advice on how to deal with it.

"Well, are they wrong or right about you?" I asked.

"They're so wrong."

"Then it doesn't matter. We're together. We're smiling. We're happy. And we'll continue to shine because good things grow out of happiness."

"What do I do about all the emails I'm getting from the media?"

"Ignore them. Anything you tell them, they'll blow out of proportion to keep the story going. Stay cool and take the high road. The lies will fade. The truth lasts forever."

She nodded, smiled, and squeezed my hand. "You're right. Why should what's outside have an effect on what's inside? I like the bubble we're in, and I'm not letting anyone burst it."

Back when I was going to Dances with Spank, getting lucky meant taking someone home that night. In this moment, I learned what getting lucky *really* was.

Not long after, I asked Eniko to move in so we could be closer and she could begin a relationship with my kids.

Despite all the drama, I never turned my back on Torrei. Even when things got ugly, I still remembered that she had stayed with me through the hardest times, supporting me when I'd needed it most. I went into divorce court saying that I was a high-income earner and, despite whatever my attorney said in the filings, the court should give her whatever it saw fit. When the decision was made, I didn't argue. I didn't debate it. I just said: "Okay, Your Honor."

I don't know why it took me so long to go through with the divorce. I guess I hadn't expected to fall in love again.

87

IF YOU NEVER TALKED TO STRANGERS, YOU'D NEVER TALK TO ANYONE, SINCE EVERYONE IS A STRANGER BEFORE YOU TALK TO THEM

Here's another way in which something that seems negative can be interpreted positively: If people are saying critical things about you, it means you're worth talking about. And if they're wrong about you, even better, because it means you're worth making stuff up about.

With *Laugh at My Pain*, it no longer made sense to follow the same plan of recording a show and selling it to Comedy Central. A third cable special would be a lateral move, not an upward move. It wouldn't get me anywhere.

I decided to raise the bar and release the special as a theatrical film rather than a television program. I knew very little about the business side of movies, so when I asked people what they thought of the idea, they said some variation of "Shut up, Kev, you dumb!"

"That's what Eddie Murphy and Richard Pryor and all the greats did. Why is it dumb for me to do?"

"Cause you don't know nothing about releasing a movie."

That was true. Then again, I'd gotten this far by being willing to stretch myself. Around the time you're eighteen, nature stops the process of growing in your body. So if you want to keep growing after that, you have no choice *but* to stretch yourself on your own and increase your thinking, your capabilities, and your accomplishments. It's a scary thing to take the risks and make the sacrifices necessary to keep growing, but it's better than living a life in which you don't fulfill your potential. The worst-case scenario is that it doesn't work. The best-case scenario is that it does. Whatever happens, life goes on and so does the laughter.

I formed a production company, HartBeat Productions, and began working toward this new goal. You only learn by doing. Everyone's inexperienced when they start anything new.

One morning, I was at the Los Angeles airport waiting for a flight to a *Laugh at My Pain* show when a cocky guy with a great big wall of teeth came up to me. It looked like he put a lot of care into his appearance. Each item of his clothing—from his black fedora to his brown dress shoes—were impeccable. But none of it matched. I remember thinking: *That's the best worst-dressed guy I've ever seen.*

"Hey, Kevin!" He stuck out his hand. "I'm a movie producer and I've had a lot of success, and I'd love to sit down with you for a second."

"Okay."

He sat down next to me and introduced himself as Will Packer, then told me about the movies he'd done—*Takers*, *Obsessed*, *Stomp the Yard*. "I got another movie in the works right now," he went on. "I would love to talk to you and just have a general conversation."

I thought for a moment about whether I wanted to exchange phone numbers with him, then decided that it couldn't hurt. When he reached out the next day, I told him that I didn't have time to meet, but he could drop by one of my shows if he wanted to. I didn't think anything would come of it, so I didn't tell my manager or agents about it.

But just like with the Shaq special, I was wrong. Often, it's been the opportunities I most undervalue in my life that end up providing the most value.

Will hopped on a plane to Dallas the next day and came to my show there. The next morning, we met for breakfast. As could be expected with anyone who approached me in an airport to pitch doing business together, he was a talker.

He began by telling me that he'd been following my career and was aware of everything I'd been doing. Then he made his pitch, but it was all hypothetical statements, vague promises, and future hype: "This is gonna be real big, and if you wanna be part of this, I got you."

In these situations, I don't necessarily focus on what someone *says*. I look at who they *are*. And Will seemed to have a lot of attributes that I shared, things that had gotten me to where I was. He was a people person. He was passionate and dedicated to his craft. He seemed like a hard worker. And, like me, there was nothing he felt he couldn't handle or do.

"I've worked with Clint Culpepper over at Screen Gems, and we do great business, big movies," he went on. "I want you to star in this movie I'm putting together. I got the rights to *Act Like a Lady, Think Like a Man*. Steve Harvey's book. Huge bestseller, a phenomenon. Biggest book of dating advice for women out there. Have you read it?"

"I'm not exactly the target audience."

"Here's a copy. Read it and let me know if you want to be involved. I think you're the guy for it."

"Okay."

"I should have the script and stuff soon, but I just want to know if you're interested. If you are, I can put this thing together and make amazing things happen for you."

He showed me a bunch of numbers about how profitable the movie could be. I felt like I'd heard this story before, but I was willing to take a chance that maybe this time it would have a different ending. "I hope your word is as good as you say it is," I declared as we parted ways that day.

"All I know is how to deliver, baby," he answered.

Whatever amount of confidence that response was intended to instill in me, it accomplished the exact opposite.

I read the book that night. Rather than seeing it as a betrayal of men, like some guys did, I respected most of the advice—for example, the part about how it was important to understand a man's dedication to his career goals. There was also a section about waiting ninety days to give a man the "cookie," as Steve Harvey called it. I wondered if Eniko had used this tactic on me. If she had, then I owed this book a lot.

I called Will back the next day. "Hey, man—so who else is in the movie?"

"Right now, brother, you're the talk of the town. I wanted to get you first and then build it around you."

"Well, you've got me. Let's build it."

"Great, great, I'll send you this script as soon as it comes in."

I didn't hear from him for a while and the project faded from my mind, until Will called out of the blue. "We're ready. The *Think Like a Man* script is done. It's incredible—you'll love it. I want to get it to you. You're our anchor on this, man!"

I read it, called him back the next day, and told him the writer had done an amazing job of turning a self-help book into an ensemble dating comedy. "Great," he responded. "Then we're gonna start casting so we can shoot this baby."

"You might not wanna use that expression."

"You're funny, man, genius. Let's knock this outta the park. Who should I talk to? Who's your representative?"

I'd never actually told Dave Becky about Will. I wanted to wait until it was real—and now it was. In the meantime, I had some serious instigating to do.

88

KEEPING MY GUARDIAN ANGEL BUSY

Since the shows had moved up to theaters and arenas, there was constantly money in my pocket.

So what happens when a risk taker who's not good with money gets a lot of cash?

He does dumb shit with it.

Most of that involved getting someone on my team to do something stupid. It all started when we were at a Fuddruckers somewhere in the South. I bet Wayne three hundred dollars that he couldn't eat two one-pound burgers without throwing up. The cocky motherfucker ordered his two burgers with bacon, mayo, the works. Halfway through the second one, he started feeling sick, and by the last bites we could see him working to control his gag reflex.

He won the money, then lost it all a few days later by pouring a shitload of vodka into a red plastic cup and betting me three hundred dollars that I couldn't drink it all.

I may be short, but I have the liver of a tall man. Back then, I could down twelve shots and still get on stage to perform without missing a beat. I won that three hundred, but the next morning, I had a *Seriously Funny* DVD signing.

Eniko was with us, and she couldn't wake me up, so she ran to Wayne for help. He smacked the shit out of me until I got out of bed. I was still wasted, and covered in vomit and urine. Eniko then won my devotion forever: She put me in the shower, dressed me, and got me ready for the signing. I'd like to say that I'd do the same for her, but I'll never know, because I out-drink her every time.

I arrived at the signing drunk and belligerent, and sat behind a folding table. A woman made her way over with a baby in one hand and a DVD in another. "Hurry it up, mama, I don't got all day," I snapped. She approached nervously. I quickly signed her DVD, then shouted, "Now get that ugly baby outta here!"

I'd lost the ability to censor myself. To a guy who was lingering at the table: "C'mon, man, nobody wants to talk to you. Go back to your park bench." To a woman who was taking a photo with me: "Get your arm off of me, lady. You look diseased." And the next person: "Look at those goddamned pants. I'm not signing no DVD for nobody wearing those stupid-ass pants. Take them off and go to the back of the line."

Eniko kept trying to calm me down, but the fans just thought I was doing my act. "Oh, man, that Kevin's so funny! He's crazy!"

I wish we'd taped that signing. It could have been the next special: *Laugh at My Drunkenness.*

We were on fire with challenges after that, until we bet John two thousand dollars that he couldn't finish a bottle of Hennessy without throwing up. When he passed out upside down in the rental car, vomited, wet himself, and almost died, it was a wake-up call.

From that day forward, we decided to stop doing bets that were about hurting each other. Instead, we made bets to help each other. All the touring was killing Wayne slowly: He was three hundred and thirty pounds, and always sick. He had high blood pressure, sleep apnea, you name it. He snored so loudly that if he napped on a plane, the other passengers couldn't sleep.

"Let's make a bet right now," I said to Wayne. "I'll put up ten thousand dollars to your thousand that you can't lose forty pounds in the next six months. If you lose fifty, I'll throw another five grand on top of it."

"Man, that ain't nothing. I can lose sixty."

"Then I'll add another five thousand."

"Done."

Wayne took off sixty-five pounds and kept going after the bet ended. I gladly paid him the twenty thousand dollars. His entire lifestyle changed after that. Instead of money being a motivation for smart people to do stupid shit, I saw that money could be a motivation for stupid people to do smart shit as well.

If that sounds like I'm being mean by calling Wayne stupid, he's earned it. He still owes me money, so I can call him what I want till I get it back. Wayne, if you're reading this, pay what you owe and I'll remove this paragraph from the next printing of the book. John, you too. I'm watching y'all, and now so is every reader of this book. They'll know you've both paid up when this paragraph disappears.

But I'll bet you a hundred dollars it doesn't.

89

THIS CHAPTER STILL GETS ME EXCITED, PEOPLE

Eventually, the time came for the big show: the one for movie theaters, the one for comedy history. I'd put three quarters of a million dollars into this moment, making it the biggest bet I'd ever made. The setting: the Nokia Theater in Los Angeles.

I scheduled two shows—that way, I'd have a backup take of each joke. This ended up saving my ass.

Because of everything at stake, I had so much on my mind that I spoke too quickly on the first night and parts fell flat.

Afterward, I made adjustments, prayed, went back for show two, and did one of the best sets of my life. No metaphors here, just gratitude.

"Can you believe this shit?" I asked the guys afterward. "We're gonna get to go see this at a movie theater!" At the end of the day, I'm still the excitable kid from Philadelphia who never got to do anything fun.

Since much of the set was about my childhood, I returned to my old neighborhood to film a short documentary about the environment I grew up in. I wanted to show that the people and places I spoke about were real.

I went to a family meal at Shirrel and Preston's house, the same place where I was stuck in the kitchen snapping peas as a child. Most of my mom's family were there, and as I was telling them I wouldn't be who I was without them, I started crying. I never told them why I got so choked up, but it's because my mom was the glue that held the family together. Since she'd passed, I realized that I'd barely spoken to our relatives, and I didn't want them to think that this meant I didn't love them.

Meanwhile, Will Packer was backing up his big talk with equally big actions. He introduced me, as promised, to Clint Culpepper, the head of Screen Gems, a production company responsible for thousands of films and shows. Clint somehow remembered me from a small part I'd done two years earlier in a drama about marriage and God based on a T. D. Jakes book, *Not Easily Broken*.

My friend Morris Chestnut had gotten me the part of his friend in *Not Easily Broken*, and he ended up cast in *Think Like a Man*, along with Romany Malco, who'd gotten the part I wanted in *The 40-Year-Old Virgin*.

During the first day of filming, after I did a few takes that followed the script, the director, Tim Story, said, "Hey, man, we got you because you're funny. You got anything you want to try in this scene? Do this one for you."

reat experience, because
on stage. So many of my
sn't given the freedom to
last seven years on the

m said, "Let's do a Kevin
my Jell-O," because I had
he takes that ended up in
h off to Ron Artest of the
g to snatch the ball out of
ngle me in the air while I
of the most memorable

yer. Nobody was selfish.
ery scene we tried to set
comedy heaven.
On one hand, I felt like
ered so many disappoint-
nd tried to be careful not

I prepared for the release
ut my concert movie on
following had soared to
ople with a single Tweet
ned.
tomorrow (which, by the
e, because if there was no
te it). Nearly every post I
ed everyone's feed with
ntil it became a trending

there was a tomorrow. I
press junkets, talk-show

interviews, billboards—and decide

that stood out.

I'd gotten to this point in my care

engage with comedy fans and show

even though this was a movie, it dic

charm offensive like I'd done in my e

My Pain was released, I popped up

bought tickets, popcorn, and drinks

movie. I thanked each person for cor

it a memorable experience.

Since so much of the film was a

miere, where he proved to everyon

kept calling out to celebrities using

come here and take this photo, sucka

When she didn't respond, he go

played on *Martin*. Call her by her re

around."

"Oh, she just one of them Hollyw

or I'll knock you on yo' ass."

In its first weekend, *Laugh at My*

It was the tenth biggest film at the

tremely rare for a stand-up comedy

put it on more screens the following

went on to generate nearly eight milli

Seven months later, *Think Like*

myself that I'd remain cautious, m

script, cast, and director—and I fe

mances.

I beat the streets up and did sur

thing I could think of. *Think Like a M*

opening weekend, knocking down *Th*

million dollars, it ended up making r

dustry was predicting. "Sony pictures is in shock!" the trade papers proclaimed.

It was not just an unbelievable success; it was a new beginning. And after hundreds of Hollywood meetings and auditions and pitches, it all happened because of a guy I ran into at the airport.

Life Lessons
FROM SUCCESS

You don't need my advice anymore. If you're
successful, then it's your turn to give the advice.
Unless you lose your success, in which case
you gotta start over at chapter one.

With Jay Z and Chris Rock at Madison Square Garden

90

HELLO, I'M BACK

It was a massive homecoming party.

Every trade magazine in the industry was writing about the success of *Laugh at My Pain* and *Think Like a Man*. Dave's phone was ringing off the hook. Interview offers came rolling in. Most of the articles began something like, "You've probably never heard of Kevin Hart, but he is fast becoming one of the biggest comedians in the business."

It showed me what a bubble Hollywood exists in: If more people bought tickets to my show than to any other comedy tour that year, then how would it be possible for people not to have heard of me?

What those journalists were really saying was that *they* had never heard of me. It had taken seven years of touring to work my way back to being a "newcomer" in Hollywood. The difference was that before I was a newcomer with a dream, now I was a newcomer with the leverage of an audience.

Suddenly, the people who didn't want to meet with me after *Soul Plane* and *The Big House* wanted to have lunch; the seeds I'd planted over the years grew into offers; and the people who'd rejected me forgot they'd ever turned me down. There were times when I'd sit in a meeting thinking: *I'm not new. I've been here for* years. *Y'all don't remember? I was in here auditioning and you cut me off and said, "Okay, that's enough, sir."*

It was a trip, but I didn't take it personally. Ultimately, casting me—or any actor—in a major role is an investment. And you don't want to put money into a company when it's peaked and is on its way down; you want to get on board when it's on its way up. They were doing their jobs by looking for a safe investment, and I was doing mine by being one.

Because I now controlled my career, I no longer had to make bad choices because I didn't have any other option, or I needed the money, or I was desperate to hear a *yes*. I could choose projects because I wanted to do them and they were right for me. For most people, mixing desperation and decision-making is like mixing vodka and painkillers—a dangerous combination.

After all the meetings, all the offers, all the let's-make-a-deals and we-want-to-be-in-the-Kevin-Hart-businesses and our-lawyers-will-call-your-lawyers, I decided to work with a true closer—not just someone who would throw money or a good script at me but someone who was willing to fight every step of the way to get a project made, released, and properly promoted. Someone whose work ethic I personally trusted: Will Packer.

Why end a relationship that's working and growing? Will believed in me when I wasn't number one at the box office, and that was something I would never get to experience in a new relationship again.

In the meantime, there were a lot of *other* new things to experience on this ride. Everything was flying by at warp speed. It felt like this . . .

ohmygodyouwantmetohostalltheseawardsshowsinfrontofthepeoplei-
lookuptookayijustinsultedallofthemandgotinthemiddleofdrakeandchris-
brownsbeefhopetheydonthatemewhattheygavemeatvseriesfromitididnt-
evenneedtopitchitorauditionornothinganditsgoingforfiveseasonsisold-
outtwodaysatmadisonsquaregardenlittleoldmedamnstalkerswhatdoyoudo-
aboutthemnowcomediansilovearehatingonmethatdoesntfeelnecessary-
imgonnacallthemandseewhatsupwiththatmanimthrowingaroundway-
toomuchmoneygamblingbutiguessivealwaysthrownaroundmoneyjustatadif-
ferentlevelshitbeckyscallingandsaturdaynightlivewantsmeafteralltheseyears-
butmanimdrinkingmorethanishouldandalmostfuckingupmylifeandthe-
livesofinnocentstrangersjesusivedonesomestupidstupidshitinthisbooklets-
seewhatelseididntevenmindwhenthenorthkoreansorwhoeverhackedsonys-
emailsandclintculpeppercalledmeawhorebutitsbusinessandnothingtodo-
withmeasapersonsowerestillgoodfriendsmantheressomuchmorelikeper-

forminginamotherfuckingfootballstadiumcanyoubelieveitareyouactually-
stillreadingthisohandletsnotforgetgoinginternationalbutmostimportantly-
neverbeingtoobusytobeagreatdad.

Let me explain by slowing this down and breaking off a few of the most
impactful pieces, starting with . . .

91

KEITH, I'M IN NEW YORK AND DOING THE GARDEN, SO WHO'S THE DUMMY NOW?

When Will Packer came to me with a follow-up to *Think Like a Man*, I agreed
to do it. But I told him that I needed to get back on the road first and stay connected with the comedy that had made the movies possible.

Where *Laugh at My Pain* was about my past, the new tour, *Let Me Explain,* was a celebration of where I'd made it to from those twisted roots, how
grateful I was to get there, and my willingness to set the record straight on the
rumors that had spread along the way.

The tour sold five times as many tickets as *Laugh at My Pain,* filling over
half a million seats in the end. The highlight of the *Let Me Explain* tour—and
of this entire period of my life—was selling out two nights at Madison Square
Garden in New York City.

I reached out to three of the people I most admired—Jay Z, Chris Rock,
and Keith Robinson (who in so many ways made this possible)—and asked if
they could come to the show to share this moment with me. They were all
down, except Keith, who had better things to do.

Chris congratulated me, then shared some advice: "It's a big world, so
don't get stuck performing over and over for just one small piece of it. People
in every country love to laugh. Get out of America and tell your jokes to the
world."

Even though I was about to perform what I thought was the show of a lifetime, I saw how small my vision still was: I thought my comedy was universal because I was able to play for every type of crowd in America, and I'd done a few European shows. I hadn't considered that what I thought was *the world* was just a tiny percentage of it.

As I was in my dressing room with Chris, Jay Z walked in, wearing three gold chains to my one.

"This is a big moment for you." He nodded his head approvingly. "A big moment."

"It really is."

"Know how I know it's a big moment?"

"Because you know where I came from?"

"Because *I'm* here."

His words didn't seem arrogant: They were just true. This was my moment. Hova was in the house. It was all happening.

Suddenly, my dad burst into the dressing room. "Oh, man, that's Jay Z right there! Got to get a goddamn picture. Motherfucking Jay Z and Chris motherfucking Rock. Y'all motherfuckers got to give me a picture!"

He whipped out an old plastic camera from the seventies, with a flash cube that he had to stick on top and a thumb-wheel that he spun to advance the film. He fiddled with it for a long minute—*click, click, click*—then started taking photos, each one accompanied by a blinding flash—*click click click* POP *click click click* POP.

Whatever magic the moment had was gone. We all slinked away politely.

When I walked on stage that night, the applause thundered through the arena. I stood there and took it all in. It was unbelievable. "I'm happy," I told the crowd. "I want to explain why I'm happy. First of all, my divorce is final . . ."

A couple of months before the film came out, I was invited to host *Saturday Night Live* and promote it. Twelve years after getting rejected by the show, I found myself crammed into Lorne Michaels's office with some three dozen writers and cast members, working on an episode. The writers pitched their ideas to Lorne, he narrowed them down to about fifty sketches, and a couple of days later, we ran through them all. For my monologue, I didn't want to give away the material from the movie, so I ended up sharing the story of my failed *SNL* audition.

Spending that week working on the show reaffirmed my faith in the idea that everything happens for a reason. If I'd been added to the cast when I'd first auditioned and performed my horrible impressions on national television, I'd probably be selling sneakers today.

When *Let Me Explain* came out in theaters, it was more than four times as successful as *Laugh at My Pain*, pulling in thirty-two million dollars and reaching number eight at the box office.

What's harder than achieving success is achieving consistent success. But what's even harder than achieving consistent success is achieving consistently bigger successes. The reverberations of that second concert film took me to the next level, because now I was respected not just in comedy circles and Hollywood circles but in business circles.

The first thing I found at that next level was script stalkers. Before this, people used to hand me scripts; but now, they were threatening me with scripts. A few guys set up meetings with networks by claiming to work with HartBeat Productions. Another script stalker reached out to everyone in my crew and, when that didn't work, went after their family members—even hiring Joey's son to work as a party DJ in order to hand him a script for me.

The creepiest stalker of them all kept popping up backstage at concerts with fake credentials and pretending to be part of the entourage. I once caught him harassing Eniko, trying to get her to convince me to make his movie.

We eventually had to take out a restraining order on a few of these guys. The lesson is that you can hustle all you want, but you're not gonna get anywhere if you're hustling with a delusional mind.

"The most disappointing thing about making it as a comedian," I told Eniko afterward, repeating something Chris Rock once said, "is that you don't get sex groupies like rappers and athletes. You get business groupies."

92

STILL HAVING TROUBLE WITH THIS PARTICULAR LIFE LESSON

This is the point where, in most memoirs, celebrities reveal how they sabotaged their rising fame and success. The flaws in their character become magnified by the spotlight, and they start messing with a drug and develop an addiction that takes them back down to the bottom.

That's pretty much what happened to me. The drug I got hooked on was a very powerful one. The kids these days call it: the Xbox.

I had already experimented with some *Madden*, which turned out to be the gateway drug to the hardest stuff of all: *NBA 2K*.

I'd been touring for so long with the Plastic Cup Boyz that we'd grown tired of clubs and after-parties. Most of us were in serious relationships, and our tolerance for the bullshit had faded to zero.

Instead, after every show, we'd meet backstage and begin the ritual.

"Yo, let's get to the hotel room!"

"Y'all set up the game?"

"Yeah, let's play."

"Hey, who got the records?"

"I got 'em. Did y'all set up the profiles?"

"I bet five hundred I'm gonna beat you with only Dirk Nowitzki."

With everything I get into, I don't have a halfway setting. It's all or nothing. I have to either be the best or give everything I've got trying. Soon we were taking our Xbox and TV to the arenas and setting up in the greenroom so we could play before and after each show. People would come backstage to party with us and end up just watching us shout, argue, and cut each other down as we played *NBA 2K*.

When we were kicked out of the arena, we'd rush to the hotel, the bus, or the plane as quickly as possible so we could get back to playing the game.

Often, we'd sit up playing all night. I remember looking up at one point and saying, "Yo, we been playing this game for sixteen hours!"

Addiction is a nasty disease. Your tolerance builds up, and soon you need a bigger, more dangerous high. We eventually found that high: Guts.

Guts is a fast-paced poker game in which players are dealt a hand of two to four cards, and each has the option of either saying "guts" (if they think they have the best hand) or folding (if they don't). Because of the way the betting works, if five people say "guts," the pot can quadruple in one round. The game is fast-paced and money changes hands rapidly, so we started keeping a record book and settling our debts with each other at the end of the tour.

I don't have a better way to explain what goes on in a game of Guts other than to bring you into one that's going on right now, on a private plane somewhere over Fresno:

Wayne: This fucking game. John's head is gonna hurt when he sees this five-thousand-dollar tab he got.

Kevin: I'll just take it out of his pay. Let him run up that tab forever. It don't matter to me. I'll eventually get what he owes me.

Spank: I owe him three thousand. He's the only one that don't pay, so that's why I'm not paying him.

Nate: You're not recording this, are you?

Writer: Of course I am.

Spank: I don't care, you can put this in the book. Shit, I ain't gonna read it.

Wayne: Remember that time on the last day of the tour, when you went to the bank and got thirty grand to settle with everybody?

Spank: Yeah, I pulled out five thousand and started playing. Then I got out the rest and lost it all before I got a chance to pay anybody what I owed.

Writer: Your wife must want to kill you for doing this with your salary.

Spank: She don't know.

Wayne: If you think they tell their girlfriends or wives what them pots be up to—hell no.

Spank: You gotta only tell them about the wins.

Na'im: I stopped playing as soon as I noticed that the person who needs the money the least always wins.

All heads turn to look at that particular person.

Kevin: What?! I'm a lucky guy. That's why you all roll with me.

I'm the type of guy that Las Vegas was built for because I'm an optimist. Someone who's practical, like Na'im, will make a little money at the blackjack table, then stop. He'll look around the giant, luxurious casino and see that it was built by people's losses.

Me, I'll make a lot of money, then keep going because I think it's my lucky day and nothing can stop me so I need to go bigger. And every time I go bigger, I lose it all.

When I go to Vegas today, the casinos love me. They give me a free panoramic penthouse suite with a Jacuzzi and assign me a complimentary hostess. I feel so important, but when I leave, I realize I've lost enough money at the casino to book that "free" room for the entire year—and pay the "complimentary" hostess's salary and benefits. I'm always leaving casinos, pointing to chandeliers and couches and telling the staff, "I just paid for that."

I tell my kids that working hard earns you the right to play hard. No matter what happened in this intense period of my life, work always came first. But just because you work smart doesn't give you the right to play stupid. And I played stupid. Real stupid. I could have lost everything I'd worked for because of one mistake I kept making and not learning from.

93

ALCOHOL

When I'm drunk, I think everything is a toilet.

This doesn't mean that I will go to the bathroom just anywhere. I'm not an animal. I don't even like to touch the door handle on the way out of a public bathroom. I've seen Spank ignore the soap dispenser, wet his hands, and then dry them on his pants one too many times.

But when I'm wasted, anything with a door looks like a bathroom to me. And anything with a lid or an opening looks like a toilet. So I'll piss wherever I think a bathroom is or should be.

I've peed behind the bar in my house because I thought it was a urinal. I've peed in hotel closets, thinking I was walking into a bathroom. I've even peed in my daughter's potty.

And I can honestly say that one time in Vegas, I pissed in Eniko's purse. I remember saying to myself: *Oh, it's a toilet with a zipper. I got it. I'll just unzip this piece and I'm good to go. I wonder when they started making these.*

In the morning, Eniko was furious: "Why'd you piss in my bag?!"

"I didn't pee in your bag."

"Yes, you did!"

She showed me the inside of her purse: Everything was soggy and smelled like asparagus. I promised never to do it again. A week later, I pissed in her Louis Vuitton luggage.

Another time, I got out of bed, walked to the bathroom, lifted the toilet seat, peed, and put the seat back down for Eniko. Then I went back to bed, feeling good about having been so considerate. I woke up the next morning in a puddle of my own piss.

It turned out that the whole trip to the toilet happened in my head. I was so drunk I thought I was in the bathroom and wet the bed.

If you want to know what birthday present to get for the comedian who seems to have everything, the answer is rubber sheets.

Despite what you may be thinking right now, I didn't have a drinking problem. Drinking had a problem with me.

The difference is that someone with a drinking problem abuses alcohol. In my situation, the alcohol abused me. I only drank when I was out with friends (which was all the time—because who goes out with enemies?) and I never felt like I got drunk.

Alcohol impairs people in different ways, and with me, it impaired my ability to tell that I was drunk. No matter how many shots I did, I still thought I was sober. Even if I was vomiting, I'd think I caught the flu from someone at the bar. I'd only find out how drunk I was the next morning, when Eniko told me where I'd pissed.

Because of this, I'd get behind the wheel after a few drinks and think that I was completely sober and perfectly fine to drive. The best thing that ever happened to me was getting a DUI. This isn't funny in any way, because I could have killed someone. It's disgusting to think of the number of times I've woken up in the parking lot of a drive-through with half a burger in my lap, thinking, "Oh, shit, I'm still fucking here?"

I almost killed myself and Dennis Rodman one night. We were driving down a hill, and I fell asleep at a stop sign. My mother, or some angel who protects assholes, must have been looking out for me, because when I woke up, my foot was still on the brake. If it wasn't, we would have rolled down that hill and smashed into someone's house, and North Korea would have lost the only American it liked.

The same angel was looking out for me the night I crashed into a fence and a metal post speared straight through the engine of my Range Rover. The car was still running, so I reversed it, sputtered into the street, and kept driving. I forgot about the accident, until I saw smoke billowing from the hood. When the engine died, I examined it and called AAA: "Hey, I need help. Someone stuck a sword or something into my engine."

The next thing I knew, I was woken by a firefighter knocking on the window and yelling, "You're sleeping in the middle of the highway!"

It was amazing that he didn't call the police—and that no one turned me in a few weeks later, when I crashed into a highway median, left my car there, and took a taxi home.

What the fuck are you doing, Kevin? I thought when I saw my car smashed against the concrete median early the next morning. *Are you trying to really fuck up your life? Is that what you're trying to do?*

But it took the DUI to really wake me up.

I was on the freeway driving home from a club with Eniko, and she was trying to lower my pants. I veered a few times outside of the lane in the process, and we got lit up.

I started to pull over, figuring I'd deal with this inconvenience and then we'd go home to pick up where we left off. My next thought was, *I gotta put both hands on the wheel in plain sight. But my pants are down. How can I pull 'em up without getting my junk blown off?*

Fortunately, the cop told me to pull off at the next exit, which gave me enough time to get myself situated.

"I pulled you over because you were swerving all over the road," the officer said, taking my license and registration. "Have you been drinking?"

"No, sir. I'm leaving the club. I had a good time, that's all."

"Sir, step out of the car!"

What? I stepped out of the car.

"Put your hands behind your back!"

Shit, no no no no. I put my hands behind my back, and he snapped the handcuffs over my Rolex Tridor Special Edition Masterpiece watch with a diamond dial. I'd started one obsessive collection since the money started coming in, and that was watches. This Rolex Tridor Special Edition Masterpiece with a diamond dial happened to be my favorite. So I requested, as politely as possible: "Sir, can you please be careful of my watch with those handcuffs?"

He tightened the handcuffs two more clicks—directly over the dial of the watch.

I thought maybe he hadn't heard me, or he didn't understand how important this piece was to me. "Sir, could you be a little more careful with the handcuffs? That's a Rolex Tridor Special Edition Masterpiece with a diamond dial."

He twisted a key in the handcuffs and loosened them. Just as I was thanking him, he clicked them down tight again, directly over my Rolex Tridor Special Edition Masterpiece. Right away I knew he'd scratched the diamond dial.

Eniko saw the look on my face. "Babe, don't say nothing," she begged.

I said something. "Dude, I just asked you not to do that!"

"Stop resisting arrest!" The cop shoved me hard against his car.

"Please, Officer, just let him go." Eniko half-begged, half-cried. Then, to me: "Baby, just do what he wants."

In my tequila-soaked mind, the guy was a bully and I wasn't going to get pushed around by a cop abusing his power. But the truth was, if I were in his position, and there was a rich, drunk asshole who cared more about his Rolex Tridor Special Edition Masterpiece and its diamond dial than about the lives he was endangering on the freeway, I'd probably do the same or worse.

"Oh, so you're *that* guy?" I went on with my dumb self. "Going out every night to take out your shitty life on everyone you pull over? I'm coming along peacefully, so don't hate on me just because you don't have my life."

"Nobody's worried about your life. I just don't like assholes."

"So I'm an asshole now, because I tell you to be careful of my watch? No, what makes me an asshole is when you run this registration and see this car ain't leased, it's *owned*."

I was already a stupid asshole for driving intoxicated, but now I was a Hollywood asshole for bragging intoxicated. Eniko was hysterical: "Stop! Shut up! Just do what he wants!"

The cop looked ready to beat my ass right on the side of the highway. "Go ahead, take me to jail," I went on with my stupid Hollywood-asshole mouth. "I'll be out in a couple hours."

His partner brought over a breathalyzer and interrupted my tirade. "We need you to blow."

"Fuck no, I'm not blowing! I know the law. Why would I blow? I ain't blowing. Take me to jail!" I turned to Eniko. "Babe, just drive the car home. I'll see you later."

"She's been drinking too. Unless she wants to join you in jail, she better find another way home."

"You're gonna make me leave my lady out here? I would suggest you figure out a way to get her home safely!"

He pushed me into the squad car and it quickly became apparent that he wasn't going to be taking my suggestion. "Babe, call somebody!" I yelled pathetically after Eniko.

They took the keys and left Eniko standing on the curb near the freeway exit ramp, shouting, "Babe, I'll come get you!"

At the precinct, some of the officers recognized me. "Have you been drinking, Mr. Hart?" one of them asked.

"Yes. I'm not gonna blow, though."

"Okay, why don't you sleep a little and figure out what you wanna do."

I slept for a few hours, and then blew. I was past the legal limit, which is .08 percent, but it was better than what would have happened if I'd blown the first time. That shit would have come in at goddamn .8 or something.

When they released me from jail the next morning, I still wasn't sober. Eniko, who'd ended up calling Wayne to drive her and the Mercedes home, came to the station to meet me. As I walked with her to the car and felt the sun on my face, a TMZ cameraman came running up: "Hey, what exactly happened, dude?" He said that the police report claimed I was driving over ninety miles an hour and almost hit a gas tanker. I couldn't remember a gas tanker, so either the cop made it up or I'm an idiot. Actually, either way I'm an idiot.

If I'd had any chance of hiring a good lawyer to get the charges dismissed, I lost it with my response: "I was actually drunk, so there's no arguing that."

I never attempted to fight the charge or make it into a racist-cop incident. It was a *dickhead* incident: Two guys on the side of the 101 freeway competing to see who could be the biggest dick. I won. It ended up costing me a lot of work, including a Bud Light deal worth ten million dollars. But I look back on the arrest today and think, *I'm a better, smarter man because this happened.*

If it hadn't happened, I might have kept drinking and driving until I killed someone. Sometimes it takes experiencing consequences to your actions for you to learn that they're wrong. And by then, it's often too late.

Because of that night in jail, I learned my lesson and quit altogether: I stopped driving.

I still drank, but I hired a driver to get me home afterward.

He quit when I pissed in his hat.

94

FROM THE HART

After getting that DUI, my commitment to health and fitness truly began. I wanted to be a better person for Eniko and for my children, and that meant taking better care of myself.

I started rising earlier in the morning, eating healthier, putting myself on a stricter schedule, and working out more regularly and systematically.

As my body became stronger and healthier, my mind became stronger and healthier as well. I began to clearly see all the ways I was at fault for the destruction of my relationship with Torrei: The constant infidelity, dishonesty, and negative talk—and, as the man in the situation, no matter what she was doing to me physically, it was never okay for me to put hands on her. That's a shame I'll have to bear for the rest of my life. These were the actions of a weak man—morally weak, emotionally weak, physically weak, everything weak.

Torrei noticed the change in me. When I was on the phone, trying to get more time with the kids, I no longer got mad when she refused to let me take them for a weekend trip. Other times, she'd say something that felt cruel to me, and I wouldn't react. I'd just rationally let her know that I disagreed with that statement. I was as surprised by this new me as she was.

A relationship is a system created by two people, so when there's a shift in one person, there's inevitably a shift in the other. Instead of battling on the phone, Torrei and I began doing something we'd rarely done for a decade: speaking *with*, instead of *against*, each other. It became clear that I had been fighting to deprive Heaven and Hendrix of a mother and she had been fighting to deprive them of a father. The only people we were hurting in this battle were the two people who mattered most: our children.

We may not have learned to like each other, but we at least learned to tolerate, respect, and accept each other. From that starting point, and through many more conversations, we were able to get to a place where we could co-parent in a way that was healthy for our children without ever going to court to battle for custody.

And what was that way? It was simply and finally putting the kids' needs above our own. If I wanted them to come hang out with me on set for a month over the summer, we were able to discuss that in a way that was about what was best for them, and not about what was wrong with me or unfair to her.

The day we made this shift was the day we grew up and became good parents. It took years of separation and divorce to bring us closer together, but today I put Torrei on a pedestal because she's their mother and I will never knock her off that. Even if she makes a decision that I disagree with, I will never contradict her in front of the kids. At most, I may tell them, "Whether it's right or wrong, in this particular case, that's how your mom feels." This way, they see me respecting their mother in the same way I expect them to respect her.

After all we've been through, it's amazing to write those words. I've supported Torrei beyond what the courts ordered. I've bought her a house, a truck, and as much as possible so that the kids feel as comfortable and have as many opportunities in her world as in mine. In the meantime, Torrei has come to develop a cordial relationship with Eniko and has accepted her as a loving part of the kids' lives.

Running parallel to my entire comedy career, there's been a relationship career that took just as long and just as much work to succeed in. My kids have never seen Eniko and me fight or argue in any way. I'm not proud that it took me so long to create a healthy environment for my kids, but I am proud to have matured and showed them what adult relationships should look like.

Once, when I'd said something that unintentionally hurt Eniko's feelings, Heaven dropped into my lap and said, "Daddy, are you and Miss Eniko upset with each other? You've both been quiet."

"I was a little upset. I'm about to go and apologize."

"Yes, please do that, Daddy."

"Okay, I'll go apologize now."

It touched my heart to see how important it was to her that we got along. At the same time, it broke my heart to know why that was so important to her. I'm determined to dedicate the rest of my life to repairing whatever damage the past may have done to them, to Torrei, and to her mom's credit.

95

IN WHICH I LEARN THAT THERE'S A GIANT GAP BETWEEN WHAT YOU IMAGINE YOURSELF DOING AND WHAT YOU'RE CAPABLE OF DOING, AND IT HURTS PRETTY BAD WHEN YOU FALL INTO THAT GAP

In the two and a half years after *Think Like a Man*, Will Packer and I went on to make four more films together. I had a functional home family, I had a dysfunctional road family, and now I had a supportive set family. Despite all the meetings I was taking, I kept working with Will because the relationship was thriving and the films kept getting bigger.

The project that most excited me was *Ride Along* with Ice Cube, who, like me, had worked hard and on his own terms to break into the film business as an outsider. It was an action comedy, which I thought meant that I'd get to shoot people and jump off buildings and blow shit up. So I was disappointed to learn that they'd hired a stunt double to do all the fun stuff instead of me.

"Why do you need someone else? We're just jumping off a hill onto that rail, right? I can do that."

Crew members glanced at each other and rolled their eyes as I tried to talk my way into doing my first stunt by myself. I recognized that look, because it's the same one my friends give each other when I'm gambling and say, "I'm on a streak! Let me play just one more hand."

Finally, Tim Story sighed and gave in. "Please, just don't hurt yourself."

I began doing my own stunts whenever I could, until we shot a scene where I was supposed to jump, land on my back, roll, and pop back up in a classic action hero move.

But as soon as I hit the ground, my spine connected with the floor so hard that the camera operators winced. I jumped up like I hadn't hurt myself. I was too proud to admit that, clearly, there was a craft to this work that stuntmen knew and I didn't.

"Nice. Let's get one more take of that," Tim directed.

"You know what? Let's have the stuntman do this one, just so we can get a different version of it."

"Sure, Kevin."

From that moment on, every time there was an action scene, I was the first one saying, "All right, where's the stuntman? There he is. I see him right there, eating hot dogs. Somebody tell him to put the hot dog down. Bring him over. It's fine, I don't need to do this one."

When it came time to plan the marketing for *Ride Along* I sat down with Universal, who were distributing the film. Chris Rock's advice rang in my head, and I asked them to let us travel internationally to promote the movie.

"I'm not saying throw a bunch of money at it," I reasoned, "but let me go overseas and try to sell this product. If I can get an introduction in these countries, I'll be able to build up a fan base and tour in more places, which will also help our future movies together."

Universal let Cube and me travel to Europe and Australia to do media and promotion, and everyone won. With a budget of only twenty-five million, *Ride Along* held down the number one spot at the box office for three weeks and went on to make one hundred and fifteen million dollars domestically and twenty million internationally. The next two films that Will and I did together (*The Wedding Ringer* and *Think Like a Man Too*) went respectively to number two and one at the box office on their opening weekends—and soon, instead of being the newcomer, I was the guy that everyone couldn't get rid of.

I was an overnight success that was only sixteen years in the making.

96

CAN'T STOP WON'T STOP CAN'T STOP WON'T STOP CAN'T STOP WON'T STOP CAN'T STOP WON'T STOP CAN'T STOP WON'T STOP CAN'T STOP WON'T STOP CAN'T STOP WON'T STOP CAN'T STOP WON'T STOP CAN'T STOP WON'T STOP CAN'T STOP WON'T STOP OKAY I'M STOPPING NOW

On Pattison Avenue in Philadelphia, there's a landmark that casts its shadow over the city. I've seen it on television. I've been there many times. And on a hot, humid Sunday, I was there again, but in a spot I'd never set foot in before.

I stood in the center of Lincoln Financial Field and craned my neck, looking at four ascending levels of seating that blotted out the city and the freeway in all directions. This is where Philly sports fans have come for years to worship the Eagles like a religion, where Chad Lewis made the ankle-breaking catch that won them the NFC title game in 2005, where Donovan McNabb threw the last-minute twenty-eight-yard pass that came to be known as the 4th and 26. And where in just a few hours, fifty-three-thousand people would be coming to see one man tell jokes. It was the climax of the *What Now?* tour, which wasn't even over and had already become the highest-grossing comedy tour in history.

My thoughts turned to my mother. She'd never come to a show of mine, but I knew that she would have been at this one. Somewhere and in some way, I felt she would still be watching tonight, to see her son become the first comedian to ever sell out an NFL stadium. When I talk of my accomplishments and my work ethic, it is so that she will hear, and smile, knowing that all the hardship she suffered to keep me from throwing my life away was not in vain.

That night, illuminated by millions of watts of lighting, I stood on stage and talked about a life I never thought I'd have: a soulmate I was on the verge of marrying; two beautiful children who turned out happy against all odds; a house where I can provide all the things for my kids that I never had, like actual rooms to themselves; my father, who I once thought would die on the streets, visiting the grandchildren who love and adore him; renting a motor boat for a family vacation, and driving it without crashing into anything.

Every story to me was a small miracle.

After the show, I donated several hundred thousand dollars from ticket sales to build playgrounds around Philadelphia in my mother's name—especially in the forgotten, decaying areas where she struggled to find safe ways to keep me busy. My hope is that her name lives on forever in the city just like her spirit does.

After the show, I had one more big hurdle to cross: the ocean.

I'd been to a few foreign countries, but I'd never left the so-called Western world. I was scared of getting arrested and thrown in a prison with just a hole in the dirt to shit in. I was scared of getting a rare disease that would make my blood hot enough to cook me from the inside. I was scared of getting captured by terrorists and of my beheading becoming number one at the jihadi box office. All I knew is what I read. I didn't have any experience.

I debated whether or not to go to these parts of the world, until finally, I said, "Fuck it. If I want to be global, that means I need to actually *go* all over the globe."

Before leaving for my overseas dates, I went to see a doctor, who told me that I needed to get a bunch of shots to protect me from diseases like yellow fever and hepatitis B. I reconsidered my ambitions.

Me: Do I absolutely need those?

Doctor: Yes. By injecting you with small amounts of these viruses, you'll produce antibodies to prevent you from getting sick over there if you're infected.

Me: So you're saying that you're gonna give me yellow fever now, so if I catch it over there, I'm immune to it cause I got it?

Doctor: Yes, that's basically how it works.

Me: Why can't I go over there without the virus, not catch it, and come back okay? Or go over there, catch it, come back, and then you give me the antidote to get it out of my body?

Doctor: Mr. Hart, you won't experience any symptoms with these shots. It's just a low-grade version of the virus.

Me: But why would I want the disease in my body? If I told you I was gonna go out with someone who had herpes, you'd say, "Wait, come in and see me so I can give you herpes first?"

Doctor: Mr. Hart, these are standard immunizations that all travelers get.

Me: It doesn't make any sense. If I let you give me the shot, I have a hundred percent chance of getting the disease. But if I don't get the shot, there's still a chance I might not get it, right?

Doctor: . . .

Me: It's like telling me you're gonna break my leg so when I go play soccer, I'll be used to getting a broken leg. Naw, man, I'm not letting y'all mentally manipulate me into thinking this makes sense. I'm rolling the dice. If I get sick, you just better fix me when I come back.

The trip took me to Africa and the Middle East for the first time. Learning about apartheid, seeing where the marches took place, and going to Nelson Mandela's jail cell was a powerful history lesson, teaching me that it is never wrong to fight for what is right.

Along the way, I learned that the fears and stereotypes I had about other countries were nonsense. Outside of minor differences that were all surface level and all cool to learn about, people there were just like people here. Life there was just like life here. So much ignorance comes from a lack of experience, and these trips showed me that we are all brothers and sisters—and we need to always remember that. Because if one person is hurting, then we are all hurting.

The most amazing part of the tour—besides not getting sick—was visiting the royal family of the Bafokeng people. They gave me an African name, Mpho, which means *gift*. "We give it to you because you have the gift of making other people laugh," they told me.

This simple gift has brought me to places I never expected to go, given me just about everything I have, and taught me most of what I know. But only because I never gave up on it. Everybody wants success in something, whether it's in work, love, play, finances, family, or an inner struggle. But success doesn't come instantly. Life has a process of rejecting you to test you and prepare you to win.

Steve Harvey lived in his Ford Tempo and showered in gas stations when he couldn't get enough comedy gigs to cover his rent. Halle Berry slept in a homeless shelter in New York when she was auditioning to become an actress. Even James Cameron, one of the richest directors in Hollywood, was reduced to living out of his car when he was trying to sell the screenplay for *The Terminator*. The list goes on and on.

How you handle rejection is very similar to how you'll handle success. If you're strong enough to handle rejection without taking it personally, without holding a grudge, and without losing your passion and drive, then you'll be strong enough to reap the rewards. But if you're too weak to handle failure and disappointment, then you're too weak to handle success, which will only end up damaging your life and happiness.

If life is a struggle, then struggle. If you get rejected, get rejected again. If your dreams are smashed, keep dreaming. Just keep your eyes on the prize—and always remember that you have to fail to win.

Unless you're at a blackjack table in Las Vegas with me, in which case you should remind me that this advice applies only to games that aren't rigged, and that the Bellagio doesn't need any more fountains.

EPILOGUE: LIFE LESSONS FROM LEGACY BUILDING

One day you won't be here, but your legacy will.
Even if the earth is gone, you contributed to that.
If you'd done something different, maybe the planet
would have survived another minute, another year,
another millennium. Everything you do matters.
So treat it like it matters.

With Heaven, Hendrix, and Eniko

97

BUILDING NEWER, BETTER MODELS

Growing up, the best thing I ever had was nothing.

All the experiences I disliked in my childhood—sleeping in the hallway, not having a car, and being too poor to afford a haircut—were essential to building my character.

I remember going to the homes of other kids and looking around with envy: "You got grass? Wait, you got steps *inside* your house? And you got *two* bathrooms?"

My kids will never have that experience.

One of the first challenges I faced when I began earning enough money to over-provide for myself and my kids was how to raise them with the same qualities my mother instilled in me. Because if you give kids whatever they want, you create monsters who go out into the world and say, "Gimme." And the world says, "No."

However, when your children are flying on private planes and traveling with Daddy's security guards, they can quickly lose their grounding in reality. So I constantly tell Heaven and Hendrix about my childhood; why we're fortunate to have this lifestyle; and that in no way, shape, or form are they on Easy Street for life.

"Nothing's been given to us," I explain. "Everything that we have came from hard work. You're a part of it because you're my kids, but when you're no longer kids, it's up to you to go get your own stuff. You don't have to be your dad, but you're gonna have your dad's will and you're gonna know that whatever you put your mind to, you can achieve."

One of my biggest regrets is taking my education and opportunities for granted in my youth, and being content with just barely getting by. Today, I often think: *Damn, what if?*

What if I'd put one hundred percent into learning when I was growing up? Maybe I'd have accomplished more.

What if I'd gone to the University of Pennsylvania? Maybe I would have been able to add Professor to the front of my name.

What if I'd given more of a shit about swim team? Maybe I could have been the first black man under five foot five to win an Olympic gold medal for swimming.

I will never know the answers to these questions, because I fucked off parts of my life and shut certain doors that were open to me. As a father, I'm dedicated to making sure that my children don't have those same regrets. Our conversations about it usually go like this:

Me: Baby, why did you get a B?

Heaven: I don't know, Dad. That class was tough for me. How'd you do in math? Were you good?

Me: Nope.

Heaven: What'd you get?

Me: A lot lower than a B.

Heaven: So sometimes it's okay to get lower than a B?

Me: Nope.

Heaven: Why not, Dad? You did.

Me: Because your job is to be better than me. Getting a B is fine, but you should never be content with a B. You should always wonder why you didn't get an A. Because you know what happened to Daddy? Daddy got lucky and stumbled into something that he had no idea would end up working out like it did. You don't have to get lucky. You can know what you wanna do and walk straight into it. Do you understand?

Heaven: I do, Dad. I don't want to disappoint you.

Me: I'm never disappointed. I want *you* to be disappointed. Don't be upset because you think your dad is gonna be upset. You should be upset for you.

Education is the only area where I spoil my kids rotten. When it comes to opportunities to get better, I am the deliverer.

Whatever they're interested in—and sometimes whatever they're not interested in—I will provide every possible way for them to excel. There are times when my house is like the Make-A-Wish Foundation, except my kids seem to wish they were somewhere else. My biggest failing as a parent is being unable to get my children to appreciate some of the incredible teachers they have access to.

Hendrix: Can I go play my *Skylanders* game?

Me: What? David Beckham is teaching you how to kick a soccer ball right now.

Hendrix: Yeah, I know, but he's boring.

Me: Son, that's David Beckham—one of the best soccer players in the world. Go take this goddamn lesson!

Hendrix: Ugh, Dad, don't make me do this.

Heaven: I don't wanna learn to dance right now.

Me: But that's Beyoncé. She wants to teach you some moves.

Heaven: Yeah, but I'm over her.

Me: No, no, you can't be over Beyoncé! Just show me "Run the World" one more time from the top.

Hendrix: Dad, I don't think that guy knows what he's doing.

Me: That's Chris Paul. He knows what he's doing! He's the best point guard in the NBA.

Hendrix: I know, but Mr. Klein at camp says I should do it like this.

Me: Mr. Klein isn't a nine-time NBA All-Star! What are you talking about, son?

Hendrix: I like the way Mr. Klein does it better. I'm just gonna go play on the iPad.

One day, I brought my kids to Philadelphia so they could see the house I grew up in. I was prepared for them to be shocked, to be scared straight, to wrinkle their little noses and say, "How did you survive?"

But that's not what happened. My daughter looked at the house and the neighborhood, then turned to me and said, "I like it here. Can we stay?"

That's when I knew that the lessons on humility and appreciation had sunk in. Since then, I don't get as much time to teach them as I want to. Not because I'm working so hard, but because, at ages twelve and nine, they're busier than I am. Just yesterday, this is the conversation I had with them.

Me: Hey, guys, wanna go get ice cream?

Kids: Can't, Dad, got soccer practice.

Me: All right, we can go when you're done with practice.

Kids: Can't, Dad, after that we're meditating. We're learning how to meditate.

Me: Uh, what about tomorrow?

Kids: Well, we gotta see, Dad. We might have spin club.

Me: You got spin club? What, kids do that now?

Kids: Yeah, Dad.

Me: Well, let me know when you have time for your father.

Kids: Sure, Dad, we'll try to fit something in.

I believe that my work is done. In fact, there's a distinct possibility that I may have gone overboard.

98

THERE'S ALWAYS MORE

The other side of success is the backlash.

"Oh my God, Kevin Hart is doing too much. When is he going to sit down? How many movies is he trying to do? I'm getting sick of him. It's too much. He needs to relax."

But who works hard just so they can relax? What was the point of the blood, sweat, and tears that I put in on that road from Philadelphia to New York and all across the United States if I don't keep going?

Success is not an excuse to stop; it's a reason to move the goalposts farther out and accelerate. There is no destination, just a journey. And that journey is to keep building on top of what I'm building.

When my comedy career got going, that meant it was time to get my acting career going. Now that my acting career is going, it's time to get my writing, producing, and directing careers going. And then I'm ready to become a better CEO of my companies. I want to excel in the day-to-day operations, hiring, managing, preparing budgets, forming corporations, selecting health insurance plans, and, especially, understanding taxation.

A few years ago, I rented a single office and conference room on the fifteenth floor of a building in Encino. I walked in with Harry and Joey on that first day and said, "This is HartBeat Productions: you two, me, and this here office!"

"You don't need to waste your money on a place like this," Joey said.

"Man, it's not a waste, because we're gonna be in here working. I'm talking from sunup to sundown. This office is an investment in us creating our own TV shows, our own movies, our own social media team, and our own start-ups."

Within a couple of years, we expanded to fifteen employees and took over half the fifteenth floor in the building. I now run four companies—HartBeat Productions, HartBeat Digital, New Generation Promotion, and the Laugh Out Loud Network—out of that space. I recently rented the whole damn floor: I don't even have enough people for the other offices yet, but I know that I'm gonna grow into them. And once I fill the floor, I'll work to fill the building. There's always more.

Here's a recent example of this approach that means a lot to me: One morning on the *What Now?* tour, before my daily run, I posted a tweet telling people to meet us in the park and run with us. Three hundred people showed up and ran through the streets of Brighton, Massachusetts. In the next city where I tried it, three thousand people showed up. After that, it was five thousand people, and then sixty-five hundred people getting out of bed early and doing something healthy together.

From there, I contacted Nike and set up a meeting with their executives. I walked in with proof of the impact I was having on people's fitness. I told them that I wanted to use my influence to help people make the decision: *I want to start running. I want to start exercising. I want to take care of myself.*

"Put me in a position to do it," I said, "and I promise I'll do it in a way that's never been done before." They listened and, as a result, I became the first comedian ever sponsored by Nike. Together, we launched the Nike Hustle Hart sneakers—and the Move with Hart campaign that, to this day, motivates people to run on our official Sunday RunDay.

I willed the dream I had at eighteen years old, before I ever discovered comedy, to come true: I'm finally working for Nike. If you grind hard enough and stay true to yourself, all your dreams will come true—even the ones you've forgotten about.

This book is not the story of my life—it is the story of my foundation. The construction of my life is still in progress.

I refuse to relax. I refuse to get comfortable. I refuse to sit down. (Okay, sometimes I sit down, but when I sit down, I'm still working.) I'm on a quest to find the ceiling of what's possible in this life and raise it, so that my children and their children and their children's children will look at my accomplishments and go, "Holy shit."

I'm chasing after that Holy Shit Effect.

If this sounds arrogant, that's because it is. If you don't believe in your own greatness, no one else will. You're limited only by your doubts, your fears, and your desire to fit in rather than stand out.

And there's room in this world for all of us to stand out.

99

THE BLUEPRINT

Life is like a pack of cards. There are fifty-two cards in a deck, but only four of them are aces. The goal of life is to make your way through a crowded deck where the odds are stacked against you and draw an ace.

Looking back over the decades covered in this book, I've picked out eight qualities that put me in a position to draw aces. These characteristics don't work alone. Like a recipe, they only create success when combined together in just the right amounts.

1. **Persistence:** More than anything, my willingness to be persistent is responsible for the success I've had. My mindset is: It's okay to fail, but it's not okay to quit. Struggle, rejection, failure, and doubt break most people. Your goal is to learn from these challenges without letting them diminish your motivation. The secret to accomplishing this is simple: Let yourself be driven by your will to succeed rather than your fear of not succeeding.

2. **Patience:** The companion to persistence is patience. It drives away the anger, disappointment, and resentment when success doesn't happen overnight. Patience is understanding that your moment will come at the right time, and your job is to get ready for that moment. Because if it comes when you're not prepared, then it vanishes just as quickly. Know that your patience will always be tested, and if you can pass that test, you will be tested again and again, until the rare few left standing reap the rewards.

3. **Class:** It's easy to get bitten by what I call "the false-reality bug" and start looking down on other people. Class, to me, is having a high level of humility and likability—and knowing that all human beings are equal and worthy of respect, understanding, and consideration. Even if someone has done something that seems harmful to you, you still have the option of

handling it in a classy way by responding logically instead of emotionally. Class is an investment that will pay off your whole life, because the people you interact with can become your greatest allies or your greatest foes. There are no positive consequences to showing up anywhere with an attitude.

4. **Commitment:** Whenever I do a performance, a film, or any type of production, I sign a contract. That contract spells out in specific words an obligation that I'm under. It includes being in a specific place at a specific time on specific dates for a specific number of hours. In other areas of life, the details may not be written out on paper, but if there's a commitment, there's a contract. If you have a child, that's a contract. Your friendships and relationships—those are contracts. Your career, your projects, your goals, your dreams—all contracts. The most important contract of all is your word to others and to yourself. If you do not honor your contractual obligations, then other parties won't honor theirs either, and you won't get the results you want. Though you always have the option of renegotiating your contracts, you don't have the option of breaking them unless they're a danger to you or others.

5. **Learning:** The key to learning is to shut your mouth. Observe, listen, evaluate, and then choose. Every experience you have is a gift created to teach you a lesson. If you learn and implement that lesson in your life, then you get to receive the next gift. If you don't learn from it, then that same lesson will keep coming back to you, over and over, until you die standing in the exact same spot where you started, blaming others for something you should have done yourself long ago. In this world, there is nothing but life lessons. Pay attention to them and the world will open itself up to you.

6. **Passion-Centered Competitiveness:** This is the engine that drives all of these qualities. Having a passion—something you love that gives your life meaning and focus—is just the beginning. (If you haven't found your passion yet, don't overthink it. Just start doing *something* you enjoy.) The key

that turns passion into directed action, though, is competition. It can be competition with yourself, with others, or even with history. After I found my passion, I saw how much others before me had accomplished and I competed to get to that level. When I got there, I saw how many talented people were trying to get to my position, so I began competing to stay ahead of them. The important thing to realize is that you're not competing *against* anyone, you're competing *with* them. There are four aces in every deck, and there are an infinite number of decks.

7. **Positivity:** What you put out is what you get back. If you want to achieve positive goals and experience positive relationships, then put out positivity. If someone else is putting out negativity, then maneuver around them like you would a puddle on the ground. If you respond with negativity, you will only get dragged into the mud. It is a talent to stay positive and avoid negativity in the face of a sometimes cruel, unfair, and indifferent world. Cultivate that talent. It's the secret to living a happy life.

8. **Discomfort:** This last quality is specifically for the high achievers. If you want to get far in life, then never get too comfortable. Don't stop, don't rest, don't be satisfied. As soon as you get comfortable, you're pressing a brake and halting your forward motion. It will be hard to accelerate again afterward. This may seem like advice that goes against almost every self-help book ever published, but it is work that gives our lives meaning. That's not an original idea; that's in the Bible. "One who is slack in his work is brother to one who destroys." When you look back on your life, it should mean something. You should be able to say: "Wow, I made an impact on the world when I was there." And you don't create change by being comfortable.

Behold these truths that I have given you. Go forth, prosper, and don't blame me if any of this advice doesn't work. Blame yourself for following the advice of a guy who tells jokes for a living. Surely there's someone wiser you could have chosen to listen to, like a professor or a philosopher or the Dalai Lama or the wisest person of them all—the person reading this book.

With E, Joey, Spank, Harry, Wayne, Na'im, and Terry

ACKNOWLEDGMENTS

Thanks to the following metaphors for making it possible to write about comedy:

- Murdering, killing, destroying, assassinating, slaughtering, exploding, slaying, shredding, gutting, ravaging, smashing, battering, clobbering, pounding, wrecking, cracking, crippling, exterminating, decimating, terminating, obliterating, demolishing, annihilating, massacring, mutilating, crucifying, liquidating, nuking, vaporizing, blasting, bombing, crashing, tanking, dying, choking, and laughing one's ass off.

- This book is also dedicated to all the lives that have been lost slinging jokes. To the Richard Pryors, the Redd Foxxes, the George Carlins, the Bernie Macs, the Patrice O'Neals, the Charlie Murphys, and many more—thank you for blazing a trail.

Thanks also to these individuals for helping put this beast together:

- Everyone already named in the text of this book. (You already got your shout-out. Don't expect another one back here.)

- Dawn Davis, Lindsay Newton, Judith Curr, Yona Deshommes, Paul Olsewski, David Brown, Kimberly Goldstein, Paige Lytle, Navorn Johnson and the team in Copyediting, and all the good folks at 37 INK/Atria Books who we stressed the fuck out.

- Marc Gerald and Ethan Stern for pulling the strings behind the scenes.

- Laurie Griffin for the design heroics.

- Everett "E" Fitzgerald, Terry Brown, and Boss, three of the newest and ugliest members of the Plastic Cup Boyz road crew.

- Phoebe Parros, Benjamin Smolen, Brian Fishbach, Roni Brown, Charlene Lee, Molly Lindley, Ingrid Strauss, Tenn Strauss, Rico Rivera, Thomas Scott McKenzie, Alex Vespestad, Nikki San Pedro, Jane Adair Lauderbaugh, Anthony Errigo, Phillip Jacquet, and Christina Swing. You know what you did. Don't do it again.

American Express, if you're reading this, please run my credit again. I wrote this entire book just to send a message to you: *I'm now ready to handle the responsibility of a credit card.* I went out to dinner with Trey Songz last night, and he has a black card. That motherfucker is publicly on record singing about giving his card to random women and letting them max it out. That violates your terms of service. So why does he have one and not me?

Finally, thanks to you for reading this entire book, even the acknowledgments. Seems like you don't want this story to end. Fortunately, it's just the beginning . . .

Baby's Arrival

Name Kevin Darnell
Hart

Born at 10:13 A.M. o'clock

on July 6 19 79

Place Temple Hospital

Doctor Dr. Patricia Sullivan

Nurse

Comments At the time of his
birth Temple's nurses and hospital
workers were on strike. The R.N's
and doctors were very nice. Especially
Dr. Sullivan. They kicked me out at
five days.

Family Tree

Paternal	Maternal

Nancy Hart

Father's name   Mother's name

Henry Witherspoon   Barbary Hart

Grandfather's name   Grandfather's name

Robert Witherspoon   Richard G. Hart

Grandmother's name   Grandmother's name

Mary Witherspoon   Elouise G. Hart

Great Grandfather's name   Great Grandfather's name

HATTIE HART   MARSHALL GLOVER

Great Grandmother's name   Great Grandmother's name

NANCY SIMS   HATTIE POLTY

First Visitors

In the hospital his first and only visitor was his second cousin Shirel. She came to visit and also helped us to come home.

At home the next visitor was Preston. He and Shirel came to take us out shopping.

Next one to see him was his cousin Rita and her kids. Then his aunt Mae.

He was also visited by his Uncle Roe and Aunt Stella. His Uncle June came by to visit also.

My girlfriend Roz from work came for a visit with her two children.

His grandmother didn't see him until he was about three weeks old and his Aunt Patsy and cousins Daryl, Anthony, Michele and brother Kenneth until he was almost six weeks old, about 5 lb.

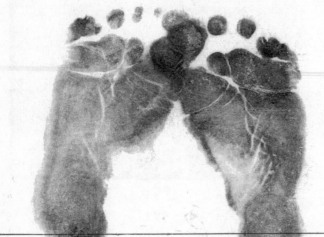

Baby's left foot   Baby's right foot